A Procession of Prayers

A Procession of Prayers

PRAYERS AND MEDITATIONS FROM AROUND THE WORLD

John Carden

MOREHOUSE PUBLISHING

Compilation © John Carden 1998

For copyright information on individual prayers see pp. 329–39.

First published 1998 by Cassell
First U.S. edition published in 1998 by
Morehouse Publishing
P.O. Box 1321
Harrisburg, PA 17105
Morehouse Publishing is a division of the Morehouse Group.

A catalog record of this book is available from the Library of Congress.

ISBN 0-8192-1752-2

Cover design by Trude Brummer
Cover image: Scala/Art Resource, NY. Ceiling of the Hall of the Labyrinth, Palazzo
Ducale, Mantua, Italy
Typeset by Pantek Arts, Maidstone, Kent.
Printed and bound in Great Britain by
Redwood Books, Trowbridge, Wilts

Contents

	Introduction	1
1.	The Advent Mystery	4
2.	The Mystery of Numbering	15
3.	Nativity: The Mystery of Poverty and Riches	23
4.	Christ's Presentation in the Temple in the Presence of the Elderly Simeon and Anna	34
5.	The Mystery of Christ's Epiphany to Wise Men	45
6.	A Sorrowful Mystery: The Suffering of Holy Innocents	57
7.	The Flight into Egypt	68
8.	The Mysteries of Nazareth:	79
	Annunciation	79
	Childhood	82
	Adolescence	86
	Anointing	91
9.	The Mystery of the Baptism of Christ	97
10.	Stations in the Wilderness	105
11.	The New Route:	114
	The call to follow	115
	Teaching and preaching	117
	Healing	120
	Rest and refreshment	124
	Storm on the lake	127
	Well of living water	132
	Encounters with death	135
	Homeless and at home	137
12.	The Shadow of the Cross	144
13.	The Mysteries of Christ's Entry into the City	152
14.	Mysteries of the Upper Room	165
15.	Gethsemane	178

16. The Stations of the Cross 189
    I   Jesus is tried and condemned 192
    II   Jesus takes his cross 201
    III   Jesus falls 208
    IV   Jesus meets his mother on the way 214
    V   Simon of Cyrene helps Jesus carry
           the cross 220
    VI   Veronica wipes the face of Jesus 227
    VII   Jesus falls again 234
    VIII   Jesus speaks to the women of Jerusalem 242
    IX   Jesus falls a third time 249
    X   Jesus is stripped 256
    XI   Jesus is crucified 262
    XII   Jesus dies 273
    XIII   Jesus is taken down from the cross 278
    XIV   Jesus is buried 284
17. The Resurrection Mystery 294
18. The Mysteries of Commissioning and Ascension 309
19. Mysteries of Pentecost 319
    Sources and Acknowledgements 329
    Index 341

Introduction

Situated just off one of the ancient roads leading into Rome, the volcanic-ally created lake of Bracciano, 50 kilometres north-west of the city, is wide-ly thought to have once served as a stopping-place for the Roman legions. Here war-weary troops cleaned their armour and chariots, watered their animals and rested themselves prior to their triumphal entry into the capi-tal. Popular with present-day Romans, Bracciano and its lakeside towns are among the many resting-places which lay astride the network of roads in the days of the Imperial empire.

Inspired by this ancient Roman practice of providing such 'stations' along every major route, the universal Catholic habit of observing special places at which to keep company with our Lord on his journey to the cross – known as Stations of the Cross – is a familiar one.

Perhaps less familiar, however, is the way in which, in more recent years, Christians of many different lands, in considerable numbers, and covering a wide spectrum of confessional allegiance, have been drawn to other incid-ents in the life of Jesus in the Gospels – his infancy; his family's flight into Egypt, with the inevitable stopping-places along the way; his time of test-ing in the burning desert; his presence in the storm; his entry into the city; his imprisonment; his burial; right through to the assurance of his contin-ued presence in the final commissioning and empowering of his followers – and in this way have been relating what they perceive to be the saving con-cerns and activities of Jesus throughout the whole of his earthly life to their own needs and to those of the world around them. This Procession of Prayers and meditations has its origin in these events.

These saving events, often referred to in traditional spirituality as mys-teries, seem to have demanded a much more corporate and practical response from contemporary Christians than appears to have been the case in the past; and whole Christian communities as well as individuals have increasingly come to see these events as speaking in very concrete and direct ways to matters of wide social concern.

In each of these mysteries, however, the wonder of God's love lying at the heart of every such episode in the life of Jesus remains hidden until such time as he chooses to disclose it; sometimes slowly, in the manner of a gradually unfolding flower (an image used frequently in a number of the prayers); sometimes unexpectedly and strangely: but always calling for a response from the believer.

A response not unlike that demanded by the writer of the epistle of John when he reminds his readers that their way of life, as befits those to whom has been entrusted the mystery of Christ, must conform to that of their Lord. 'Because', as he puts it, 'in this world we are as he is' (1 John 4:17). Words which were taken up and expounded many centuries later by the French Benedictine, the Abbé Columba Marmion, when he spoke of the mysteries of Christ becoming the mysteries of his followers.

This present procession of prayers, therefore, drawn from all around the world, takes the entire life of Christ as its itinerary; pausing, sometimes briefly, sometimes at greater length, at significant points along the way, much in the same way as Roman travellers would have done along their roads, or as do present-day travellers, whether along hidden tracks, or at service stations on motorways. The hope is that this journey, undertaken together, will help to bring a world-wide dimension to bear on the themes and seasons of the Church's year; serve as a companion to lectionaries and existing prayer cycles, and be a source-book for those who seek to achieve a greater sense of solidarity with their fellow Christians everywhere.

My own early steps along this route were taken, many years ago now, in company with Christians in Pakistan; and were followed by wider travel in Asia and the Middle East in the service of the Church Mission Society. Later, and following a memorable incumbency in an English parish, my wife and I spent a brief period caring for a small international Christian community in Jordan, travelling on roads to this day still dotted with Roman milestones and pilgrim stations. Subsequently we accepted an invitation from the World Council of Churches in Geneva, to edit the second edition of the Ecumenical Prayer Cycle *With All God's People*.

Along this way, Bracciano and its adjoining lake – with which I began – holds a special place in the affections of our family. For two years one of our sons lived in a house by its shores. From time to time we were reunited as a family there; swam in the cool waters; encountered women in black saying the rosary in street processions; suffered frustration at the hands of its local bank; ate and talked under the trees, and together worked our way through some of life's mysteries, sorrowful as well as joyous.

It will be apparent from the very individual – some might say, idiosyncratic – manner in which the prayers and reflections have been selected, and in some cases written, that this book is not just another anthology but the record of a personal pilgrimage in which questions of theological correctness or liturgical purity or the niceness of English language are less important than the enrichment and invigoration gained by travelling in such company. Pausing with fellow Christians in the diverse cultural and climatic, economic and political circumstances in which they follow Christ today, I have found myself again and again marvelling at the simplicity and directness of many of their petitions; pulled up short by their transparency and firmness of faith; reduced to silence by some daring phrase used in prayer or meditation; excited by some unexpected and fresh insight brought to bear on the Gospel narrative, and shamed at the poverty and inadequacy of my own following.

All that remains now is for me to express grateful thanks to all who have contributed to this procession, and who have helped it on its way: to my family, and in particular to my wife Margaret for the part she has played in marshalling the straggling elements and encouraging me on. Our indebtedness – to the Church Mission Society, to the sub-unit Renewal and Congregational Life in the WCC, to churches and to fellow Christians in many different countries – will be apparent in the prayers and meditations that follow.

1

The Advent Mystery

'The light shines in the darkness, and the darkness has never mastered it.' (John 1:5)

1   O God we are in great darkness
When we heard of Jesus we saw a light far off
Do not let anything put out that light
But lead us nearer to it.

(Africa)

Identifying with the mystery of the light described in John's Gospel, that went on shining in the darkness, one lifelong apostle to the Muslim world speaks of the undue haste in which many of us pass over the Old Testament readings in the Christmas season, and even the seemingly obscure early verses in the Prologue of John, in our impatience to get on to the great denouement of John 1:14 'And the Word was made flesh and dwelt among us.'

But this, he claims, is to deny the validity of the mysterious light which through many centuries went on shining, shining, shining in the darkness. To do this is to ignore those intimations of an eternal presence, discernible in so many places and situations, which have enlightened and inspired and activated men and women of many faiths over the centuries.

2   O mysterious One to whom we always look,
lighten our hearts as the sun throws light upon the dark
 bushes around us.
May we always reflect your radiance so that those who
 have not known you may see you in us.
In the name of the Great Light we ask this.

(Africa)

3   Darkly and dimly have we known
    that you are near and everywhere.
    We hear you in thunder and waterfalls.
    We feel your presence in the prayer and the dance:
    with the old men under the tree,
    the young men in their age group,
    women in the market place.
    In full have you participated;
    darkly and dimly have we known this.
    Our pale brothers from over the seas came;
    with the book of life they proclaimed the good news.
    This is Him, we have felt His presence.
    This is Him, we have heard in the council.
    Though darkly and dimly this was Him!
    For joy we shouted, this is Him!
    No, said our brothers,
    This was not Him.
    In darkness have you been sitting:
    listen to the word or you perish.
    Away from the market place.
    Away from the party and the council.
    Away from the trade union.
    Away, away! Away, brothers, away.
    Away, away from the world.

                              (Africa: Bethel A. Kiplagat)

4   The prodigious expanses of time which preceded the first
    Christmas were not empty of Christ: they were imbued with
    the influx of his power . . . Let us have done with the
    stupidity which makes a stumbling-block of the endless eras
    of expectancy imposed on us by the Messiah; the fearful,
    anonymous labours of primitive man, the beauty fashioned
    through its age-long history by ancient Egypt, the anxious
    expectancies of Israel, the patient distilling of the attar of
    oriental mysticism, the endless refining of wisdom by the

Greeks: all these were needed before the Flower could
blossom on the rod of Jesse and of all humanity. All these
preparatory processes were cosmically and biologically
necessary that Christ might set foot upon our human
stage . . . When Christ first appeared before men in the
arms of Mary he had already stirred up the world.

(Pierre Teilhard de Chardin, 1881–1955)

5 Awakening to the presence of God

Leader: By your word, O Light of this whole universe,
we live, move and have our being.
As you have illuminated the hearts
of people at many times in the past,
we pray, eternal God, for your awakening within us.
From delusion to truth, and unto your righteous way.

People: Lead us, Source of all, our Father and our Mother.

Leader: From darkness to light and into your gracious will;

People: Lead us, O Christ, our Friend and our Brother;

Leader: From death to eternal life and into your infinite joy;

People: Lead us, Divine Spirit, enlivening Power within, for we
seek your awakening touch.

*(South India: from a eucharistic liturgy incorporating
words from the Brihadaranyaka Upanishad, c. 600 BC)*

6 Almighty God, you bring to light things hidden in darkness
and know the shadows of our hearts; cleanse and renew us
by your Spirit that we may walk in the light and glorify
your name, through Jesus Christ the Light of the world.
Amen.

(Kenya)

7   As our tropical sun gives out its light, so let the rays from
    your face, O God, enter every nook of my being and drive
    away all darkness within.

    (Philippines)

8   Art Thou a stranger to my country, Lord?
    My land of black roots and thick jungles
    where the wild boar sharpens his tusks,
    where the monkeys chatter in the trees,
    and the peacock's shrill note
    echoes through the mist-clad hills;
    my land of brown, caked river mud
    where the elephant and the leopard come to drink,
    and the shambling bear with his dreamy eyes
    sees the porcupine shedding his quills;
    my land with its friezes of palmya palms
    etched sharply against the blue mountains;
    my land of low-lying plains
    with its miles of murmuring paddy fields
    that stretch in undulating waves of green
    to the distant horizon;
    my land of sapphire skies and flaming sunsets,
    my land of leaden grey skies piled high
    with banks of monsoon clouds;
    my land of stinging rain, of burning heat,
    of dark nights, of enchanting moons
    that dance behind the coconut fronds;
    my land of tanks and pools
    where the lazy buffalo wallows
    and the red lotuses lie asleep?
    Nay, Thou art no stranger, Lord,
    for the wind whispers of Thee
    and the waters chant Thy name.
    The whole land is hushed in trembling expectancy,
    awaiting Thy touch of creative Love.

    (India)

9   Great Lion of the grasslands!
Ahunuababirim: when you see him your heart thumps.
Lion of the tribes of Israel!
Kurotwiamansa: the Leopard,
whose cubs cannot be caught!
Etwi: the cat with the royal mane!
Okokuroko: the Powerful One,
among women and men, the most beautiful of all!
Lion of the grasslands!
We call to you, 'Come!'

(Ghana: invocation of Jesus of the Deep Forest)

10   O Christ the Light of the World
We thank you that your light shines among us.
Draw us ever closer to you
So that free from sin
We may show forth the light of your
    glory in the world.

(Torres Straits, Australia: commemoration of the arrival of the first Christian missionaries)

11   O You who are our great Chief, light a candle in my heart
that I may see all that is within,
and sweep the rubbish from your dwelling place.

(Africa: a schoolgirl's prayer)

12   A litany of darkness and light

Voice 1: We wait in the darkness, expectantly, longingly,
anxiously, thoughtfully.

Voice 2: The darkness is our friend.
In the darkness of the womb, we have all been nurtured
and protected.
In the darkness of the womb, the Christ-child was made
ready for the journey into light.

All: **You are with us, O God, in darkness and in light.**

Voice 1: It is only in the darkness that we can see the
splendour of the universe –
blankets of stars, the solitary glowings of distant planets.
It was the darkness that allowed the Magi to find the star
that guided them to where the Christ-child lay.

All: **You are with us, O God, in darkness and in light.**

Voice 1: In the darkness of the night, desert peoples find relief from
the cruel relentless heat of the sun.

Voice 2: In the blessed desert darkness, Mary and Joseph were
able to flee with the infant Jesus to safety in Egypt.

All: **You are with us, O God, in darkness and in light.**

Voice 1: In the darkness of sleep, we are soothed and restored,
healed and renewed.

Voice 2: In the darkness of sleep, dreams rise up.
God spoke to Jacob and Joseph through dreams.
God is speaking still.

All: **You are with us, O God, in darkness and in light.**

Voice 1: In the solitude of darkness, we sometimes remember those
who need God's presence in a special way –
the sick, the unemployed, the bereaved, the persecuted,
the homeless;
those who are demoralized and discouraged,
those whose fear has turned to cynicism,
those whose vulnerability has become bitterness.

Voice 2: Sometimes in the darkness, we remember those who are
near to our hearts –
colleagues, partners, parents, children, neighbours, friends.
We thank God for their presence and ask God to bless
and protect them in all that they do –
at home, at school, as they travel, as they work, as
they play.

All: **You are with us, O God, in darkness and in light.**

Voice 1: Sometimes, in the solitude of darkness, our fears and concerns, our hopes and our visions rise to the surface. We come face to face with ourselves and with the road that lies ahead of us.
And in that same darkness, we find companionship for the journey.

Voice 2: In that same darkness, we sometimes allow ourselves to wonder and worry
whether the human race is going to make it at all.

All: **We know you are with us, O God, yet we still await your coming.**
In the darkness that contains both our hopelessness and our expectancy,
we watch for a sign of God's Hope.

(New Zealand)

13 Come, Lord,
and cover us with the night.
Spread your grace over us
as you assured us you would do.
Your promises are more than all the stars in the sky;
your mercy is deeper than the night.
Lord, it will be cold.
The night comes with its breath of death.
Night comes; the end comes;
but you come also.
Lord, we wait for you day and night.

(Ghana)

14 Put your ear to the ground
and identify the noises round you.
Predominant are

anxious, restless footsteps,
frightened footsteps in the dark,
footsteps bitter and rebellious.
No sound as yet
of hope's first footsteps.
Glue your ear to the ground again.
Hold your breath.
Put out your advance antennae.
The Master is on his way.
Most likely he will not get here
When things are going well.
But in bad times
when the going's unsure and painful.

(Brazil)

15   O Father God
I cannot fight this darkness by beating it with my hands
Help me to take the light of Christ right into it.

(Africa: for all in trouble)

16   Make us, we beseech thee, O Lord our God, watchful in
awaiting the coming of thy Son, Jesus Christ our Lord; that
when he shall come and knock, he may find us not sleeping
in sin, but awake, and rejoicing in his praises; through the
same Jesus Christ our Lord.

(South India)

17   Lord,
oil the hinges of my heart's door
that it may swing gently and easily to welcome your coming.

(New Guinea)

18   Let all the fire-heaps clap their hands
and scarred earth join the song!
Let broken brigalow and stones
with joy come dance along!

Throw off your grey and weeping face
you sad old coolibah,
and send out summer shoots of green
that chant the Gloria.

For where the ironbarks shattered lie,
and twisted she-oak heap,
where once the dozers chained the scrub,
for joy the old trees weep.

And lift your face to that bare hill,
a mighty thing, yet small;
the old black stump has grown a shoot,
a tender Sign for all.

For if that stump so black and dead
where fires have charred the earth,
can bear a baby shoot so green,
you too can have new birth!

So clap your hands and shout for joy,
who sad and dead appear;
and know that when the black stump grows,
your Saviour now is here!

> *(Australia. The prophet Isaiah speaks of the coming*
> *Saviour as a little shoot coming from a stump that appeared*
> *to be dead (Isaiah 11:1). In this 'Carol of the*
> *Cleared Field', Aubrey Podlich sets the scene*
> *in Australia.)*

19   I believe with perfect faith in the coming of the Messiah,
and even though he tarry, every day I await his coming.
*(Ani Ma Amin: ancient song sung by Jews on the
way to the gas chambers)*

20   The grass has turned brown.
These are the days
When Christmas is not far off.
(Japan: haiku poem)

21   Bright moon, scattered stars; so solitary is creation. The
universe which God has created is especially silent on this
night. It waits with bated breath for the Lord of Creation
to return. The universe belongs to God, it is his home.

Silence reigns supreme. The flowers of the field sway gently
in the moonlight. This night, the vast earth awaits the
homecoming of our Creator God. The vast earth and open
fields belong to God, they are his home.

Bethlehem lies dreaming. In his gentle mother's arms, the
babe sleeps peacefully this night. The City of David awaits
the homecoming of David's descendant. The town of
Bethlehem belongs to him, it is his home.

My bones, my flesh, my blood, my lungs and my heart,
were all made by his hand. This night, my heart is at peace,
awaiting my Creator's return. My heart belongs to him, it
is his home.
(China)

22   Almighty God, grant that as we your children are bathed
in the new light of your incarnate Word, so may that which
shines by faith in our minds blaze out likewise in our
actions. Amen.
(Gregorian)

23   God of power and mercy, you call us once again to
celebrate the coming of your Son. Remove those things
which hinder love of you, that when he comes, he may find
us waiting in awe and wonder for him who lives and reigns
with you and the Holy Spirit, one God, now and for ever.

(Canada)

24   God comes down to us like the sun at morning,
wounded to the heart by our helplessness.
Let us proceed in his strength
to love and serve one another.

(Philippines: Asia Youth Assembly)

2
The Mystery of Numbering

1   When the Lord draws up the record of the nations:
    he shall take note where every man was born.
    (Alternative Service Book, Church of England: Psalm 87:5)

*'In those days a decree was issued by the emperor
Augustus for a census to be taken throughout the Roman
world. This was the first registration of its kind; . . .
Joseph went up to Judaea from the town of Nazareth in
Galilee, to register in the city of David called Bethlehem
. . . and with him went Mary, his betrothed, who was
expecting her child.' (Luke 2:1–2, 4–5)*

2   Nations were registered in the name of Caesar Augustus,
    and we the faithful are registered in your divine name.
    O Incarnate, O Lord who are born, great is your mercy!
    Glory to You.
    (Greek Catholic Church: December Vespers)

3   On the day when men were counted
    God became the Son of Man.
    (Sri Lanka)

One of the most telling images in the film *Schindler's List* is that of the
portable tables and chairs, and the assortment of old typewriters, ink pots,
sheafs of paper and rubber stamps, which constituted the stock in trade of
the functionaries who prepared the lists for the transportation of Jews to
those infamous concentration camps.

Though not so maliciously applied as in that awful numbering of the Holocaust, nevertheless registration of one kind or another is frequently required by governments and those in authority in many parts of the world today; and often leads to considerable harassment of innocent people. Sometimes the demeaning procedure of fingerprinting is involved, or intrusive questioning, or the carrying of identity cards; and most often it is the very vulnerable – migrant workers, refugees, tribal and indigenous peoples, minority communities and other marginalized groups – who are required to submit to these indignities.

In the case of the compulsory registration of Joseph and Mary in the Gospel story, there is no indication of ill-intent on the part of the emperor Caesar Augustus in ordering this numbering; yet it was the necessity to go to Bethlehem which put the Holy Family under the jurisdiction of Herod, and therefore at risk at the hands of a despotic ruler.

For their part, biblical writers seem to have a great liking for registration. They list the generations, count the tribes, number the people and add up the redeemed; yet at the same time they also do their sums quite differently from the the way the world does its counting, singling out insignificant people for special attention, and giving the lie to the power of large numbers.

In the attention which he devotes to each individual, Jesus embodies this gospel mystery that in the sight of God every single hair on the heads of each of his children has been counted and is valued (Luke 12:7). Jesus' whole life declares that this is the evaluation which ultimately counts.

4   O God, you who have numbered even the hairs of my head, think of me when these things come. Amen.

(Prayer based on Luke 12:7)

5   Lord Jesus, yourself the insignificant one who escaped the attention of this world's statisticians, and lived and died to give us a new way of numbering our fellow human beings; calling a negligible number of men and women to be your followers; blessing five barley loaves and two small fishes for the feeding of a multitude; giving significance and value

to the one over against the ninety and nine; promising your
presence to the two or three who gather in your name;
teach us likewise to do our arithmetic with you.

6   O God, save us from counting heads
     but save us also from not counting at all.

7   Thank you, Lord, for counting me one of your sheep
     Teach me, Lord, to count better, like you.

                                                    (USA)

8   To count the crowds that fill the street
     statistics are the measure.
     I am a tag without a name,
     a chest without a treasure.
       Just call me by my name
       Just call me by my name
       Just call me by my name, O Lord,
       Just call me by my name.

                                              (Singapore)

9   O Lord, we thank you for numbers:
       numbers to promote order
       numbers to further scholarship
       numbers to facilitate business
       numbers by which countries make reasonable provision
         for their numerous peoples.

     But Lord, we repent us of our numbers:
       when they are used to accuse
       when they are used to imprison
       when they deface personality made in the image of God
       when they restrict true freedom
       when they involve riot squads and secret police.

O Lord, you who were numbered at birth
and yet are the first and the last
accept and purge our use of numbers. Amen.

*(Pakistan. The second verse of this prayer relates to the numbers
of particular sections of government rules under which arrests are
made and freedoms curtailed. Such rules vary from time to time
and country to country, but the concern remains constant.)*

10   A litany of naming and numbering

Jesus, born and throughout life subject to the restraints and
indignities imposed by an occupying power, look upon the
many people in the world today who find themselves either
numbered against their will or else entirely lost sight of by
their fellows.

Kyrie eleison.

For the scattered people of the world: refugees; fugitives
from famine, drought or war; orphaned children; migrant
workers; country people flocking into overcrowded cities to
escape the stagnation and poverty of village life.

Christe eleison.

For members of minority communities for whom the
carrying of distinctively marked identity cards has become
mandatory practice in a number of countries in recent years.

Kyrie eleison.

For people deprived of their land and identity in countries
where they were the original inhabitants, who now find
themselves exposed to ways of life which impose impossible
burdens upon them.

Kyrie eleison.

For aliens of many nationalities forced to submit to the
humiliating processes of fingerprinting, stripping and hostile
questioning from officials of the countries to which they
seek admission.

Christe eleison.

For all who implement government regulations, count numbers, administer quotas and make decisions concerning the fate of their fellow human beings.

Kyrie eleison.

(Various countries)

11   There are times when we unprivileged people
          weep tears that are not loud but deep,
          when we think of the suffering we experience.
      We come to you, our only hope and refuge.
      Help us, O God, to refuse to be embittered
          against those who handle us with harshness.
      We are grateful to you
          for the gift of laughter at all times.
      Save us from the hatred of those who oppress us.
      May we follow the spirit of your Son Jesus Christ.
                    (South Africa: prayer of a Bantu pastor)

12   Dear Lord,
      who yourself once experienced what it is like to be a
      member of an invaded and subject nation: look with mercy
      on the inhabitants of those many countries whose culture
      and way of life has been discounted and exploited by later
      arrivals; and by a process of apology and forgiveness restore
      to them the freedom to live henceforward in ways which are
      in accordance with your Father's rich and varied provision
      for the different members of his diverse human family.
                    (Prayer for the world's indigenous peoples)

13 O God, you have spoken to us through the story of Ruth, sojourner in a foreign land, and were yourself present among us in Jesus to gather and welcome all those who were cast out and adrift from their societies; stir us and speak to us afresh through the migrant people of our time. Amen.

(Canada)

14 When she has to go to a foreign land 'to ease the burden of the family', Lord, calm her terror on the ear-bursting plane;

a girl of different colour in strange clothes, humiliated by what they call her with their eyes, be her protection on her arrival;

on her knees cleaning floors, with names like 'beggar' in her ears, Lord, hear the prayer of her aching knees;

sweating at the stove preparing food, Lord, heal the raw, sore hands of the young 'cook';

holding the child of another woman, Lord, create some bond of love as he screams at his 'nanny ayah';

just a 'servant girl', carrying loads with both her hands and on her head, Lord, comfort her through meeting fellow-servants at the market;

and at last when the day's work is done and she falls asleep to dream of home, may she hear her mother whispering 'little daughter'. Open her inward eyes to know she is your daughter.

To all migrant workers, Lord, give the blessing Jesus promised to the meek, for 'The souls of the righteous are in the hand of God, and the torment of malice shall not touch them'. Amen.

(Prayer for Sri Lankan women migrant workers)

15   Jesus, you lived in exile in Egypt: be with all migrant workers and protect their families.

(Central Africa: Ukaristia)

16   O Lord,
we remember those many needy people in our world today who, because of the prospect of finding corn in Egypt, leave their homes and families in search of work in other lands. We pray for all such migrant workers; and especially for the young men and women of the Philippines; that in times of loneliness and difficulty they may be sustained by thoughts of home; by considerate employers; by the fellowship of the Church; by the presence of friends; and that above all they may be assured of your presence, and aware of your protection.

(Prayer for young Filipino migrant workers)

17   O God who, looking with compassion upon your travel-weary people of old, and seeing them as sheep without a shepherd, sustained and provided for them in their need; be with all such in our world today, and help us to count and care for them in the way shown to us by your Son, Jesus Christ. Amen.

(Prayer based on Mark 6:34)

18   Almighty God,
protector of Mary and Joseph and the unborn child
on their weary pre-natal journey to Bethlehem;
be with all whose job it is
to interrogate travellers arriving on our shores.
Help them to recognize your image in each arriving person
and to receive them accordingly,
in the name of Jesus. Amen.

(United Kingdom)

19   Lord, touch with your fingers those who are so demeaned
       and restore to them their rightful dignity.
       (Japan: prayer for aliens subjected to compulsory fingerprinting)

20   Lord, may it ever be kept in mind
       that your kingdom is open to all;
       and that every feature of every face,
       every hair of every head,
       every smallest swirl of pigmentation
       that makes each one of us different from the other
       is loved and valued and important in your sight. Amen.

21   In our contentment, O God, help us to see the uprooted
       people of the world who drift like shadows, nameless and
       homeless; that we may share with them part of our loaf, for
       bread is to be broken and shared.

                                                        (Hawaii)

22   O God, in every age and to every race you reveal yourself to
       the childlike and lowly in heart, and write their names in
       the book of life; give us the simplicity and faith of your
       saints, that loving you above all things, we may be what
       you want us to be, and do what you want us to do, that we
       also may be numbered with all your saints in glory. Amen.

                                                        (Traditional)

3
Nativity: The Mystery of Poverty and Riches

'You know the generosity of our Lord Jesus Christ: he was rich, yet for your sake he became poor, so that through his poverty you might become rich.'

(2 Corinthians 8:9)

1   It is right that human beings should acknowledge
      your divinity.
    It is right for the heavenly beings to worship your humanity.
    The heavenly beings were amazed to see how small
      you became,
    and earthly ones to see how exalted.

(Prayer of St Ephrem the Syrian, 306–373)

2   Wise Creator, when you sent our Saviour Christ to be a helpless child, you purposefully darkened his divine vision. You left him but one eye, and that entirely human. Help us to see, through him, the true worth of human insight when it is perfected, and the true love of a God who would blind himself, simply to bear the name 'Emmanuel'.

(United Kingdom: a mother's prayer, reflecting wonderment at the unique individuality of her new-born infant, with just one eye open, looking directly at her)

3   Down in a slum a new born babe
    stirs in her sleep.
    She wakes, she looks,

she looks into my eyes.
She looks into my eyes
and I know we have hope.
I know we have hope.

(India)

4 The theme of the fortnight-long confirmation class was that
Jesus was born poor and humble and shares our life; and
the question was: Why? The women present were all poor.
None had much formal education. Most were migrants
from rural areas. All knew real hardship. They could easily
identify with a poor family on the move whose baby had
been born in harsh circumstances. Indeed, a one-minute
reading of Luke's account of the nativity provoked a
one-hour discussion of the injustices, humiliations and
hardships that the mothers themselves had experienced.

They discussed the terrible health services available in the
area and how a local woman's baby had been born while she
was waiting in a queue to see the doctor. (The baby died.)
They exchanged accounts of having to wait in shops while
better-dressed people were served first, and how as domestic
servants they were treated without respect by their mistresses.
They spoke of the high price of food in the local shops.

After an hour of such talk the catechist put the question:
'Why did Jesus choose to be born poor and humble?'
'Maybe', said one woman, a mother of ten of whom three
had died and only two were working, 'it was to show those
rich people that we are important too.'

A ripple of excitement passed through the room. Was God
really making such a clear statement about their humanity?
About their rights as people? The discussion progressed, but
with an electric charge in the air. Half an hour later a young
woman said 'I think we still haven't got the right answer to

the first question!' A complete hush. 'I think', she went on,
'I think God chose his son to be born like us so that we can
realize that we are important.'

(Brazil: account of an experience in a
confirmation class on the outskirts of São Paulo)

5   Lord, thank you for revealing the mystery of your truth and
love to the poor.

(Korean social worker in Pakistan)

6   Blessed are you, O Christ child, that your cradle was so low
that shepherds, poorest and simplest of earthly people,
could yet kneel beside you, and look, level-eyed, into the
face of God.

(Prayer used in Uganda)

7   God looked where in the world he might display his face
He pitched his tent in human fields, no other place.

(Persian poet, Hafiz)

8   God of God . . .
only the sound of an infant
crying in the night.
A familiar, homely, human sound
like the sound of hooves on flagstones,
like the rattle of chains tethering cattle,
like the crunch of straw in the mouths of oxen,
like the rustle of hay tossed into a manger.

Light of Light . . .
only the light of a star
falling on an infant in a crib
like the light in a shepherd's lantern

like the light in the eyes of a mother
like the light in the learning of the wise men
like the light that lightens each dawn.

Very God of very God . . .
only a pillow of straw
and an infant in rags and tatters
like the weather-worn blankets of shepherds
like dusty, travel-stained garments of travellers
like old cloths thrown to a beggar
like cloths stuffed in a stable window
to keep the draught out and cattle warm.

God is with us,
terribly, simply with us.
And the shadow of men and women
with arms outstretched to take him
fall across the manger
in the form of a cross.

(India)

9   O Lord, in company with those earliest visitors to
Bethlehem, grant that we too may see the ladder of the
cross leaning against the stable, and thankfully incline it
towards ourselves.
*(Prayer inspired by an Indian artist's depiction of a ladder in the
shape of a cross leaning against the stable of the nativity)*

10   Dear Lord
may your light
shine on me now
as once it shone
upon the shepherds
as they kept their flocks
by night!

(Japan: leprosy sufferer Ozaki)

11 O Lord, thank you for humbling yourself to be born in a manger and to become the son of a carpenter. We thank you for bearing our sin and agony. You died for us and rose again from the dead for us. We thank you for bringing new birth and everlasting life for us. You are the light of the world, the hope of human beings and our salvation. We ask you to let us truly rejoice with those who rejoice, to weep with those who weep, and to bring your light to the world.

(Taiwan)

12 We celebrate with joy your coming into our midst;
we celebrate with hope your coming into our midst;
we celebrate with peace your coming into our midst;
for you have come to save us.
By your grace we recognize your presence in men and
    women everywhere;
by your power you free us from all that stands in the way
    of your coming kingdom;
through your strength our lives can proclaim joy and hope;
through your love we can work for peace and justice.
You are the source of our being
You are the light of our lives.

(Latin America)

13 O God, who before all others called shepherds to the cradle of your Son; grant that by the preaching of the gospel the poor, the humble and the forgotten may know that they are at home with you.

(South India)

14 Lord God, in the birth of Jesus,
you show your preference for all that is humble and poor.
May this mystery save us
from illusions of grandeur and power,
and lead us to love simplicity of heart,
through Christ, our Lord. Amen.

(France)

15 Jesus, you were rich, yet for our sake you became poor:
move those who are wealthy
to share generously with those who are poor.

(Central Africa: Ukaristia)

16 O God, to us whose vision of the poverty-turned-riches of
your son's nativity has inspired an intense concern for the
poor and needy, grant us also to look into the homes of the
poor of the world, to share their hopes, their sayings, their
customs, their hospitality, and to recognize that we are
enriched by their wisdom and knowledge and by the beauty
of their lives.

(Prayer inspired by some words of Henri J. M. Nouwen)

17 O God,
grant that we may not seek the child Jesus
in the pretty figures of our Christmas cribs;
but rather look for him
among the undernourished children
who have gone to bed tonight with nothing to eat;
among the poor newsboys who will sleep
covered with newspaper in doorways.

(El Salvador: prayer based on some words of Oscar Romero)

18 Wake up
little baby God
thousands of children
have been born
just like you
without a roof
without bread
without protection.

(Chile)

19 Almighty God, whose son came to earth to dwell with the
lowly and simple, with the victims of violence and crisis,
and with the outcasts and rejected of society; may we keep
the same company.

(Pakistan)

20 I am the child who lives on the streets;
Pray for me.
I am the child in a refugee camp;
Pray for me.
I am the child hidden away in an orphanage;
Pray for me.
I am the child trying to find my parents;
Pray for me.
I am the child dying of hunger;
Pray for me.
Share your music, your education, your riches with me.
Share your shoes, your food, your blankets, your fuel,
    your toys with me.
Share your ideas, your imagination, your skills, your time,
    your dreams with me.
Share your world with me.
It should be mine as well.

(United Kingdom: Children's Aid Direct)

21   Christ of a cold December,
quicken us to remember
poverty in a stable,
need, like the sting of snow.

(Aotearoa, New Zealand)

22   In the bleak midsummer
dusty winds made moan,
earth stood hard as iron,
water dirty brown;
dust was blowing,
dust on dust,
dust on dust . . .
in the bleak midsummer
not so long ago.

(Uganda: a re-writing of some familiar words)

23   God our midwife . . .
Contain in your hands
the breaking of waters,
the blood and din of your birth:
then, through our tears and joy, deliverer,
your wrinkled, infant kingdom may be born. Amen.

(Christian Aid)

24   O God, we pray that you have mercy on women who have
had recurrent miscarriages and still births, that your healing
miracle might bring joy into such homes. We pray in the
name of Jesus Christ our Lord. Amen.

(Nigeria: a woman's prayer)

25 Heavenly Father,
we thank you for your love
especially to women who work with poor people,
teaching, nursing, and helping women during their labour.
We pray you to give them wisdom;
guide them always to fulfil their duties without difficulties.
Lord, be with those they work with
and send your Holy Spirit to give us love to help all people.
We pray you to lead us,
through Christ, our Saviour. Amen.

(Prayer of Sudanese women)

26 O Lord Jesus Christ, who enjoyed the comforts and
makeshift toys of a poor child, bless, we pray, the parents of
children in poor families, and give them all that is needful
for their child's growth and contentment.

*(In Dürer's 16th-century painting of the Madonna and Child
the infant Jesus is shown clutching a comfort rag.)*

27 Lord,
may the memory of teenage mother Mary
inspire Christians to reach out
to welcome babies born of teenage mothers
and to provide young people
with the homes that will encourage mature,
stable, loving relationships.

(USA)

28 Thank you for Christmas
And what the Salvation Army did.

(USA: a delinquent teenager)

29 Behold how the angels sing:
Glory in the highest,
peace on earth.

Love has taken a name and a form, and,
becoming meek for his helpless creatures,
has come to earth.

The finger on which the sun is set as a diamond,
he puts to his mouth
and plays with in the small cowshed.

O Christ, give to us this mind,
that as the finger turns and beckons
we too may respond.

(India: words based on a Marathi hymn)

30 Who started the rumour that one needs a lot of money to remember, to rejoice, to celebrate the birthday of the one who chose to become poor for us?

(A worker among the poor in Mexico)

31 Lord God, Father of Jesus Christ, be present, we pray, at our Christmas celebrations which honour the birth of your Son, and make them fine and full; make our greetings sincere and our giving real; make our eating and drinking a delight without their becoming an excess; enliven our relationships, both within our families and beyond them, with the spirit of the Christ Child. Amen.

(United Kingdom)

32   Give us hope to look forward to the challenges
    of tomorrow.
Give us courage to face the hardships without losing hope.
Give us faith so that the joy of receiving Christ will lead us
    to serve our brothers and sisters.
Give us appreciation for the gifts that we have received,
    that we may use them responsibly,
    daring to offer friendship, service and love to others.
Give us, O Lord, Christmas throughout the year. Amen.

(Korea)

33   The Virgin today gives birth to him who is above all
creation; and the earth offers the cave to him whom none
can approach. Angels and shepherds sing glory, and wise
men journey with a star, since for our sake he who is
eternally God has come as a new born child.

(Eastern Orthodox: Kontakion for the Nativity of Christ)

4

Christ's Presentation in the Temple in the Presence of the Elderly Simeon and Anna

'Then, after the purification had been completed in accordance with the law of Moses, they brought him up to Jerusalem to present him to the Lord . . .

There was at that time in Jerusalem a man called Simeon. This man was upright and devout, one who watched and waited for the restoration of Israel, and the Holy Spirit was upon him . . .

There was also a prophetess, Anna . . . She was a very old woman, who had lived seven years with her husband after she was first married, and then alone as a widow to the age of eighty-four. She never left the temple, but worshipped night and day with fasting and prayer. Coming up at that very moment, she gave thanks to God; and she talked about the child to all who were looking for the liberation of Jerusalem.'

(Luke 2:22, 25, 36–38)

1   O Lord Jesus Christ, who as a child was presented in the temple and received with joy by Simeon and Anna as the Redeemer of Israel: Mercifully grant that we, like them, may be guided by the Holy Spirit to acknowledge and love you unto our lives' end; who with God the Father, in the unity of the Holy Spirit, lives and reigns God, world without end.

(Church of South India: Feast of the Purification)

2   O God, grant that your spirit may move us to enter
your temple. Open our eyes that we may see your saving
grace, and stretch forth our hands to receive the Lord
who has come.

(China)

3   Lord our God,
as Simeon awaited the salvation of Israel,
you granted him the joy
of recognizing Christ in Mary's arms.
Strengthen the light of faith in us
that we may contemplate the divinity of your Son.
He humbled himself to raise us up to you,
and he reigns with you
for ever and ever.

(France: Cistercian Vespers)

4   Praise be to God, I have lived to see this day.
God's promise is fulfilled, and my duty done.
At last you have given me peace,
for I have seen with my own eyes
the salvation you have prepared for all nations –
a light to the world in its darkness,
and the glory of your people Israel.

(Nunc Dimittis)

5   Old Simeon had had a long life and now at last he had seen
the wonderful thing for which he had been waiting for
years. But he never intended his joyful utterance to be
translated into an Anglican lullaby accompanied by a slow,
dragging, soporific chant. He is calling upon the Lord to
send him out now. The words have a missionary intent; and

they are meant for young and old alike. Let us be sent out now, not with droopy lids and stifled yawns, but seized with a vision of salvation.

It has been prepared for years and has come to its fruition in Christ. But because Christ is true for every age it is also true that for every age there is a preparation of the gospel 'before the face of all people'. We come back once more to what God is preparing in the experience of those who do not acknowledge him; the people who adhere to the new religions of Japan, those who wrestle with existentialism in a South American university, or with nationalism in Africa, may all be undergoing a kind of preparation for the gospel. It all adds up to a light to lighten the world in its darkness. The message, if it is truly the message of Jesus Christ, is one for outsiders.

In many of our churches the lighting is arranged so that it draws attention to the central figure of our worship, the cross or the likeness of Jesus; and this is expressing something true. But in reality where Christ himself is the light he does the shining, and the spotlight is directed upon the poor and outcast; for this is where our Lord is most at home and this is where his mission is enacted.

(United Kingdom: meditation on the Nunc Dimittis)

6   Lord, you choose such strange people to be the vehicles of your grace. At times the touch of your fingers is so light and lovely and graceful. You go on surprising me. I don't ever want to get so old, or tired, or wise that I cannot be surprised by you. You have taught me never to take anyone for granted. They will come, you said, from the east and the west, from the north and the south, to sit at the feast of your kingdom, while the children of the kingdom might be cast out because they never really knew you. Help me today, Lord, to receive your grace and to recognize your sons and daughters, although they may be so anonymous.

(India: a response from Canon Subir Biswas to receiving a letter and a visit from two old people at the time of his last illness in a Calcutta hospital)

7   Lord Jesus, looking up as you once did into the eyes of the elderly Simeon and Anna, sensing their warmth and welcome; grant that we too may recognize and affirm the rich gifts of the elderly in our midst and submit ourselves to their loving embrace; as you, Lord, together with the Father and the Holy Spirit, watch and wait and welcome, ever world without end. Amen.

8   Father, there are those among us who like Simeon
have worked all their lives in your service.
Thank you for all they have taught us
and demonstrated to us of your kingdom.
Keep them fresh in their faith
and a continued inspiration to the young.
Make us sensitive to their growing physical needs
and give us a generous spirit in serving them.

(Prayer from Pakistan)

9   God who breathes life,
we thank you for all that has been done
by people past retiring age.
Thank you for John of Patmos, and for Anna and Simeon,
for the older people who keep communities together
in the countries of Central Africa and other places,
for the Mabels and Alfs who keep the churches ticking.
We thank you for the wisdom that experience offers:
may we acknowledge it.
We thank you for lives lived,
and continuing.

We ask for endurance and humour
against the infirmities and frustrations of age.
When the steps on to buses seem to get higher and higher,
when the shops seem further and further away,
when seeing the family is more demanding;
may help be close at hand.

And when we meet those who are dying,
we ask for their peace.
Help us to look into their faces,
with thin-veined ears,
with mouths slack and damp,
with clouded eyes;
and see people like ourselves,
romantic, hopeful, angry, giving;
people for whom a hanky
given for a drip on the chin
can be a love token;
people vulnerable as we are and will be;
people loved by you.

(Prayer suggested for use by members
of the United Reformed Church of Great Britain
on International Day for Elderly People)

10   Lord God, Eternal Father,
You have ordered the seasons of our lives.
We thank you for the elderly,
for their experience of life,
for their wisdom
and for all they did for us when we
were dependent upon them.
Now they are old and their strength is failing.
Show them the need for things to change.
Enable them to adopt new ideas.
Help them to feel wanted and loved.
Help us to give them the respect they desire

and the care they need.
Unite us all in the circle of Christian love and care.
For Jesus' sake. Amen.

(Kenya: prayer for old people)

11 We thank God for your life, service and sacrifice
We thank God for your faith in Christ
We thank you for running the race set by God
We thank God for your contribution to us and to the world.

We need you to remind us of sacrifices made for us
We need you to remind us of old values
We need you to remind us of our heritage in Christ
We need you to give us of your invaluable experience for
   our growth and development.

Forgive us if we have ignored you as persons
Forgive us if we have ill-treated you
Forgive us if we have used you for our own selfish ends
Forgive us if we have underestimated you as children of God.

You are golden
You are precious to God and to us
You welcome us into a circle of friendship larger than ourselves
You are important in God's sight.

(Malaysia: prayer-poem for old people)

12 Lord Jesus,
welcomed in infancy by the elderly widow Anna;
moved to compassion by a sorrowing widow in Nain;
touched by the giving of a poor woman in the temple;
mindful of your widowed mother at the cross,
and accepting the faithful support of widowed women
   among the travelling companions of your earthly life;
we ask you to bless and to accept the ministry of all of
   those who are widowed in Rwanda in these days,

and called to take on responsibilities formerly undertaken
by their menfolk.
Give them friends and a community to cherish both them
and their gifts;
and a lively sense of the communion of saints to encourage
and support them;
for your loving mercy's sake. Amen.

(Prayer based on 1 Timothy 5. The Association of Widows
of the Genocide of April 1994 supports the many
widows left to care for their family survivors
and to rebuild their devastated homes.)

13   Let the cry of widows, orphans and destitute children reach
your ears, O most merciful loving Saviour. Comfort them
with a mother's love, shield them from all harm and danger,
and bring them at last into your presence in heaven.

(England: John Cosin, 1595–1672)

14   O God, our heavenly Father, who does not want us, your
children, to be in sorrow, come down now and be with our
brothers and sisters who have lost their husbands/wives.
Comfort them during their hard times, when they are alone
at night or day; be with them to encourage and strengthen
them. May they pass their days here on earth in the
assurance that they will join you in your heavenly kingdom
where there will be no more sorrow, weeping or pain. Amen.

(Prayer of a Nigerian woman)

15   Open your hand and think on God's grace. To you are
freely given all the blessings of this life, placed in your open
hand. The gift of life itself; the love of parents; health and
vigour of body; joy of friends; enrichment of education; all
given into your open hand. Freely given is work, marriage,
children. But now, because we are susceptible to this
spiritual disease, when a gift is given, our reaction is to

close the hand, to keep the gift so that it might not slip away. But just as surely as God gives, he comes to claim the physical things; a parent, a marriage partner, our work, our physical health, at last life itself. And when the hand is closed, God's taking back hurts us. But keep the hand open. For as surely as God comes to take back that which he has given, it is only so that he might give us a greater gift.

(Meditation from Africa)

16 O Christ, my Lord, sometimes I wonder what you would have shown us of God's love of men and women, had they not crucified you but let you live on to old age. Surely you would have shown us how to accept the diminishments, the failing powers, the humiliations of old age. Your remark to Peter by the Sea of Galilee (John 21:18) tells us that you observed the limitations suffered by the old; and even now, dear Lord, you whisper in the hearts of your listening disciples the words you spoke to Paul 'My grace is sufficient for you, for my strength is made perfect in weakness.' Perhaps, dear Lord, the increasing weaknesses of age mean that we are being hollowed out of the physical, the material, the temporal, so that we may be filled with the eternal, that our mortality may be transformed into immortality.

(Bishop George Appleton)

17 Ageless God, let me not
just grow old.
Let me grow.

(USA)

18 Bless, O God, my weatherbeaten soul.

(West Indies: prayer of an old man)

19   Ancient gumtrees

Lord, your ancient, noble red gums
  scattered across the grass lands
  of southern plain and valleys,
never fail to move me,
awakening a mood
of admiration, awe,
and meditation.

Their weathered, warped limbs,
  gnarled and distorted
  like the arthritic limbs,
  hands and fingers,
  of one most dear to me,
insist on reaching
out and up
in some defiant ballet
of divine celebration.

Immense trunks,
  bent in a long-past
  sapling-youth
  by prevailing winds,
  and scarred from storms
  which centuries ago
  tore out limbs,
invite me to touch
and gently feel the texture,
or rest my cheek
in love.

Fed by massive, mis-shapen roots
  which, before my life began,
  had already explored
  the ground of their being
  and found it sufficient,
these old folk, Lord,

of your other kingdom,
share with me
the secret of grace.

(Australia)

20 O God, it was you who called me
and sent me to this place.
You know all about me –
the days I have lived
and the days that are left to me.
If it is your will to call me home
I leave the decision to you.

*(Rwanda: prayer of an Anglican priest, kidnapped
and shot during an incursion of terrorists in 1964)*

21 I have come a long way and sometimes my going has been too
slow, but now I have come to the ending of the way and I see
my resting place. I thank you my God for the long life you
have given to me your unprofitable servant. I rejoice in it
because it has enabled me to work hard and long in your field.

(Fiji: prayer of an old pastor)

22 O God, whose love has kept me vigorously and joyfully at
work in days gone by, and now sends me joyful and contented into silence and inactivity, grant that I may find happiness in you in all my solitary and quiet hours. In your
strength, O God, I bid farewell to all. The past you know: I
leave it at your feet. Grant me grace to respond to your
divine call, to leave all that is dear on earth, and to go out
alone to you. Behold, I come quickly, says the Lord.
Come, Lord Jesus.

(India: prayer of a priest in old age)

23   Lord God, you kept faith with Simeon and Anna
     and showed them the infant King.
     Give us grace to put all our trust in your promises,
     and the patience to wait for their fulfilment;
     through Jesus Christ our Lord. Amen.

(England: Eucharist of Candlemas)

5

The Mystery of Christ's Epiphany to Wise Men

'They opened their treasure chests and presented gifts to him: gold, frankincense, and myrrh.' (Matthew 2:11)

1   May it please you, O God,
      to accept this oblation to the birth of our Lord Jesus Christ;
      and thanks to this union, may we please him;
      for he rules over our nature.

                                        (Ambrosian Liturgy)

From earliest times the mysterious identity of the travellers from the east, and the origin and significance of their gifts, have led men and women of many different countries and traditions to identify their ancestors in the faith with the wise men of the gospel.

Local traditions, therefore, have the wise men coming from places as diverse as Iran, Afghanistan, India, China, the Philippines and the United Arab Emirates, and one legend even routes their journey through Europe! All find grounds for believing that the gifts and oblations of the magi originated in their particular country, and hold this journey to be a very important part of their spiritual and cultural inheritance. Artists, poets and hymn writers have added their weight to these traditions by portraying the wise men as members of different races and cultures.

Countless other Christians world-wide with no possible claim on such traditions have also sought to identify with different elements in the story – with the journey of faith, the offering of gifts, the gestures of homage and worship – and in this way have claimed their own share in the revelation of Christ to the nations.

2   O God our Creator,
in you alone are the riches of life.
We come from the East and we come from the West
believing we follow, on our different roads,
the same star to the same place.
May we share what we know of its light,
learn from each other the way to the stable,
worship you, our only wealth,
and serve the world with Gospel gold.
We make our prayer through Jesus Christ our Lord.

(Sri Lanka; United Kingdom: Companion link prayer)

3   O Christ, whose adoration at the hands of wise men of old speaks to us of the Spirit's unceasing activity in preparing the hearts of men and women to receive the good news of the word of God; renew in your Church an eagerness to carry your gospel to the whole world so that all creatures may adore you, the Lord of the universe.

(Orthodox)

Another interpretation of this mystery – favoured by some Christians – is that the wise men were the magicians of the ancient world, and that their gifts were in fact the tools of their trade offered up in submission to Christ; their rule of magic having been brought to an end by his coming. A reality which is expressed in many African prayers, not least those relating to the practice of juju and witchcraft.

4   You know, dear God
my people still believe much in juju.
But I don't believe in it any more,
since I believe in you.
But sometimes
I am afraid of it.

You are much stronger than juju,
Halleluja, Halleluja,
you are my God,
mine, mine, mine.
My great God,
strong, strong, strong.
My loving God,
loving, loving, loving.
My redeemer, my saviour,
my father, father, father.
My hut,
my shadow,
my redeemer, my redeemer, my redeemer,
You are my cave,
my door and my weapon,
when now
evil ones are making juju against me.
But you are still stronger,
much, much stronger.

(Ghana)

5   The witchdoctors tremble
and the magicians die
their work become as ashes.

But the word of Jesus is alive
harder than a stone,
sparkling more than any diamond.

From East to West
from North to South
from America to Madagascar.

Black or floury white
red or maize yellow
your Word gladdens all our hearts.

(Central African Republic)

6

Priest: From the attacks of wizards and witches
Congregation: Good Lord, deliver us
Priest: Over those who employ spirits against us
Congregation: Good Lord, give us victory
Priest: Over all bad and wicked juju-men
Congregation: Good Lord, give us victory.

*(African Independent Church. For wizards and witches
and juju, some might wish to substitute astrology,
horoscopes, seances, ouija boards and tarot cards.)*

7 Lord Jesus, whose birth, death and resurrection heralded the
end of the power of evil, have mercy upon all who have
recourse to fortune-tellers, and to magical and superstitious
practices in order to give meaning and direction to their lives;
and grant that they, with the wise men of old, may lay down
all such preoccupations, and worship you, who with the Father
and the Holy Spirit, are alone worthy of devotion and trust.
Amen.

8 The green mamba dies at the sight of Jesus
The cobra turns on its back, prostrate!
Jesus, you are the Hunter who has gone into the deep forest
In search of the evil spirit which has troubled hunters for
   many years.
You have killed the evil spirit, and cut off its head!
The drums of the king have announced it in the morning
All of your attendants lead the way, dancing with joy.

(Ghana: invocation of Jesus of the Deep Forest)

9 Lord of all might and majesty,
   bind the power of the Evil One
   block the progress of the Evil One
   banish the presence of the Evil One
   and free his prisoners.
Through the holy name of Jesus.

(United Kingdom)

10

Minister:	All our problems
People:	We send to the setting sun.
Minister:	All our difficulties
People:	We send to the setting sun.
Minister:	All the devil's works
People:	We send to the setting sun.
Minister:	All our hopes
People:	We set on the Risen Son.

(Kenya: traditional Turkana blessing – accompanied by a sweep of the arm, to the west at the first three responses, and to the east at the last)

11   Heavenly Father, who led the Wise Men by a star to your Son, born on earth for us; as we study the stars, turn our hearts and wills to you, the Creator, and to your Son our Saviour, Jesus Christ our Lord. Amen.

(United Kingdom)

12   O God, who by a star guided the Wise Men to the worship of your Son, lead, we pray, to yourself the wise and the great in every land, that unto you every knee may bow, and every thought be brought into captivity; through Jesus Christ our Lord.

(Church of South India)

13   Two thousand years have slipped by
like freshets in the Ganges
since St Thomas came to our land.
Here, though the cross is lifted
amidst the paddy fields and coconut palms,
and white-clad Christians flock to the churches
when the bells call them to worship;
our wise men have not yet seen the star,
and the manger of Bethlehem
is not yet the cradle of our land.

But Christian hope never dies
and the ends of the strands of destiny
are held safe in the hands of God.

Pass it on to the ends of the earth!
Christ is the answer – Ours! Yours!

(India)

14   Christ, the saviour of humankind, is the great light which
shines upon all peoples. But the very first to be called to
worship the holy infant were the wise men from the East.
Why them, in particular? Was it that the ancient cultures of
the East had received more of God's revelation and were
thus better prepared to accept Christ? Or was it that the
East stood in greater need of Christ because of the endless
river of tears which is its history? I do not know. Perhaps
the answer lies in the star that lit their path.

What I do know is that the East, in its recent history, has
been hammered on the anvil of extreme adversity, there
forged and tempered for over a hundred years. Precisely
because of this, should not the East be able to offer up an
even more refined gold when it worships Christ? Out of this
pain and agony, should not the East be ready to bring forth
even more fragrant frankincense and myrrh?

The wise men have already returned home, because people
from the East have a deep sense of attachment to their native
places. And yet, they haven't really gone far from the manger.
Don't you see them still, kneeling over the infant?

(China)

15   May Jesus Christ, the king of glory
help us to make use of all the myrrh that God sends,
and to offer him the true incense of our hearts;
for his name's sake.

(Germany: Johannes Tauler, 1300–61)

16 From a pure virgin by divine command appeared the
  light that lighteneth man's days.
A brilliant star proclaimed the glad event in the
  far heaven shone its ardent blaze.
The Persian magi saw the effulgent star, illumining
  the sky like solar rays.
Towards Bethlehem with joyful steps they sped to
  offer him their precious gift and praise.

  (Translation of words by the modern Persian poet,
  Hamidi, in the Church of St Simon the Zealot, Shiraz, Iran)

17 O merciful God, who in sending your Son into the world
granted unto certain Magi from the East the honour of
admission to the presence of the blessed babe; grant that
we, the Persians of this century, may enter into the holy
inheritance of our forefathers and bow before him who
with you and the Holy Spirit lives and rules, one God for
ever. Amen.

  (Iran: Collect for Epiphany)

18 O Lord almighty, who has mysteriously revealed to the
sages of old your ineffable presence in the depths of the
heart, grant to us and also to those of our brothers and
sisters who follow in their footsteps, that being led by your
Holy Spirit in this inward journey, we may discover there,
in the light incorruptible, your divine Son, Jesus Christ our
Lord, ever and ever. Amen.

  (Prayer of a North Indian Christian ashram
  for their neighbours of other faiths)

19 Even the most common changes
  in our lives
  are difficult:

to repair a leaking tap,
to start a more efficient book-keeping,
to re-arrange a room,
to clean a cupboard,
to write a letter,
to come to a reconciliation
and shake a hand.

It is often not done;
though the light appeared,
the idea flashed,
the star shone,
it was not followed,
nothing happened.
All remained the same.

Those three men
were wise,
because when they saw
that new star
indicating
    a new life,
    a new king,
    a new ruler,
    a new child
    they followed faithfully
    notwithstanding
    all the risks.

Let us follow it
too
until
we arrive.

(United Kingdom)

20   Give us, O God,
      the wisdom that comes from being willing to take risks,
      to follow intuitions and to travel in strange company

to that place where the ultimate wisdom lies revealed,
even Jesus Christ our Lord.

*(Lebanon: prayer inspired by the story
of a journey of faith taken together by
members of three different communities)*

21 O small Lord of the whole world
to whom at your Epiphany
came wise men
offering gifts of gold, frankincense and myrrh:
India's gifts came late
travel-worn, flood-drenched, dust-covered
yet still on time
for burial, if not for birth.
By hands of Mary: spikenard (very precious)
grown on Himalayan hills.
From Joseph (who also gave a tomb),
a winding sheet from hottest Sindh
for that cool body.
Of birth, they say, this land sees more than most,
of death, still more;
its constant meeting place at dawn and dusk
some little corner of hard-baked earth
where young and old (in Indian ways) are laid to rest.

O Lord,
with Mary's outpoured balm
and Joseph's burial sheet
given by this land;
accept also the costly offering
of the courage and fortitude of its many people,
and bless both gift and giver
with your risen, anointing presence.

*(Pakistan. This prayer, prompted by frequent funeral visits to
cemeteries in Pakistan's North West Frontier Province, arises
from a tradition that the cloth offered by Joseph of Arimathea
was made of the finest cotton produced in Sindh, and that
spikenard was extracted from plants grown in the
foothills of the Himalayas.)*

22 O God, who by the guiding of a star led the Wise Men to the holy crib, we thank you for guiding us to this blessed, quiet and hallowed place. Grant us seasonable weather, a prosperous journey, and guard us that we may arrive safely at our destination, both today and also beyond this life, through Jesus Christ our Lord. May the souls of the faithful, after the tensions of this world, rest in peace.

(United Kingdom: prayer of an unknown visitor to the ancient Anglo-Saxon church of Gregory Minster in the valley of Kirkdale, North Yorkshire)

23 We intercede before you for beloved Hindustan,
And our prayer is the same
As that of ancient seekers after you:
  'From darkness lead us to light,
  and from shadows to reality.'

Mercifully grant that the millions of this land,
Forever engaged in arduous pilgrimages
In search of peace and satisfaction,
May at last lay down their weary burdens
At the feet of Him who gives rest and peace
To all those who labour and are heavy laden.

May they come at last to the haven of peace,
Even Jesus Christ,
And find in him your own response
To their age-long quest.

To that end, may the frankincense of India's meditation,
The myrrh of its renunciation and sacrifice,
And the gold of its devotion,
Be laid at the feet of Jesus Christ,
And may He be crowned Lord of all. Amen.

(India)

24   And so, that is why, at nightfall when my people are asleep, kneeling barefoot, close to the altar of my little chapel, I become their intercessor – like Abraham, Jacob, Moses, like Jesus. A stick of sandalwood sends forth its fragrance, the symbol of all of those who today are worn out with their labours in suffering, or in love. And I am there, weighed down with all the faults of my people, afflicted with all their sorrows, heavy with all their hopes – all of those who today have fallen asleep thinking only to meet a Judge – to them I present him as their Saviour, and I introduce them to the eternal Nuptials. All those little children who were born this day I make children of God. All the prayers said today in the homes, the mosques, I transform into an 'Our Father'. My heart is nothing more than the melting pot, where, in the fire of Christ's love, all the dross of my people is turned into gold – and through my lips it is the whole of Afghanistan who cries that 'Abba' to the Father that the Holy Spirit inspires.

(Afghanistan)

25   O God, our Father, Creator of the Universe, whose Son Jesus Christ came to our world, pour your Holy Spirit upon your Church, that all the people of our world, being led through the knowledge of your truth to worship you, may offer the gold of intellect, the frankincense of devotion and the myrrh of discipline to him who, with you and the Holy Spirit, lives and reigns forever one God, world without end. Amen.

(Sri Lanka)

26   Let us present our offerings to the Lord, with reverence and godly fear.

(Church of India, Pakistan, Burma and Ceylon:
Invitation to the Offertory)

27

The representative of the West says: We offer to you, O King of earth and heaven, the gold of our costly service. Take the labour of our hands, the skill of our minds, the power of our organization. Purge us of pride, and stir us from sloth, that we, being refined by your grace, may become advocates and workers for your Kingdom, now and hereafter. Amen.

The representative of Asia says: We offer to you, our Lord and God, the incense of our worship and our prayer. You, by the gift of your Holy Spirit, have hung forth a star in the lowly heaven of every Christian soul; grant us with eager feet to follow wherever it leads, until our questioning hearts are blessed with the vision of yourself, our Heaven and our Home. Amen.

The representative of Africa says: We offer to you, O Man of Sorrows, the myrrh of your Church's sufferings. When we have nothing else to give, this offering remains. Where you are on the cross, there also may your servants be. May your perfect sacrifice avail to make our light afflictions redemptive in the world, that sharing the fellowship of your sufferings we may rejoice in the power of your resurrection, now and for ever. Amen.

(Ghana: adapted from a prayer used at the Assembly of the International Missionary Council, 1956)

6

A Sorrowful Mystery: The Suffering of Holy Innocents

'When Herod realized that the astrologers had tricked him he flew into a rage, and gave orders for the massacre of all the boys aged two years or under . . . So the words spoken through Jeremiah the prophet were fulfilled: "A voice was heard in Ramah, sobbing in bitter grief; it was Rachel weeping for her children and refusing to be comforted, because they were no more."'

(Matthew 2:16, 17, 18)

1   God keep you, O finest flowers of martyrs, who, at the dawn of life, were crushed by the persecutor of Christ and flung like petals before a furious wind.

You, the first to die for Christ, tender flocks of martyrs, now dance before the altar, now laugh candidly with your palms and garlands.

(Orthodox)

Herself the mother of a child with a severe mental handicap, a distinguished theologian has written of the occasion when she took her child to a Christmas celebration in an unfamiliar place and among unknown people. Feeling somewhat uncomfortable on her son's behalf lest he make a noise during the service, she suddenly became aware in the chapel of the presence of a statue of Our Lady. Pondering on how Mary might regard their presence there, she questions her in the words of the following poem which forms part of the introduction to her exploration of the theology of human suffering:

2   Mary, my child's lovely.
        Is yours lovely too?
        Little hands, little feet.
        Curly hair, smiles sweet.

        Mary, my child's broken.
        Is yours broken too?
        Crushed by affliction,
        Hurt by rejection,
        Disfigured, stricken,
        Silent submission.

        Mary, my heart's bursting.
        Is yours bursting too?
        Bursting with labour, travail and pain.
        Bursting with agony, ecstasy, gain.
        Bursting with sympathy, anger, compassion.
        Bursting with praising Love's transfiguration.

        Mary, my heart's joyful.
        Is yours joyful too?

                                        (Frances Young)

In the concluding section of her moving book, Professor Frances Young's answer to that question, reached after a good deal of theological reflection and much heart-searching, is unequivocally 'Yes'.

Confronted with the slaughter of innocent children, and aware that Mary's son was spared on that occasion only that he might face a future death that would enable him to identify with the sufferings of children of all time, our hearts too are full to bursting with the emotions – pain, agony, sympathy, compassion, angry questioning – described by Frances Young in respect of the needs of her own child. Her parallel experience of the mystery of such pain transfigured into praise and joy is also reflected in the thoughts and prayers that follow, as it has been in those of all suffering ce-lebrants of the Feast of Holy Innocents throughout the centuries.

3   Blessed Lord,
     whose life in this world began with the slaughter of the
     infants of Bethlehem, show compassion, we pray, on all
     who suffer and grieve because of the cruelty and injustice of
     the world, and teach both them and us that by your grace
     life's most bitter and painful things can be redeemed and
     turned to your praise.

4   I love you Lord Jesus.
     I do not reject you even when I get nervous once in a while,
          – even when I get confused.
     I love you with my arms, my legs, my head, my heart.
     I love you and I do not reject you, Jesus.
     I know that you love me, that you love me so much.
     I love you too, Jesus.

     (France, L'Arche Community: prayer of a mentally handicapped
     young man from Cork, Ireland. 'And as he prayed',
     writes Henri Nouwen, 'I looked at his beautiful, gentle
     face, and saw without any veil or cover his agony as
     well as his love. Who could not respond to a prayer like that?')

5   I meet him every moment
     your Son and our Brother Christ.
     Hunger causes physical, mental and moral damage.
     When I see the children of my people,
     the Silent World,
     wasted away, stomach distended,
     heads enormous and often very empty,
     retarded as if it were missing,
     it is Christ that I see.

     Mother, we understand each other so well
     that I have no need to explain
     or ask you anything.

I shall keep your statue
with the deformed Child
as in life, as in our world,
in which egoism breeds monsters.
Even when the Third World
gains a head and a voice,
the Child will continue to be headless
as a remembrance of the days of sorrow
that will belong for ever in the past.

> *(Brazil: Dom Helder Camara addressing the Virgin Mary on*
> *seeing a stone statue of her cradling in her arms an infant*
> *Christ whose head had been knocked off)*

6 Like you, Jesus,
who chose to be born in a difficult age
full of ambition and selfishness,
I, too, am fated to live
in a difficult moment of my country's history
when the poor are hated and to believe in you is a crime.
That's why it's hard to be a child,
and why today I ask you to hear me.

Like you, Jesus,
who, while still a child, the powerful wanted to kill,
today hundreds of children are tortured and murdered
together with their parents;
they burn our homes and fields,
many of us are left orphaned
and we flee to the mountains to hide,
without either food or clothing,
and with the memory of fire and of death
engraved for ever on our eyes.

This Christmas, infant Jesus,
I, who have heard the good news of the gospel,
want to thank you
for having been born poor and vulnerable to danger,

because that way you are present in me
so that wherever I am, inside or outside of Guatemala,
I become the hope that survives all massacres.

(Guatemala: prayer of a refugee child in Mexico)

7   I saw a child today, Lord, who will not die tonight, harried
into hunger's grave. He was bright and full of life because
his father had a job and feeds him, but somewhere, everywhere, ten thousand life-lamps will go out, and not be lit
again tomorrow. Lord, teach me my sin. Amen.

(Christian Aid: prayer of an African Christian)

8   Christ,
whose life in infancy was saved while others died, help us
to be sensitive towards those many circumstances in our
present world where many of us live and flourish at the
expense of others who die. Let not the death of innocents
around the world rest too easily upon our consciences, but
strengthen in us the resolve to search out all those places
where innocence is at risk at the hands of poverty, disease,
ignorance, market forces, exploitation, neglect and human
cruelty. Amen.

9   God almighty,
in your greatness you stooped to share human life
with the most defenceless of your creatures.
May we who have received these gifts of your passion
rejoice in celebrating the wordless witness
of the holy innocents to your Son our Lord.

(England: Eucharist for Holy Innocents)

10 Dear Lord, I pray for innocent babies who are handicapped. They may feel out of place, rejected and not wanted, but through loving parents and friends and neighbours show them that you really love them, Lord, so that they grow to know and follow you faithfully. Through Christ, I pray. Amen.

(Prayer written by a group of Ugandan women)

11 'His widespread wings will fill the breadth of your land, O Immanuel.' This was the cry of the prophet Isaiah which he had seen in a vision.

Where the waters of the river overflow its banks,
I entreat you Immanuel,
spread your wings and protect your children from the flood!
Where famine yet rages,
I entreat you, O Immanuel,
spread your wings, protect your children from starvation!
Where the butcher's knife sheds the blood of innocents,
I entreat you, O Immanuel,
spread your wings, protect your children that their corpses
    shall not cover the wilderness!

O Immanuel, you provide for the birds of the air, how can you allow humanity, created in your image, to die on the barren earth? Abel's blood cried out to you from the earth, and you sought after him. Can you then allow the blood of innocents to be shed?

O Immanuel, spread your wings, I entreat you,
fill the breadth of your land and cover the children who
    dwell here!

(China: based on Isaiah 8:8)

12   God of the dispossessed,
      defender of the helpless,
      you grieve with all the women who weep,
      because their children are no more;
      may we also refuse to be comforted
      until the violence of the strong
      has been confounded,
      and the broken victims have been set free
      in the name of Jesus Christ. Amen.

(United Kingdom: Janet Morley)

13   Almighty God
      surround us with your presence.
      Grant us a vision of our city;
      a city of justice where none shall prey on others.
      A city of generosity,
      where vice and poverty shall cease to exist.
      A city of companionship, a city of peace, a city of love.
      Hear, O Lord
      the silent prayer of our hearts,
      for the capture of the person or persons
      responsible for the deaths of our children
      and for those who are missing.
      Hear our prayer, O Lord,
      in the name of your son Jesus. Amen.

(USA. This prayer, following the unsolved murder of black children in the city of Atlanta in 1981, has continued to be used on behalf of street children murdered, misused or missing in many other cities around the world.)

14   Good Jesus,
      as with mixed feelings we contemplate
      your escape from the fate
      of the other innocent infants of Bethlehem;

so we also share the mixed emotions
of relief and thankfulness, grief and guilt,
felt by those parents whose children survived
the massacre of infants in Dunblane.

And as we weep with those in Dunblane
who mourn the death of their children;
we remember those who grieved over your death,
but eventually entered into the experience
of your living presence.

And though the manner of your death,
for which you were preserved from infancy,
speaks few words, offers no easy explanations,
and answers no questions,
our trust is that over the course of time
it will heal the wounds
and ease the sorrows of your people
in this and every place.

To this end, good Jesus, hear our prayer.

(Scotland. In Dunblane, Scotland, on 13 March 1996,
sixteen small children and their teacher were shot dead in their
primary school. 'With distraught mothers hurrying towards
the school, with hardly a word exchanged between them, the
road to Dunblane Primary School on that fateful Wednesday
morning seemed like the road to Calvary.')

Expressing in a single word the grief and sense of outrage felt on account of the atrocities which society allows to be committed against successive generations of its innocent children, a card accompanying a bunch of flowers left outside the school after the massacre simply asked: Why?

Echoing the lament of the Hebrew women and the questioning prayer of psalmists and prophets, and of Jesus himself on the cross, many contemporary Christians in different parts of the world have come to regard lament and questioning as vital elements in their response to events in the world around them.

15 Almighty God,
you have brought us together in this place
we have asked each other many questions
and heard many answers.
Help us to live with the questions
that have no ready answers,
save in the love of Jesus Christ our Lord.

(Prayer on a visit to East Germany, 1980)

16 **The killing of the children: a litany of intercession**

A sound is heard in Ramah,
the sound of bitter weeping.
Rachel is crying for her children;
she refuses to be comforted;
for they are dead.

Pray for the holy innocents of Israel,
victims of fear and anti-Semitism.

Lord have mercy upon us, Christ have mercy upon us.

A sound is heard in Gaza,
the sound of bitter weeping.
Pray for the holy innocents of the camps,
victims of displacement and injustice.

Lord have mercy upon us, Christ have mercy upon us.

A sound is heard in Mogadishu,
the sound of bitter weeping.
Pray for the holy innocents of Somalia,
victims of war and famine.

Lord have mercy upon us, Christ have mercy upon us.

A sound is heard in Sarajevo,
the sound of bitter weeping.

Pray for the holy innocents of Bosnia, Croatia, Serbia,
victims of hatred and hysterical stupidity.

Lord have mercy upon us, Christ have mercy upon us.

A sound is heard in Bangkok,
the sound of bitter weeping.
Pray for the holy innocents of Thailand,
victims of lust and poverty.

Lord have mercy upon us, Christ have mercy upon us.

A sound is heard in London,
the sound of bitter weeping.
Pray for the holy innocents of Britain,
victims of indifference and greed.

Lord have mercy upon us, Christ have mercy upon us.

A sound is heard in our own town,
the sound of bitter weeping.
Pray for the holy innocents in our midst,
victims of violence and selfishness.

Lord have mercy upon us, Christ have mercy upon us.

> *(Scotland: taken from a litany of the Iona Community.*
> *The full litany includes many other countries and needs.)*

17 Lord Jesus, as we celebrate your birth at Christmas, and
join in the associated festivities, we remember those
innocent victims of all ages who are slaughtered on our
roads as a result of drink and careless driving.

Lord, it is so painful for their relatives and friends to lose a
loved one in such a violent and needless way. Like Rachel,
they weep and refuse to be comforted. Lord, we ask that
you will give them comfort and strength.

Help all of us, in our giving and receiving of hospitality, to drive
on our roads with thoughtfulness and consideration. Amen.

> *(United Kingdom)*

18   God, what kind of world is this
that the adult people
are going to leave for us children?
There is fighting everywhere
and they tell us we live in a time of peace.
You are the only one who can help us.
Lord, give us a new world
in which we can be happy
in which we can have friends
and work together
for a good future.
A world in which there will not be
any cruel people
who seek to destroy us and our world
in so many ways. Amen.

(Liberia: a child's prayer)

19   We remember today, O God, the slaughter of the holy
innocents of Bethlehem by King Herod. Receive, we pray,
into the arms of your mercy all innocent victims; and by
your great might frustrate the designs of evil tyrants and
establish your rule of justice, love and peace, through Jesus
Christ our Lord, who lives and reigns with you, in the unity
of the Holy Spirit, one God, for ever and ever. Amen.

(Episcopal Church of the USA)

7

The Flight into Egypt

'So Joseph got up, took mother and child by night, and sought refuge with them in Egypt, where he stayed till Herod's death.' (Matthew 2:14–15)

1   God of grace and providence,
    Lord of our going out and of our coming in,
    we pray for Egypt,
    shelter of the Holy Family from the old tyranny of Herod
    and first resting place of the manger of the eternal glory.
    Bless her land and people,
    once entertaining unawares the earth's redeemer.
    Make the Church in Egypt
    the patient means of your purpose
    and ready custodian of the peace of Christ,
    ever left with his servants
    and ever passing through and from them
    for the saving of the world.
    We pray in his name. Amen.
                        (Kenneth Cragg: one-time assistant bishop in Egypt)

A stone recently unearthed by workmen engaged on routine repair work on the Bethlehem to Jerusalem road, and traditionally held to be the rock on which Mary rested, has led to the discovery in that place of the mosaic floor of an early Byzantine church commemorating the flight of the Holy Family into Egypt – an event sometimes known as one of the seven sorrowful mysteries of Mary. Thus, from very earliest times the mystery of Christ's exile in Egypt, as recorded by the Gospel writer Matthew, has held an honoured place in the imaginations and devotions of Christian people.

For believers in Egypt, for instance, it has long been a matter of considerable pride that their land and forebears once offered refuge to the Holy Family. For others in today's world, finding themselves among the millions in flight from drought and famine, war and oppression, the mystery of Christ's flight into Egypt has become an essential ingredient of their spirituality, the subject of their story-telling and the substance of their prayer and lamentation and song.

Indeed, for many Christians the reality of exile and flight has become so commonplace that, as in the case of a prayer from South Africa, personal acquaintance with at least one refugee is taken for granted. Sensitive and close acquaintance with a particular refugee is also evident in the prayers of a sponsor in the USA who struggles to enter into the hurt and need of the exile, while resisting the temptation to do things for him which might best be left undone, or be left to God to do in his own time and in his own way.

Uniting their prayers and actions on behalf of today's fugitives with those of Jesus and his parents in the mystery of their flight into Egypt, and in this way seeking to strike the right balance between doing and not doing, is the clear intent of those who wrote a number of the prayers that follow. Others identify strongly with the Holy Family – or with one or another of its members – in the wide range of emotions which they must have experienced during that flight. Many spiritual writers and artists have discerned special qualities in the response of the Holy Family to these painful events, including, according to Charles de Foucauld, 'contemplation and adoration and joy'. This insight might alert the users of these prayers to the presence of similar qualities and spiritual gifts in the lives of many contemporary refugees, in a manner which reflects the sorrowful and joyous nature of this mystery.

2   O God of the ever present crosses,
      help your servants.
                                        (Egypt: 4th century)

3   I have great devotion to the Flight into Egypt. I love in my
      comings and goings to think of the journey of Jesus and his
      parents, and to unite myself to him and try to imitate their
      contemplation and adoration and joy. We, too, have the
      Beloved always with us.
                          *(Algeria: Charles de Foucauld, among
                          the Tuaregs of the Hoggar, Tamanrasset)*

4   My Egyptian heart longs, O my God, for the redemption of
my people. It has been our shame that the oppression of the
Pharaohs drove the children of Israel to the sea. But you, my
God, who free us from our sins, you who make all things
new, chose this same country as a shelter for the Holy Family
and a home to that One who was persecuted and oppressed,
that we might have life and have it abundantly.

Thank you, my Saviour, for the greatest gift you have given
me. As a little girl my heart bubbled with joy every time I was
taken to play under the tree in Materiah where you rested with
Mary, your mother, and Joseph. I loved to touch the stone
upon which your crib was placed in that dark underground
church in old Cairo. I felt your presence. I heard your cry and
laughter. I wept with the mothers whose children were killed
by Herod. I rejoiced over your safety. I praised and continue to
praise you, my Saviour and Redeemer, who take us out of
darkness into your marvellous light.

(Egypt. a Coptic Christian)

5   Lord,
I would take Mary, Joseph and the child
safely to Africa;
on hidden roads
not known to Herod
nor to any foreign power.

(Ghana)

6   Lord Jesus, who as a child was subject with your parents
to the flight into Egypt; we give thanks for this place which
once served as a sanctuary and refuge for your people from
Jerusalem, and is thereby hallowed and blessed as a place
of shelter and hospitality. We ask you to bless all who in
our day must flee from oppressive regimes, and all who

welcome them. Bless all who chronicle their plight and seek
to relieve it through prayer, publicity, gifts and political
action. O Lord, make haste to help them.

> *(Jordan. Inspired by a visit to Pella, one of the Decapolis
> cities, to which early Christians fled and found refuge
> before the fall of Jerusalem in AD 70, this prayer can be
> adapted for present-day places of sanctuary.)*

7   Help us, Lord, who are the privileged inn-keepers of our
day, to find room for those who are driven from their
homelands because of political, racial or religious reasons.
Amen.

> *(Australia)*

8   Almighty God, you whose own Son had to face the evil
plans of King Herod and seek refuge in a strange land, we
bring before you the needs of the many refugees throughout
the world, particularly those in Africa. We pray for those
personally known to us whom we now name before you . . .

> *(South Africa)*

9   Lord, our everlasting God, we pray for our family members
and relatives at large, that you may grant us peace and
mercy. We pray that we may find the new place safe. We
pray that we may find this new place in a peaceful manner
because in your presence everything is all right. We pray
that we may not find terror in this place, and that you
will give us courage and strength to overcome Satan's
temptations. We know that your Son Jesus Christ overcame
Satan; may our spirits be strong enough to overcome his
temptations. We ask this in the name of the Father, the Son
and the Holy Spirit. Amen.

> *(Prayer of four Ugandan women)*

10 Christ, who in infancy was carried to safety in the arms of your parents, have in your safe keeping all those who today must flee from danger and tyranny, and bring them safely to their journey's end. Amen.

11 O Lord Jesus Christ, who as a boy lived as a refugee by the banks of the Nile, have compassion on all the refugees in the Sudan, the land of the Niles; and help and encourage all those who attempt to relieve their distress. Amen.

(United Kingdom)

12 Like Mary, I too had to flee when they persecuted my family. They cut my husband and two elder sons to pieces, accusing them of learning communism from Catholic religious education classes. I left my home with my other three children and walked and walked until finally I was brought here. I think that Mary deeply understands the mothers of our country because she underwent what we are suffering today. She now pleads with her son for our children when we no longer have the strength to do so.

(El Salvador: a woman in flight)

13 In films sometimes people are followed.
Let the feet of the follower
become as heavy
as lead,
so that they can
no longer run.

(Germany: a child's prayer for fugitives)

14 Lord, as once you took flight into Egypt
with Mary and Joseph
and came to our continent of Africa
as a Holy Family of squatters:

Give, we ask you,
the families of the townships
peace among themselves and hope for the future.

(South Africa: the Crossroads township)

15   Jesus, you lived in exile in Egypt:
be with all migrant workers and protect their families.

(Province of Central Africa: Ukaristia)

16   Lord God, I can feel the pain suffered by this refugee;
the remembrance of friends killed on the streets,
the memories of tear-gas, beatings and cramped prison cell.
The lack of a job – another kind of hell for a person of
    independence and strength.
The lack of English – another kind of prison for a person of
    intellect and warmth.
The longing for the familiar, comforting sounds and scenes
    of home.
The realistic worry for the family left behind.

My heart is filled with the longing to comfort and soothe
    with my human warmth and words.
Lead me from this temptation.
Grant me the ability to allow freedom to this person to
    suffer pain, the consequence of past decisions.
Grant me the ability to refrain from smothering with well
    intended care.
Grant me the ability to avoid confusing and burdening this
    refugee with my own concerns and needs. Amen.

Oh God, one more person has one more idea for one more
    thing I should do for this refugee. Oh God, deliver me.
Amen.

(USA: prayers of a refugee sponsor)

17   Spirit of Jesus, if I love my neighbour
      out of my knowledge, leisure, power or wealth,
      help me to understand the shame and anger:
      of helplessness that hates my power to help.

                  (Brian Wren: opening verse of a hymn inspired
                          by a study tour to South Africa in 1973)

18   Almighty God, our Father, in the name of Jesus I come to
      you with supplications. You are Immanuel, God with us.
      You love us all. We know that you are not happy when
      your people are in desperate conditions. The hostilities have
      made us refugees in our own land. We are without enough
      clothes, not enough food, and yet our gardens are not
      cultivated because we left them, and live in camps far away.
      One day we are under burning sun; another day under
      heavy rain. Our children do not go to school.

      O Lord, help us to overcome this situation. O Lord, stop
      the fighting and resolve its original causes. O Lord, we pray
      for the restoration of peace in our country, so that we may
      go back to our own place and cultivate our gardens to feed
      our families.

      O Lord, we know that you bore our nation's sin at the
      cross. Listen and intervene quickly. Many people –
      especially children and old people – are dying every day in
      our camps. Young people are weakened every day. Lord
      Jesus, look on displaced peoples' camps and react to their
      unhygienic conditions.

      My Saviour, in you there is hope; you are the Risen Lord; you
      are the King of Kings; you are the Mighty Saviour; you are
      the Prince of Peace. Come Jesus, come and bring us peace.

                          (Rwanda: prayer of a displaced woman)

19   Almighty God, we pray for all bombed out, burned out, driven out pilgrims in this world. Forgive us our part in uprooting them. Restore their lives, renew our commitment, and make us partners with them in the rebuilding of their farms and cities, their homes and their lives. We pray in the name of him who had no place to lay his head, your Son, Jesus Christ our Lord.

(USA)

20   For refugees and other displaced persons who have been forced from homes and security, we pray to the Lord.
Lord, hear our prayer.

For the people and land from which refugees have fled, we pray to the Lord.
Lord, hear our prayer.

For the humane and constitutional treatment of refugees in our nation, we pray to the Lord.
Lord, hear our prayer.

For the perception to see Christ in the strangers we welcome, we pray to the Lord.
Lord, hear our prayer.

(USA)

21   Give comfort, O Lord, to all who are torn away from their homes and their loved ones by war, famine or the cruelty of their fellows. Grant that we who dwell secure in an insecure world may be generous in caring for our displaced sisters and brothers.

'After Herod's death an angel of the Lord appeared in a dream to Joseph in Egypt and said to him, "Get up, take the child and his mother, and go to the land of Israel, for those who threatened the child's life are dead." So he got up, took mother and child with him, and came to the land of Israel. But when he heard that Archelaus had succeeded his father Herod as king of Judea, he was afraid to go there. Directed by a dream, he withdrew to the region of Galilee, where he settled in a town called Nazareth.'

(Matthew 2:19–23)

22   Holy Traveller Jesus,
you who were acquainted with the processes
of uprooting and journeying;
and who came from a people
whose songs were of removal and pilgrimage;
from earliest childhood you moved quickly
(and abruptly, with little notice; circuitously)
from Bethlehem to Egypt and back again to Nazareth;
and later, in the company of your parents,
you regularly walked the long, uphill road to Jerusalem.
Was it from such experiences
that you took your picture of your Father's house
as having within it many resting places,
and urged your followers to travel unencumbered?
Holy Traveller Jesus,
be with us in all our removing.

(Prayer based on John 14:1–4 and Luke 10:4)

23   O God,
the guardian and guide of the Holy Family
in their return and resettlement after exile in Egypt;
we thank you for the dreams and visions and songs
which sustain and guide so many returning exiles today;
and we pray that they may be fully realized.
To this end, O God, we ask your blessing and protection
   upon them;
and upon members of peace-keeping forces
and all others, who as companions and advocates
   and observers
travel with them to their journey's end. Amen.

24   Like you, Jesus
who fled to Egypt to save yourself,
I have wandered through the mountains
to arrive at this sister country
where I am called 'refugee'.

Like you, Jesus
I have left behind the country I love with my whole heart
and I want to return to it, as you did
the day when the powerful died
and peace was born again.

May we and all the children of Guatemala
who are growing up in exile, like you, child Jesus,
know how to prepare ourselves for our return
so that tomorrow we may discover how to build your kingdom,
the kingdom of the poor,
in a new Guatemala.

(Guatemala: prayer of a refugee child)

25 We still pray, we still sing
We still dream of the day
when the birds will return
and the flowers
and our lost loved ones.

We still live with the belief
that love and gentleness and faith
will blossom forth one day
like roses in winter.

We still believe that God
will be born again in our land
as we prepare the stable of our hearts
for the birth of a new people.

(Greeting from Salvadoran refugees in Honduras,
to Guatemalan refugees in Mexico)

8

The Mysteries of Nazareth

Annunciation

'In the sixth month the Angel Gabriel was sent by God to Nazareth, a town in Galilee, with a message for a girl betrothed to a man named Joseph, a descendant of David; the girl's name was Mary . . . Then the angel said to her, "Do not be afraid, Mary, for God has been gracious to you; you will conceive and give birth to a son, and you are to give him the name Jesus."' (Luke 1:26–27, 30–31)

1   May the Spirit who overshadowed Mary
come upon your Church also,
and make her the earthly sign of your love,
through Jesus, the Christ, our Lord.

*(France: Cistercian, Praise at Dawn,
The Annunciation of the Lord)*

2   O God, grant that always,
at all times and in all places
in all things both small and great
we may ever do your most holy will
and be Jesus Christ's faithful servants
and handmaids to our lives' end. Amen.

*(Bangladesh: prayer used daily by a small group
of young Bengali nuns, Christa Sevika Sangha,
the Little Handmaids of Christ)*

3   O God,
you fulfil our desire
beyond what we can bear;
as Mary gave her appalled assent
to your intimate promise,
so may we open ourselves also
to contain your life within us,
through Jesus Christ. Amen.

(United Kingdom: Janet Morley)

4   O God, you used Naomi and Ruth
simple women who thought they were nobodies,
to build your nation.
You, who chose a simple village maiden
to be the mother of your son – use me, Lord.
You, who can put down the arrogant of heart and mind,
and raise the humble and weak – use us, Lord.
Help us to be ready when your call comes
and to commit ourselves to your service.

(Sri Lanka: Fellowship of the Least Coin)

5   Lord, you have called me and I come. I have spoken with
the voice you gave me. I have written with the words which
you taught me. So I pass along the road like an over-laden
donkey, with hanging head. I am ready to go wherever and
whenever you wish. The Angelus is ringing . . .

(France: annunciation to an old woman, Luke 1:5–45)

One of my childhood memories is that of my mother keeping a box.
Although containing a rag-bag of items, the box was a treasure trove to us
children, and one to which we rarely had access, and usually only then as a
last desperate measure to keep us amused and occupied during childhood ill-
nesses, or at other times when we had reached the end of our own resources.
It contained, I recall, things like a fourpenny piece, a couple of lockets,

letters tied with ribbon, pressed flowers, a scentcard, and treasured photographs. There were highly coloured postcards of the kind sent back from the trenches in the 1914–18 war, decorations from wedding cakes, a piece of lace, and a medal or two.

And then there were other, sadder, items, which I didn't really understand: faded newspaper cuttings; a man in soldier's uniform who, I was informed, never returned from the war; a photograph of a rather sad looking lady, my grandmother, whom I never knew. There was the birth certificate of my elder brother who died in infancy, a poppy, and some cards with heavy black lines all around them.

Just such as these were Mary's memories; a mixture of sadness and joy, treasured up, and then, in response to the interest of the early Church, and during difficult days for that first Christian community, opened up so that they might be shared by the Gospel writers.

Some of these treasured memories, like those concerning the birth of Jesus and his presentation in the temple; and more painful recollections like those of the family's flight into Egypt, and the slaughter of the innocent children, have already been touched upon. Others – joyful, sorrowful, glorious – will emerge in connection with the Mysteries of the Ministry of Jesus, his Transfiguration, Journey to Jerusalem, and later with his Death, Resurrection and Ascension, all of which follow.

It is on a selection of these Mysteries, using beads as a tactile aid to meditation, that the devotion known as the Rosary is based, interspersing reflections on these different episodes in the life of Jesus and that of his mother with prayers, and in this way attempting to relate them to the life and circumstances of those who are praying.

6   Mary, wellspring of peace
      be our guide.
    Model of strength
      be our guide.
    Model of gentleness
      be our guide.
    Model of trust
      be our guide.
    Model of courage
      be our guide.

Model of patience
  be our guide.
Model of risk
  be our guide.
Model of openness
  be our guide.
Model of perseverance
  be our guide.

(Asia: from a Litany of Mary of Nazareth)

Childhood

'*When they had done everything prescribed in the law of the Lord, they returned to Galilee to their own town of Nazareth. The child grew big and strong and full of wisdom; and God's favour was upon him.' (Luke 2:39–40)*

7

Leader: Jesus, we want to grow in knowledge.
All: Help us to grow in body, mind and spirit.
Leader: Jesus, we want to grow in faith.
All: We thank you for the people of faith in bible times and in our times whose lives are an example to us.
Leader: Jesus, we want to grow in hope.
All: We pray for all who are helping to bring freedom, peace and justice in our world.
Leader: Jesus, we want to grow in love.
All: Help us to love one another as you have loved us and given yourself for us. We pray for those who today are giving their lives for others.

(Africa: prepared by women on behalf of their children)

8

Our heavenly Father and our God,
we praise you because you made us
and protect us under your wings,
like a hen protecting her chicks.

We are children and we need to learn.
Put the knowledge that is being taught us firmly in our minds.
This is the prayer of your earthly children,
spoken with lips that speak amiss.
As we bring this prayer to an end,
widen and deepen it in our hearts.
For the sake of Jesus Christ who died for us,
and whose name will endure for ever. Amen.

(Papua New Guinea: prayer of a 15-year-old girl)

9   Lord,
make what happened to Jesus
happen to us.

(A child's prayer)

10   Thank you, dear Lord, from the bottom of our hearts,
for our food and our clothes, and for everything. Amen.

(Prayer of a Palestinian child)

11   My God, I praise you, I thank you for my mother.
For all that she could give me,
for all that she gave of herself,
a true, living school of love and humility.
She revealed to me your mystery –
thank you for her revelation of your truth.

Now, O God, I pray for all the children
of Africa, of Asia,
of America and Europe.
For all the children of the world.
Give me a heart like that of a mother
the heart of a black woman for her children.

(Central African Republic)

12   O God, you are both Father and Mother, whom we love
and honour.

(USA)

13   O God, who called blessed Joseph to be the faithful
guardian of your only-begotten Son, and the spouse of his
virgin Mother: Give us grace to follow his example in
constant worship and obedience to your commands, that
our homes may be sanctified by your presence, and our
children nurtured in your fear and love; through the same
Jesus Christ our Lord.

(Church of India, Pakistan, Burma and Ceylon:
Joseph, foster-father of our Lord)

14   O Lord of life, make our lives clear spaces where children may
find happiness and law: through Jesus Christ our Lord. Amen.

(USA)

15   Our Heavenly Father,
thank you for the joy which our children bring us.
As we love them,
help us to show your love
to those who do not know loving parents.
Show us our responsibility towards them.

Especially we pray for children,
who, because they are blind, deaf, disabled
or without parents, cannot live at home,
that they, and those who care for them,
may know that they are your children
and part of the Christian family.

We ask these things in the name of Jesus
through whom we call you Father. Amen.

(Kenya)

16 God our Father, all parenthood comes from you. Allow all the children who have lost their parents to understand your love for the world; send your Holy Spirit to lead them in their ways, through Christ our Lord.

(Prayer of a Sudanese woman)

17 O God our Father,
thank you that Jesus grew up in all the normal and
unremarkable ways of a child of his time and culture; and
that knowing you with the simple love and trust of a child, he
came to respond to you in faith and obedience as your son.

Father, let us not dress up the child Jesus in false miracle
and pious fantasy, but revere him as one who went through
the same developmental processes as our children. After
his example may they enjoy the freedom to work and
play and live and grow, and thus become your mature sons
and daughters.

(Czech Republic: prayer on seeing The Child of Prague. *This
gorgeously apparelled figure of Christ, dressed as a king, in a
Prague church, gives rise to a Catholic joke in which Mary
remonstrates with Jesus, saying firmly 'I don't care who your
father is, you're not going out to play in those clothes!')*

18 O Lord, beginning from the first cry in the manger,
and sustained in the family life of Nazareth,
this mystery is to be wondered at,
and allowed to permeate the worshipping life of every
     congregation:
that you too could be young!

19 God, it may be worldly wisdom that we should grow less
dependent on our mother's anchal as we mature in age. But
teach us that it is spiritual wisdom and, indeed, your will

for us, that we grow closer to your anchal and hold on to it more fervently, day by day.

May we have your wisdom, courage and, at times, temerity to wave your anchal so high above everything else that all can discern its graceful patterns and admire its gorgeous designs.

And God, make sure that your anchal for ever flows longer and wider that it embraces all children around the world in its loving and intricate folds.

> *(India/Pakistan: prayer of a Christian couple on the birth of their daughter, named Anchal. Anchal is the name given in Sanskrit to the colourful and finely decorated end of the sari. Young children often hang on to their mother's anchal giving it the poetic significance of maternal love, protection and solace.)*

Adolescence

'When they could not find him they returned to Jerusalem to look for him; and after three days they found him sitting in the temple surrounded by the teachers, listening to them and putting questions . . . His mother said to him, "My son, why have you treated us like this? Your father and I have been anxiously searching for you." "Why did you search for me?" he said. "Did you not know that I was bound to be in my Father's house?" But they did not understand what he meant. Then he went back with them to Nazareth, and continued to be under their authority.' (Luke 2:45, 46, 48–51)

20 Jesus, you sat among the learned,
listening and asking them questions:
inspire all who teach and all who learn.

> *(Central Africa: Ukaristia)*

21 In the course of our spiritual journey, it often happens that we think Jesus is still at our side when actually he hasn't been walking with us for some time. And far more than once, when we have gone seeking him with hurt feelings, his

response has been, 'How is it that you have sought me?' But we have never understood his words, because we do not understand his heart.

We are also going to Jerusalem, but we only go at the appointed times, following the rules. We make the sacrifice, we keep our 'Passover', but when we have done what is required, we return to our own path, assuming that Christ will be with us on the way we have laid out for ourselves. The result is that day by day, year after year, we walk without God.

O Lord, help us to understand what is in your heart, to follow in your footsteps. Save us from our own stupidity, in which we expect you to follow us. Amen.

(China)

22 O God,
whose only Son was sought by his distraught family and found in the Temple; be present to all parents whose children have disappeared, or run away, or for any other reason become separated from them. In the continued absence of their children may they be sustained and comforted, and in the happy event of their discovery, may they be reunited and give thanks to you, the true home of all your children.

23 Lord God,
we pray for the young runaways of our country;
bless all who work with them, and grant:
that their hurt may be healed,
their sense of belonging increased,
their humanity enhanced,
their health and safety preserved;
and that the experience of your presence
may be made ever more real to them,
through Jesus Christ our Lord.

(United Kingdom)

24   Lord Jesus, thank you for your word in the Bible that gives me hope. I pray for all young people who have gone astray, that you will bring them back to the fold and bless them and lead them aright.

This, my son, in particular has gone off the track . . . You alone know where he is . . . Draw him out of the net he has entangled himself in and save him, for your name's sake. Amen.

(Sierra Leone: prayer of a desperate mother)

25   God, we ain't so strong
and get scared easy –
We hope you will
hang around with us
so we won't get scared
and get bad ideas
or get hurt.

(USA: prayer of a delinquent teenager)

26   God, our Father and our Mother,
we think of Joseph and Mary, searching desperately for their son and yours, until at last they found him in the Temple. Look, we pray you in your mercy, on those in many lands today who search unwearingly for a disappeared son, daughter, husband, wife or father. For their sake we beg that some may yet be found and restored to homes and families, and that at the last, these and all your children may be held safe and at peace in your keeping.

27   Loving Father,
your young and loveable Son
was found amidst the teachers of the law

listening and enquiring of them;
have pity on the young people of South Africa
who in the quest for freedom and a better future
have fled from home and forsaken their families;
sustain them in all danger,
give them your wisdom and protection
and let their every sacrifice
yield peace, justice and freedom in their day

(South Africa)

28   Lord
I could use your help.

(Prayer of an American teenager)

29   Heavenly Father,
you who taught your Son all he knew in a situation where
everything was in a state of transition, bless, we pray you,
children and teachers and parents in those many countries
where education is continually interrupted by political
instability and civil strife. Give to children wisdom in
learning from what is going on around them, and education
in church and school to equip them for the future, assured
of your Son's presence with them.

(Prayer based on some words from Madagascar)

30   O Lord, the ally and aid of the young, we thank you that
you have called us at the outset of our lives to follow you.
Grant that we may dedicate our youthful powers to your
service, and, fixing our gaze on your shining countenance
may we dutifully and faithfully serve you to the end of our
days: and this we ask of your divine love.

(Iran: prayer used by a group of young people)

31   Son of the carpenter,
      enable all young people with vision,
      courage, confidence and skills;
      may they live productive lives
      with their self-worth and dignity enhanced;
      may they become useful citizens of their country,
      and living stones in the house of God;
      unite us all in you, the chief cornerstone,
      Jesus Christ our Lord.

(The Caribbean)

'"Nazareth!" Nathanael exclaimed. "Can anything good come from Nazareth?" Philip said, "Come and see."'
(John 1:46)

32   Living as a young person in Nazareth even today is quite dull.
(Nazareth: young Orthodox Christian)

33   Almighty God, whose only begotten Son proclaimed the
      gospel in the villages of his childhood: hear our prayers for
      those who are called to live out their faith in the community
      of their birth and grant that they may be sustained by the
      peace and confidence of those who have trusted in you;
      through Christ our Lord. Amen.

(United Kingdom)

34   Lord Jesus,
      in and through those early years spent in your own
          small town in Nazareth
      you became our companion in the mediocrity of our most
          ordinary days;
      so that, in every solitary and insignificant moment,
      in every tedious and unwanted occupation,
      and in the hidden places of our greyest hours,
      we might know that you have passed this way before.

(Italy: based on some words by Luigi Santucci)

35 Blessed Jesus,
who as a young person once experienced the pull and
fascination of people and places beyond those of your own
family circle and environment, bless the questioning spirit in
all young people, quieten the anxiety of their parents, and
help parents and young people alike to see this world as
your Father's house, and the well-being of all its children as
your Father's business. Amen.

Anointing

'He came to Nazareth, where he had been brought up, and
went to the synagogue on the sabbath day as he regularly did.
He stood up to read the lesson and was handed the scroll of
the prophet Isaiah. He opened the scroll and found the passage which says,

"The spirit of the Lord is upon me
because he has anointed me;
he has sent me to announce good news to the poor,
to proclaim release for prisoners
and recovery of sight for the blind;
to let the broken victims go free,
to proclaim the year of the Lord's favour."

He rolled up the scroll, gave it back to the attendant, and sat
down . . . "Today", he said, "in your hearing this text has
come true."' (Luke 4:16–21)

36 Come Holy Spirit, grant us the Gospel of Jubilee, the good
news of liberation, freedom and unity; proclaim the release
of the prisoners of division; recover the sight of those
blinded by hatred, jealousy, greed and power; grant peace
and freedom to the poor, oppressed and lost.
(Korea: prayers for 1995 as a Year of Jubilee for Unification)

37 Creator God,
help us to remember that Jesus
always spoke for the weak and gave them
a message of hope.
Help us to accept his calling
to work for the weak and oppressed.

(Pakistan)

38 There are no prophecies. Only life
continuously acts as prophet.
The end approaches, days grow shorter.
You took a servant's form. Hosanna.

I searched for singers and for prophets
who wait by the ladder to heaven,
see signs of the mysterious end,
sing songs beyond our comprehension.

And I found people who were restless, orphaned, poor,
drunk, despairing, useless,
lost whichever way they went,
homeless, naked, lacking bread.

*(France. This poem was written among the homeless and
outcasts of Paris by Mother Maria Skobtsova, 1891–1945,
a Russian Orthodox nun, active in the resistance movement,
who died in Ravensbruck concentration camp.)*

39 O God, enable those people in oppressive poverty and in
bonded labour to struggle for their rights. Raise up those
who will fight for justice on their behalf. Let justice and
righteousness prevail.

(Pakistan)

40   O Lord and heavenly Father, we commend to your care the men, women and children of our country and of all Africa who are suffering distress and anxiety because of lack of food. Strengthen and support them, we pray, and grant that the world may grow in understanding of your ways and in sharing with each other the good gifts which you have given to us; for Jesus Christ's sake. Amen.

(Kenya: prayer for the hungry)

41   Lord, forgive me for becoming accustomed to looking at children who appear to be eight-year-olds when they are already thirteen;

forgive me for becoming accustomed to sloshing through mud puddles which I can leave behind me – they cannot;

forgive me for learning to shut out the smell of open sewers which I can leave behind me – they cannot;

forgive me for turning on my lights automatically, forgetting those who have no lights to turn on;

forgive me for telling them that 'Man cannot live by bread alone' without joining them in their struggle for bread.

Lord, I want to love them for who they are – help me;
I dream of dying for them – help me to live for them;
I want to be with them when the light breaks through –
   help me.

(Argentina: member of the Third World Priest Movement assassinated in 1974 by right-wing gunmen)

42   Creator God, our heavenly Father,
your Son was a carpenter in Nazareth:
we pray for all those who labour
in our factories and shops.
Grant them wisdom and honesty, strength and skill,

to provide for themselves
and for the needs of our country.
Look with compassion on the landless poor,
the unemployed and homeless,
the orphans and the hungry,
and grant us your power to work towards justice
in transforming their lives for your glory;
through our risen Lord Jesus Christ,
who had nowhere to lay his head.

(Kenya)

43 Lord, you came to preach the gospel to the poor, and
proclaim deliverance to the captives and sight to the blind,
drive out from our people the spirit of fear and let your
light shine upon them, O Sun of Righteousness.

(South India: daily prayer for village people
at the Christukula Ashram)

44 Jesus, divine Prisoner,
who came into your synagogue at Nazareth
proclaiming release for the captives.
Release men and women from the suspicion and fear
that pushes others into isolation and darkness.

45 When the Lord comes, he always makes for the temples,
cathedrals, churches, synagogues, mosques and monasteries
first. Change must begin there.

O Christ in the synagogue at Nazareth.
O Christ in the pulpits of our churches.
O Risen and Cosmic Christ,
O Voice of the Compassionate and Righteous God,
give us no peace
until we become renewed workers for your gospel.

(Jerusalem: George Appleton)

46 Jesus of Nazareth,
whose habit was always to take your place in the synagogue
  on the sabbath day,
inspire with your presence the life of the Church in every place,
that every congregation may be as a city set on a hill,
a reminder of your claims upon its worship and service
a powerhouse of prayer and concern
a community of love
a source of joy and comfort
and a stimulus to action
to all who gather there. Amen.

> *(United Kingdom: adapted from a*
> *prayer of Peter Green of Salford)*

47 O Spirit of the poor man of Galilee
fall upon this church.

> *(Jordan: prayer of an Orthodox Christian)*

48 Lord God,
renew your Church and
  begin with me;
heal our land, tend our
  wounds, make us one
and use us in your service
  for Jesus Christ's sake. Amen.

> *(Kenya)*

49 O Lord of the Saturday synagogue sermon,
in my buying and selling this weekend,
in my deciding, in my giving,
in my reading of newspapers, watching of TV,
talk with friends and family, give me
a leaning towards the poor
a special expectancy of finding you with those people in those
places to which your words and your heart lead you.

50 Feverishly we clung together in prayer,
in fellowship groups we confessed our sins
and condemned the world.
Together we huddled in the church
to shut away the anguish of the freedom fighters,
the agonies of the politicians,
the conflict of the present situation.
From our painted church window
we see the shadows of those dashing to and fro.
We hear the cry of the mother
deprived of her husband.
No, we cannot stand it any longer.
Dimly but clearly we hear Him cry.
A few heard the voice, stood and left the church.
The door of the church was shut behind them,
and there with Him they joined the conflict.

(Africa: Bethel A. Kiplagat)

51 Help us, good Lord, to take on in your name
the risks involved in the struggle for peace and justice.

*(France: prepared for the Ecumenical Forum of European
Christian Women)*

9

The Mystery of the Baptism of Christ

'During a general baptism of the people, when Jesus too had been baptized and was praying, heaven opened and the Holy Spirit descended on him in bodily form like a dove, and there came a voice from heaven. "You are my beloved son; in you I delight."' (Luke 3:21–22)

1   Father, dear Father, we do not understand what it meant for your Son to be baptized at the lowest place on earth; but we thank you that he was willing to become one of us in our humiliation, that we might become one with him in glory.

(United Kingdom)

2   O God,
Although we sometimes elevate and rarefy the presence of the dove at your Son's baptism, help us to remember what common, ordinary birds these were that served as an offering at your Son's presentation at the temple, and as a sign of his sonship and calling at his baptism. We thank you for all everyday birds fed by children and old people in city squares and back yards. Grant that we too may look for the confirmation of our calling in all such places, surrounded by ordinary people and mediated by such humble means. For the sake of Jesus. Amen.

3   They would circle about in the smoke-filled sky
Giving colour to the twisted gloom;
Lumps of beauty in the midst of haze;
The Holy Ghost's image above the Cwm.

The Holy Ghost sanctifying the smoke,
Turning worker to person of flesh and blood.
The cash nexus transformed in the order of grace
And the Unions part of the household of God.

(Wales: Gwenallt Jones, 'Pigeons')

4   O God, baptize our hearts into a sense of the needs and
conditions of all.

(England: George Fox, 1624–91)

5   This morning I found a pigeon's feather on the floor. I do
not know how it was left in this prison cell. For a moment I
was absorbed thinking about doves in the biblical passages,
the accounts of the great deluge and of Jesus' baptism in the
river Jordan, and so forth. I was naturally led to think of
hope and peace in Korea. I was somewhat piously asking
myself whether there will be hope and peace in the near
future. Also I was thinking of the resurrection from
suffocating social and political tensions. I trust that we all
have a new heaven and a new earth, breaking through the
cosmic sea of darkness. I am looking forward to breathing
the air of freedom under a new heaven.

(Korea: written by a Christian student of Seoul National
University undergoing a heavy prison sentence for
demonstrating in favour of the re-unification of Korea)

6   Living God, the heavens opened
and the Spirit descended upon Christ.
We pray that the faith may spread among all peoples,
and that those who believe, freed from slavery,
may recognize themselves in your beloved Son,
Jesus, our Lord.

(France: Cistercian, Praise at Vespers)

7   If people want to look into their own mystery – the meaning
     of their pain, of their work, of their suffering, of their hope –
     let them put themselves next to Christ. I cannot explain that
     mystery except by returning to Christ, who gives authentic
     features to a person who wants to be genuinely human.

                                    (Brazil: Dom Helder Camara)

8   Servant Christ,
     help us to follow you deep into the waters of Baptism;
     to link our lives with all those who grieve
     about the unjust way of our human life;
     to break free from the chains of past wrongs;
     to become fit to face your coming new age;
     to be renewed by your Spirit, anointed to preach.

     Servant Christ,
     help us to follow you deep into the waters of Baptism,
              (India: Litany of the Disciples of Christ the Servant)

9   Lord God, help us who have dipped a foot into the waters
     of life to plunge in over our heads, dead to the old ways
     and fully alive to the new, for the sake of Jesus, who gave
     his life for those He loved. Amen.

                                              (United Kingdom)

10   Lord God, gracious and merciful,
     you anointed your beloved Son with the Holy Spirit
     at his baptism in the Jordan,
     and you consecrated him prophet, priest and king:
     pour out your Spirit upon us again
     that we may be faithful to our baptismal calling,
     ardently desire the communion of Christ's body and blood,
     and serve the poor of your people and all who need your love,

though Jesus Christ, your Son, our Lord, who lives and reigns with you in the unity of the Holy Spirit, ever one God, world without end. Amen.

(Lima Liturgy: drawn up specially for the Faith and Order Commission of the WCC meeting in Lima, Peru, January 1982)

'John said "I baptize you with water, for repentance; but the one who comes after me is mightier than I am . . . He will baptize you with the Holy Spirit and with fire. His winnowing-shovel is ready in his hand and he will clear his threshing-floor; he will gather the wheat into his granary, but the chaff he will burn on a fire that can never be put out."'

(Matthew 3:11–12)

11 Come O Christ
with your winnowing-shovel.
Enter our institutions and each of our lives,
and by your presence in our midst
remove from them all that is hollow and husk-like,
nourish our bodies with wholesome grain
and give substance to our determination
to share your good gifts with all in any kind of need.

12 O God, we dedicate this threshing-floor to you. May all the grain that is threshed here be used for your glory alone. May your angels guard this place and these your servants who will here thresh the grain you have given. Grant that of all this precious grain none be lost, but that all may be used to feed your hungry children. May all that eat it know that of your grace and love you give them bread in due season. May even the little birds of your creation who shall glean their food here be conscious of the heavenly Father's care, through Jesus Christ our Lord, who is the true Bread of Life come down from heaven. Amen.

(India. Originally offered by Christian villagers at the dedication of a threshing floor, this is also used as a prayer for the purifying of the Church and its stewardship of the gifts of creation.)

13 Lord, enable us to know, not only your mercy, but your strict discipline, not only your pity and grace, but also your anger and power. May your Church, through the baptism of the Holy Spirit and through fire, be made pure and without flaw!

(China)

14 Lord,
strengthen me to bear the scorching fire of your love
so that you may find a home in my heart
in the day of your coming. Amen.

(United Kingdom)

15 In his diary, a visitor to the Holy Land writes of time spent with a Christian priest and a small community devoted to prayer, fasting and hospitality in the old city of Jerusalem, and in particular of a memorable day spent with his host in the Judean wilderness.

He describes how they were walking in the desert hills near the Jerusalem to Jericho road, in the region of Jesus' baptism and temptations. They had just come in sight of a monastery set in the cleft of a rock, deep in the side of a great valley. As they gazed down on that dramatic chasm, his companion stood forth in his faded brown cassock, eyes gleaming, and read out an incident from one of the Sayings of the Desert Fathers, originating in just such a setting as this. The story concerned Abbot Lot, who on one occasion came to visit Abbot Joseph, and sought his advice and counsel as follows:

'Father, according as I am able, I keep my little rule, and my little fast, my prayer, meditation and contemplative silence; and according as I am able, I strive to purify my thoughts; now, what more should I do?' Whereupon the old man stood up and stretched his hands towards heaven. His fingers became like ten lamps of fire, as he said to him, 'Why not become all flame?'

And, concluded the visitor, his companion, savouring the story with characteristic zest as they clambered down over the rocks, murmured again several times the words 'Why not? Why not?'

(Incident related in Jerusalem Diary, *Simon Barrington-Ward)*

16 O God, fan to flame in me and in your Church the fire of your life which has burnt low.

(Church of South India)

17 Hitherto I have lived like a clod on this earth; henceforth let me burn out for God.

(Iran: Henry Martyn of Shiraz)

18 Saturate me with the oil of the Spirit that I may be a flame. But flame is transient, often short-lived. Can you bear this, my soul – short life? In me there dwells the Spirit of the Great Short-Lived, whose zeal for God's house consumed him. Make me your fuel, Flame of God.

(Uruguay. Reflecting on the words of Hebrews 1:7 'He makes his ministers a flame of fire', this prayer, together with the question 'Am I ignitable?', was found in the diary of the North American missionary, Jim Elliot, after his death.)

19 Pray for all ministers who have borne the hot coal of his word upon their lips and in their lives.

(USA: Bidding in Washington's National Cathedral)

20   Unless the eye catch fire
       The God will not be seen.
    Unless the ear catch fire
       The God will not be heard.
    Unless the tongue catch fire
       The God will not be named.
    Unless the heart catch fire
       The God will not be known.

Everything that touches you shall burn you.
Do not ask where it will be,
or when it will be,
or how it will be.
On a mountain or in prison
or in a desert or in a concentration camp
or in a hospital or at Gethsemane.

It does not matter.
So do not ask me, because I am not going to tell you.
You will not know, until you are in it.
But you shall taste the true solitude of my anguish and of
    my poverty.
I shall lead you into high places of my joy and you shall die
    with me.
And find all things in my mercy
which has created you for this end
that you may become the brother of God
and learn to know the Christ of the burnt men.

(USA: Thomas Merton)

21   Lord,
    remind us of the truth
    that if we would be as lights in the world
    we must also endure the burning.

(Philippines)

22   In the desert of our petrified souls, without shade or water, appears John the Baptist, calling upon us to repent, and to look upon the Lamb of God who carries our sins. Then the Lord appears, sanctified by the Father's Spirit and blessed by his voice. Let us worship the Holy Trinity for the salvation that Christ brings us.

Holy Father, you called us out of the desert of our sins to share in your everlasting kingdom. Help us by the power of your Spirit to live in your presence.

Holy Son, you have by your humility blessed the waters of Jordan; bless our lives, and send your Holy Spirit to abide with us and renew us from within.

Holy Spirit, purify our bodies, sanctify us, and make us a temple where you will be permanently present.

Holy Trinity, bless our coming together in your name. Deliver us from the evil one, lead us into your truth and renew in us the image of your likeness of your being, for you are both the source and goal of our life. Amen.

(Lebanon)

10
Stations in the Wilderness

1   The word of the Lord came saying
'Go out and stand in the desert, in the presence of God.'
Then a great and awesome fire swallowed the sky,
but God was not in the fire.
After the fire came a mighty wind,
but God was not in the wind.
After the wind came blasting explosions under the earth,
shattering rock and melting sand,
but God was not in the blasting.
After the blasting came a gentle whisper
'What are you doing here?'

> *(USA. In the Nevada desert thousands of people*
> *come together each Lent to pray and to protest*
> *the evil of nuclear weapons testing.)*

2   Spirit of truth and judgement,
who alone can exorcize
the powers that grip our world;
at the point of crisis
give us your discernment,
that we may accurately name what is evil,
and know the way that leads to peace,
through Jesus Christ. Amen.

> *(United Kingdom: Janet Morley)*

'*Full of the Holy Spirit, Jesus returned from the Jordan, and for forty days he wandered in the wilderness, led by the Spirit and tempted by the devil. During that time he ate nothing, and at the end of it he was famished.*' *(Luke 4:1–2)*

3   Lord Jesus,
in your struggle with Satan in the desert,
you taught us that we do not live by bread alone.
May fasting and prayer increase in us a hunger for your word,
and dispose our hearts to welcome it,
from this day and for ever.

(France: Cistercian, Praise at Dawn)

4   Those who went freely to the desert to experience and share
the suffering and poverty that millions endured without
choice did so for one overriding reason: because God went
there first . . . And if, however mixed their motives, their
apparently useless self-sacrifice could be united with Christ's
and in some way made redemptive, as they believed his to
have been, then their prayer in the desert might not only
change their lives: it might also change the world.
     It is this above all which animated the desert people . . .
They saw prayer not as a technique to be employed and
fine-tuned, but as a life to be embarked upon in direct
imitation of Christ, sharing the poverty and homelessness
and insecurity which were once his.

(United Kingdom: Gordon Mursell, exploring
the significance of the desert people)

5   Lord,
teach us to pray
as you also prayed
in the wilderness.

(Prayer from the Sahel)

6   O God,
we pray for those places in the world
made awful by climatic conditions;
places of intense cold, and heat and drought,
places of great hardship and privation,
where man, woman and beast are constantly endangered
by the elements and environment.
We give thanks for all that sustains and helps them,
and pray that such may be multiplied
in the hands of Jesus Christ and those who serve in his name.
Amen.

(Prayer for drought-prone Botswana)

7   My God, I'm hot.
Sweat trickles down everywhere.
Clothes hang damp and crumpled.
Eyes close so soon after waking.
Feet are tired and swollen.
Tempers are short.
Rooms are dark, heavy, blanketed in heat.
Water is in short supply, and is ever lukewarm.
Arms stick to tables and saturate writing paper.

My God I'm hot.
But each drop of sweat, every temptation to irritation,
help me to offer to you,
on behalf of those who have no possibility of escape from
    the burden of heat:
        the chronically sick,
        the elderly,
        fever-ridden, pale children,
        the mother who waves the hand-fan and brushes off
            the flies,
        youngsters waiting their turn in the queue for water,
        the father who is sent heavy-hearted for a white sheet
            and a string of jasmine blossoms, for a funeral.

My God, unite my present unspeakably trivial discomfort
to the blood and sweat of Jesus in the desert and in the garden,
on behalf of this hot, dry land and its needy people. Amen.

(Pakistan)

8   O Lord,
to all who, giving themselves to the care of the poor and
handicapped of the world, find themselves confronting
fearful beasts in their own desert places; grant the
awareness of your presence and succour in that wilderness.

(After some words by a L'Arche Community helper)

9   Servant Christ,
help us to follow you into the desert,
with you to fast, denying false luxury,
refusing the tempting ways of self-indulgence,
the way of success at all costs,
the way of coercive persuasion.

Servant Christ, help us to follow you.

(India: Litany of the Disciples of Christ the Servant)

10   If a parting word may be of any help in hours of dark
trial and temptation, when the fierce heat dries the bones,
and the dark dust glooms the house, and all work seems
weariness, and you retain no strength, when Satan seems
to triumph and to send dark messages to your soul:

O, get to Christ,
live at the Master's feet.
Live in his word,
abide in him.

*(Pakistan: from a diary entry in 1893 of one
of the earliest missionary evangelists)*

11   O Christ,
guide and strengthen all who are tempted in this hour.
(United Kingdom: USPG)

12   O Almighty God,
help us not to give place to self-preoccupation,
which, snake-like and venomous,
winds its way so effortlessly into thought and action;
but to take it into the desert with Christ
and to throttle it.
(Prayer based on some words of
Temple Gairdner of Cairo, 1873–1928)

13   Grant, O God,
that in all our time of testing and self-questioning
we may know your presence
and seek your will
through the grace of Christ our Lord.

14   From the cowardice that dare not face new truth;
from the laziness that is contented with half truth;
from the arrogance that thinks it knows all truth;
Good Lord, deliver me.
(Kenya)

15   Grant, O Lord,
that I may not fail you
in the moment of truth,
of temptation,
of crisis,
of opportunity.
(Jerusalem: George Appleton)

16   Lord,
first let us hear the voice
crying in the wilderness of our own hearts

*(England: prayer based on
some words of George Fox, 1624–91)*

17   Lord, I am in the wilderness – and find it very hard. It is hot
during the day and cold during the night, and I am used to
a moderate climate. The ground is sandy, and my feet are
tired. I was excited when I started off, but now . . .

Lord, help me to go forward, not because I know where
I'm going or how to get there, but because you are with me
– Emmanuel.

(Prayer of an Indian Christian, recalling the Exodus journey)

18   Lord,
free us from falling into the sin
of believing that the slavery in Egypt
is better than the struggles in the desert.

(Nicaragua)

19   O my Lord, I am in a dry land, all dried up and cracked by
the violence of the north wind and the cold; but as you see,
I ask for nothing more; you will send me both dew and
warmth when it pleases you.

(France: St Jeanne de Chantal, 1572–1641)

20   My Lord God,
give me once more the courage to hope;
merciful God, let me hope once again,
fructify my barren and infertile mind.

(Denmark: Søren Kierkegaard, 1813–55)

21 I have chosen. And I have chosen life, and claimed your covenant, and set my face to walk your ways, towards that 'destination which God offers me'.
And then?
THUD
Flat on my silly face, miles off track, enticed away by some elementary temptation,
the same old world, or flesh, or devil,
and all my choice, and resolution, and commitment
all to do again.

And yet not all.
You take my choices, Lord, for what they are.
I could not choose except your Spirit prompted me.
And after that, it is in your salvation, not my choosing
that hope of heaven rests.
(United Kingdom: from a prayer
by Bishop Timothy Dudley-Smith)

22 Lord, grant that I may be one with you in choosing and rejecting, that I may be unable to choose or reject except as you would do.
(Germany: Thomas à Kempis)

23 If this obstacle is from you, Lord, I accept it; but if it is from the Evil One, I refuse him and all his works in the name of Calvary.
(China: a pioneer missionary)

24 Lord, our minds become bewildered and our lives frustrated by the problems of wealth and poverty, obesity and wasting, power and powerlessness, stones and bread.
We are tempted to leave the problems in your hands,
and turn away from our responsibilities.

Forgive us for wanting you to be merely the miracle worker.
Guide and inspire us at all times to do what is right,
honest, just and sincere in your sight.
Make us both hearers and doers of your word.

*(The Pacific. In some areas of the Pacific the stones have yielded
rich deposits of phosphates, and Christians face stark
choices regarding stewardship of the earth's resources.)*

*'You have stood firmly by me in my times of trial; and I now
entrust to you the kingdom which my Father entrusted to me.'
(Luke 22:28–29)*

25   Lord,
you were not only tempted for forty days down by the Jordan
but constantly all through your ministry.

Not to obvious blatant sins
but to the subtler deflections from the Father's will;
to cunning compromise which would defeat the Father's
    purpose:

As when the presence of the seeking Greeks
suggested the possibility of a wider mission
in which you might have been listened to and welcomed,
without the necessity of the cross.

As when in the Garden of Olives across the valley,
you wrestled with the doubt that death could be the
    Father's will.

Or when, in the presence of Pilate
you might have pleaded your case with your accusers;
or in those fiercest moments of pain,
acquiesced to the mocking cry of the crowd to
    'Come down from the cross and we will believe'.

Until one temptation remained –
the final test, the last claim of love,
the fiercest attack of evil –
more subtle and shattering than the rest,
when, cloaked in a blanket of darkness
came the whispering doubt:
    What if God too has forsaken you?

And at last, the battle done, the last temptation met,
faith complete, the task finished, evil defeated,
love triumphant, you said:
    'Father into your hands I commend my spirit –
    the rest lies with you, Father, dear Father.'

And then it was that by the cross with its limp body
there must surely have sounded the voice from heaven
    once more:
    'This is my beloved Son.'
    Son in call,
    Son in obedience,
    Son in love
    Son in death and in triumphant life.

(Meditation on Luke 22:28, adapted from a prayer
of George Appleton, one-time Archbishop in Jerusalem)

11

The New Route

'Here I stand knocking at the door; if anyone hears my voice and opens the door, I will come in and he and I will eat together.' (Revelation 3:20)

Telling of a visit made some years ago to Archbishop Janani Luwum in Uganda, an English bishop describes sitting with his host on the verandah of the archbishop's house in Kampala a few weeks before Janani was killed; and speaks of the archbishop telling him that for some time now he had had to travel home each day by a different route to avoid being shot. The visitor suggested to the archbishop that for his own safety's sake he ought perhaps to consider leaving the country. A foolish and unworthy suggestion, reminiscent of Peter's words to Jesus, and one that he came to regret. The archbishop replied that in this re-ordering of his life, with all the uncertainties that it had brought, God had been at work in his heart. 'Every day I have been broken before him', he said. 'How could I leave my people at this time?' 'And', recalled the visitor, 'as he spoke those words his face shone with grace and power; this man who had been broken every day.'

This story gives sharp edge to 'the new route' that many Latin American Christians have felt called to follow in recent years; a new route which for them in their very different circumstances also carries with it the real possibility of suffering and death. Starting from the promise of Jesus in Revelation 3:20, they speak of a journey characterized by a combination of 'welcome, active watchfulness, confidence and courage'; all of which are reflected in the prayers that follow.

For Jesus and his first disciples this new route was inaugurated at his baptism, testing in the wilderness and proclamation in the synagogue at Nazareth; and led by a number of circuitous paths into desert places, up a mountain, across the lake; whilst healing, teaching, preaching and doing good wherever he went. Sometimes this involved back-tracking, taking alternative routes and rejecting the ways others would have him go.

There is much evidence to suggest that Jesus regarded all such routing and re-routing, not as isolated and random events but as part of a sequence of opportunities and choices which were to lead to a growing awareness of his own messianic identity, and a closer alignment of his own will to that of his heavenly Father.

The call to follow

'Jesus was walking by the sea of Galilee when he saw two brothers, Simon called Peter and his brother Andrew, casting a net into the lake; for they were fishermen. Jesus said to them, "Come with me, and I will make you fishers of men." At once they left their nets and followed him.'
(Matthew 4:18–20)

1   Blessed are you, O Christ, who revealed your wisdom to simple fishermen, sending upon them from above your Holy Spirit, and thereby catching the universe as in a net. Glory to you O lover of all humankind.

(Russian Orthodox: Troparion for Pentecost)

2   Jesus!
You are the God of all drummers,
who is seen in the moon beating your drum.
As your young maidens dance around you,
soldiers, police and crowds of young men
leap in jubilation.
Priests and pastors in procession
thousands of them . . .

(Ghana: invocation of Jesus of the Deep Forest)

3   Lord, let it not be that I follow you merely for the sake of following a leader, but let me respond to you as Lord and Master of every step I take. Amen.

(Prayer used in Pakistan)

4   O Lord, who promised to the fishermen Andrew and Simon
Peter that they would be fishers of men, grant to us your
followers today that our nets of care and concern may be
cast as wide and as deep as your great love.

5   Lord Jesus Christ,
alive and at large in the world,
help me to follow and find you there today
in the places where I work,
meet people, spend money
and make plans.
Take me as a disciple of your kingdom
to see through your eyes
and hear the questions you are asking,
to welcome all with your trust and truth,
and to change the things that contradict God's love
by the power of your cross
and the freedom of your Spirit.

(United Kingdom)

6   O God,
help me to walk in the boots of the miner,
the shoes of the trader,
the moccasins of the trapper,
and in the sandals of Jesus Christ the Master,
and to see others as he would see them.

(Canada: an Indian prayer from the far north)

7   Almighty God,
we thank you that our living Lord,
your divine Son, has two hands;
one to point the way,
and the other to beckon us forward.
Summoned and encouraged by his Spirit
may we follow without delay.

Teaching and preaching

'So Jesus went round all the towns and villages teaching in their synagogues, proclaiming the good news of the kingdom . . . The sight of the crowds moved him to pity: they were like sheep without a shepherd, harassed and helpless.'
(Matthew 9:35–36)

8   Lord Jesus, our great shepherd,
we pray for all who teach and serve in your name:
for clergy, catechists, lay readers, teachers.
Encourage them in times of difficulty.
Keep them humble when things go well.
Strengthen them when they are tempted.
May your word be ever in their hearts and upon their lips.

(Kenya)

9   Father of all,
you have called your Church into being
in every corner of the world.
We commit to you all pastors and evangelists.
Watch over them as they travel and keep them safe.
Fire their hearts with love for you,
that they may draw many to you.

(Myanmar)

10   O Almighty God,
I am but the basket of the sower.
Grant that those
among whom I sow the seed
may look
not at the meanness of the basket,
but to the sower
who is Christ himself.

(Prayer based on some words of
St Augustine of Hippo, 354–430)

11 Wide spaces, O Lord, and rural patterns, sundry peoples and
anxious days, as of old in Galilee when the gospel first was
heard in the preaching of Jesus the Christ; look now we pray
on your Church in this land, that the word may be heard,
disciples multiplied, evils exorcized and souls healed. Give
courage, patience and strength to all who go out in your
name to serve and save their peoples, with whom, praying in
that same name, we are one, even in Jesus our Redeemer.

(Prayer for Uganda)

12 O Lord and Master, who are yourself the truth and the way,
we thank you for the fellowship of your people in which the
unknown are well known, and the stranger is at home.
Make our hearts and minds so to welcome your words that
in us they may richly dwell and from us may surely pass on
their way into all the world.

13 Lord, you made us known to friends we did not know, and
you have given us seats in homes which are not our own.
You have brought the distant near, and made a brother/
sister of a stranger.
Forgive us, Lord . . .
we did not introduce you.

(Polynesia)

14 We seek our brothers and sisters,
and find them only
when we open our hearts to them.
We must speak your word to them aright.
They must understand.
Otherwise they are lost . . .
Come, Holy Spirit,
prepare us
to enter the huts of others. Amen.

(Ghana)

15 O God our Father,
Give us a passion for your Word
and boldness in telling our neighbour about your grace.
May the Holy Spirit convict the lost
and draw them to the Saviour, Jesus Christ our Lord.

(Kenya)

16 O God,
this is the thing I most would hate:
to be casually caught
by a pin on a string
and some tired old bait.

Rather, may I be caught and held
by your wonderful story
freshly told.

(USA)

17 Lord, we pray that in all our encounters and conversations
your story may be enthusiastically told, and your loving
presence acknowledged.

18 I read
in a book
that a man called
Christ
went about doing good.
It is very disconcerting
to me
that I am so easily
satisfied
with just
going about.

(Japan: Toyohiko Kagawa)

Healing

*'At sunset all who had friends ill with diseases of one kind or
another brought them to him; and he laid his hands on them
one by one and healed them.' (Luke 4:40)*

19   Jesus, you cured by your healing touch and word:
heal the sick and bless all who minister to them.

(Central Africa: Ukaristia)

20   Mighty and Living God, your Son Jesus Christ healed the
sick and restored them to abundant life. Look with mercy
on the pain and suffering of this world and restore each
person and each nation by your healing power, through our
Lord and Saviour Jesus Christ. Amen.

*(Pakistan: prayer written by a young Christian
woman from a Muslim background)*

21   Giver of good gifts, we are waiting for you.
And the sick are waiting for medicine.
O Jesus, you have swallowed death
and every kind of disease
and have made us whole again.

(Ghana: invocation of Jesus of the Deep Forest)

22   Men hate me for the curse I bear,
    (I know it well)
But shall I heed them
Since my heart can be
    A holy temple
Where my God can dwell.

(Japan: a leprosy patient)

23   Oh Lord Jesus, you are full of mercy, and also the almighty in this world. Every day with you is better than the day before. I am aware of your presence inside, always, even though my condition is like this. Only you can share in my sufferings. Oh, I am convinced that whatever sorrow I feel, you certainly feel it too. My fellowship with you is priceless. What can we do without Jesus? You never leave your people in trouble; our debt is so big. If we look to the Saviour who suffered, we receive medicine for our souls. Amen.

(Indonesia: a leprosy patient)

24   Dear Lord Jesus,
I don't know who I am,
I don't know where I am,
and I don't know what I am,
but please love me.

(Prayer of a sufferer from Alzheimer's disease)

25   Lord you are present
You are very real to me now
May I stretch out my hand
And touch you?

(Indonesia. Inspired by the woman in Luke 7:36–38, an artist attributed these words to a young prostitute he was painting.)

26   Persons with Aids need your touch, Jesus.
They need the embrace of your Body, the Church.
The touch, the embrace
tells others it's OK to touch and embrace
and hugs are healing
overcoming distance between us
overcoming distinctions among us
an incarnation of the spiritual reality

that we are one;
if one is hugged, all are embraced together.

(USA)

27   Almighty God, our heavenly Father,
who enabled your servant Job
to go victoriously through great bodily suffering,
without denying your name, power and love,
have mercy on us, Lord,
who are stricken by this epidemic of Aids.

Stretch out your healing hand
and hold back this virus.
Strengthen and comfort, in Jesus Christ,
those infected and ease their pain of body and mind.
Send your Holy Spirit to renew us all,
and lead us into repentance and faith in the gospel.

Have mercy on us, Lord,
and on Aids sufferers throughout the world.
Give love and compassion to all who seek to assist them,
through Jesus Christ our Lord.

(Uganda: from a prayer written by Bishop Misaeri Kauma)

28   Lord, who at the seventh hour commanded the fever to leave
the nobleman's son, if there be any fear in our hearts, any
sickness of body or spirit, remove it from us also. Amen.

(Prayer based on John 4:46–54)

29   O Christ, our Lord, physician of salvation,
grant to all who are sick the aid of heavenly healing. Amen.

(Mozarabic Liturgy, AD 600)

30   O Christ,
who cast seven devils out of Mary Magdalene
cast out of our society those things,
greed, apathy, selfishness, deceit,
cynicism, prejudice, indifference,
that be-devil our lives. Amen.

31   *'So they made an opening in the roof over the place where
Jesus was, and when they had broken through they lowered
the bed on which the paralysed man was lying. When he
saw their faith, Jesus said to the man, "My son, your sins
are forgiven."' (Mark 2:4–5)*

Through a hole in the roof, O my God, I am trying to see you;
trying to tell you all that your people are suffering,
trying to ask you to bring peace,
to please stop this awful killing and destruction,
this murderous frenzy of nationalism!

*(Prayer of a Bosnian villager on entering
the shell of their ruined 15th-century church)*

32   *'The man's sight began to come back, and he said, "I see
people – they look like trees, but they are walking about."
Jesus laid his hands on his eyes again; he looked hard, and
now he was cured and could see everything clearly.'*
(Mark 8:24–25)

As children of God, we need Jesus to lay his hands upon us
a second time, because we never see things clearly. We
always tend to see upside down images.

O God, have mercy upon us;
lay your hands upon our eyes once again,
that we may see clearly the world you made for what it is.

(China)

33 Lord Jesus,
open our deaf ears and give sight to our blind eyes,
that we may receive your word of grace
and rejoice to see your coming kingdom. Amen.

(Uniting Church of Australia)

34 Everywhere he went he was doing good.
He's the mighty healer.
He cleansed the leper.
When the cripples saw him
they started walking.
Everywhere he went, my Lord was doing good.

(Sierra Leone: Krio shout)

35 Servant Christ,
help us to follow you in untiring ministry to town and village,
to heal and restore the broken body of humanity,
to cast out the demonic forces of greed, resentment,
communal hatred, and self-destructive fear:

Servant Christ, help us to follow you.

(India: Litany of the Disciples of Christ the Servant)

Rest and refreshment

*'He said to them, "Come with me, by yourselves, to some
remote place and rest a little." With many coming and going
they had no time even to eat.' (Mark 6:31)*

36 Lord Jesus, your work was hard and tiring.
You needed refreshment. And so do we.
Lord Jesus, as we thank you for work,
we also thank you for rest and recreation.

Help us to recognize that we need it as much as work,
so that we may be refreshed in body, mind and spirit.
Amen.

(Kenya)

37 Lord, we think you know our land. It is so like the country
you yourself once lived in – mountains, and sometimes
snow, contrasting with the thirsty lowlands.

You, who often went alone upon hillsides, know the
mysterious peace and beauty to be found there. You know
also the clamouring crowds waiting down below.

We wait for you today on our hillsides and in the midst of
our crowds.

(Lesotho)

38 O God,
we thank you for those moments of relaxation in the life
of Jesus:
in the presence of a child,
crossing the lake,
enjoying a party,
at ease in the homes of friends,
making a tour,
visiting new places,
going solitary,
and we ask that we too may find rest and refreshment
of body and spirit
in our moments of relaxation. Amen.

39 May you be so strong that you can be alone with God!
May the bliss of being alone with God be yours and mine!

(Japan: Toyohiko Kagawa)

40 Father,
Let my existence be ruled by a great silence.
Let my soul be listening, be given to the needs of others.
Let me be silent in my innermost being, not asserting myself.
Let my soul be detached, not grasping at anything in
    this world.
And thus overcome in my life the power of habit, daily
    routine, dullness, fatigue and fear.
Let me create within myself a carefree tranquillity, a place
    for every encounter, unreserved receptivity, and unhurried
    disposition.
Extinguish within me the feelings of self-importance and the
    last stirrings of my ego,
And make me gentle.
Let me answer thoughts and situations rather than words.
Through Jesus Christ our Lord,
who taught us to be holy as You are holy. Amen.

(Prayer of Hassan Dehqani-Tafti, one-time
Bishop in Iran, in exile)

41 Lord Jesus,
You invited us, when tired, to come to you.
Despite all your goodness to us, we do sometimes grow tired,
    tired of our work
    tired of life's routine
    tired of our failure
    tired of our sin
    tired even of ourselves.
We come to you for deliverance from our weariness.
May we find in you the source of new life
and a purpose in living it.

(Kenya)

42   Servant Christ,
help us to follow you
into the place of quiet,
to intercede for the confused, the despairing,
   the anxiety-driven,
to prepare ourselves for costly service with you;

Servant Christ, help us to follow you.

(India: Litany of the Disciples of Christ the Servant)

Storm on the lake

'All at once a great storm arose on the lake, till the waves were breaking right over the boat . . . he got up and rebuked the wind and the sea, and there was a dead calm.'

(Matthew 8:24, 26)

43   Lord Jesus,
the storm is life and life is the storm
and there is no escaping it;
but what matters is that you are in the storm with us,
a Beacon and a Presence that is sure.

(Madagascar)

44   At every moment the vast and horrible Thing breaks in
upon us through the crevices and invades our precarious
dwelling-place, that Thing we try so hard to forget but
which is always there, separated from us only by thin
dividing walls: fire, pestilence, earthquake, storm, the
unleashing of dark moral forces, all these sweep away
ruthlessly, in an instant, what we had laboured with mind
and heart to build up and make beautiful.
Lord God, my dignity as a man forbids me to shut my eyes
to this, like an animal or a child; therefore, lest I succumb
to the temptation to curse the universe, and the Maker of
the universe, teach me to adore it by seeing you hidden

within it. Say once again to me, Lord, those great and
liberating words, the words which are at once revealing
light and effective power: *hoc est Corpus meum.* In very
truth, if only we will it to be so, the immense and sombre
Thing, the spectre, the tempest – is you. *Ego sum, nolite
timere.*† All the things in life that fill us with dread, all that
filled your own heart with dismay in the garden of agony:
all, in the last resort, are the species or appearances, the
matter, of one and the same sacrament.

[*] 'This is my Body' (Matthew 26:26; Mark 14:22)
† 'It is I, fear not' (Mark 6:50; Matthew 14:27; Luke 24:36)

(Teilhard de Chardin)

45 Somewhere in this
hopeless whirlpool of life
a hand extends to help.

(Singapore)

46 God of the storms and of the calms, we praise you not
only for the times of tranquillity, but also for the times of
fury when winds twist trees and all human plans are
confounded. For a world without storms and life without
agony would give us nothing to grow on. O God, help us
to be thankful for stormy weather.

(Prayer from Hawaii, adapted)

47 Lord Jesus, you were awakened by the cry of your disciples
on a storm-tossed sea. Hear also our cry for help. There is
no justice in our land for the weak and powerless, because
the powerful and the strong have decided what is and what
is not right and just. We, the minority of the humble and
meek are tired of crying for justice and peace. How much
longer must the mighty forces of the strong dominate and
the weak suffer. Bring your justice, and grant us your peace.
Let your kingdom become a reality on this earth.

(Sri Lanka)

48   Almighty God, governor of all things in heaven and
             on earth;
         receive our supplications for protection from storm and
             cyclone.
         We acknowledge that we are unworthy of the least
             of your mercies,
         yet we humbly pray you so to hold the winds of heaven
         that we may dwell safely without fear of evil,
         through Jesus Christ, your Son, our Lord.

(Mauritius: prayed daily in the cyclone season)

49   Typhoon Ruping was raging through Metro Manila. From a
         dry corner in our house where our community tried to do
         Zen, I could hear the galvanized iron sheets flapping and
         banging on our roof. Any moment they could tear away, and
         we would be one with the wind and the rain. Water poured
         through the ceiling like a waterfall. Our windows beat back
         and forth, looking as if they, too, would come unhinged. I
         tried to pray. God stilled the storm at sea. He could silence
         Ruping, maybe not so much for our sake, but for the sake
         of thousands of squatters around us. But this kind of prayer
         could not come from my heart. Then I hoped that,
         somehow, the squatters would not get too wet or too sick.
         But, also, this prayer could not escape from my lips. So, I
         tried to be silent. After an hour of sitting, I knew that as
         soon as the typhoon abates, I must go around doing good.

(Philippines: a Roman Catholic sister)

50   God of goodness and love, in whom we human beings can
         trust in every hour of need: have mercy on all who are faced
         with fear and distress (through tempest, storm, earthquake,
         pestilence, flood . . .) We ask that help may be given to
         them compassionately and speedily, and that this need/
         emergency may be turned into an opportunity to strengthen
         the bonds of love and service which bind human beings and
         nations together, through Jesus Christ our Lord. Amen.

(North America)

51 Lord-of-the-storm
to all who live beside dangerous seas
and on the banks of unpredictable rivers
grant peace of mind
and the assurance of your presence
in each and every circumstance that may befall them.

(Prayer for Bangladesh)

52 Lord, the storm is done.
We could not keep it from coming;
we could not drive it away.
It came as a thief in the night.
Some were sleeping;
Lord, heal them, raise them from the dead.
Some were at work;
take away their fright, give them courage to pick up
    broken pieces.
The people are close to one another;
foes are now friends.
Men have been tender;
women have been brave;
children have kept their faith;
young people have matured in the storm.
It is a people, Lord,
and they are calling on your name.
Hear us, as we huddle together, Christ.
Be in our midst
as storms come and leave us.
Tell the wild winds to be still, Christ.
Tell them to be still.

(East Caribbean: prayer after a hurricane)

53 O Christ, the light of the way of my life
abide with me and show me the way.
My fellow travellers have deserted me and darkness is
   all around.
O Compassionate Christ, come, or else I will lose my life.
O Christ, the only help of the way of my life hold my hand.
When the wild storm comes in the river of my life,
when my oar is broken, and the rudder is torn
O Christ the boatman, come and take the oar lest the
   boat sink.
O Christ the boatman of the boat of my life
hold fast the oar.
(Assam: 'O Christ the Boatman!', a Bengali hymn)

54 O God our Lord, help us.
The waves and billows of our sins encompass us. Be
yourself the haven of peace that we may not sink. We want
to repent. Stretch out your hand to us, O Lord, as you did
to Peter when he was about to sink. Have mercy upon us
and lift us up into your presence.
(South India: Orthodox prayer for mercy)

55 Blessed are all your saints, O God and King, who have
travelled over the tempestuous sea of this life and have
made the harbour of peace. Watch over us who are still on
a dangerous voyage. Frail is our vessel, and the ocean is
wide; but as in your mercy you have set our course, so pilot
the vessel of our life towards the everlasting shore of peace,
and bring us at the last to the quiet haven of our heart's
desire; through Jesus Christ our Lord.
(St Augustine of Hippo)

Well of living water

'It was about noon, and Jesus, tired after his journey, was sitting by the well . . . Meanwhile a Samaritan woman came to draw water, and Jesus said to her, "Give me a drink." The woman said, "What! You, a Jew, ask for a drink from a Samaritan woman?". . . Jesus replied, "If only you knew what God gives, and who it is that is asking you for a drink, you would have asked him and he would have given you living water."' (John 4:6–10)

56   He was tired
     God, He was thirsty
     His name was Jesus.
     He sat by the well

     She came along
     She was a Samaritan.

     He asked her for drink
     He asked
     her – a woman
     A Samaritan woman at that.

     Lord open our eyes
     To look for help
     In unexpected places
     From strangers.

                    (United Kingdom: a woman working
                    in a multi-faith community)

57   Lord, grant us eyes to see your presence and peace in
     strange places and unlikely people, even in ourselves. Amen.
                                                    (USA)

58   Lord of living water, who depended on a stranger for a drink,
     help us to receive as freely as we give,

that the stranger who supplies our need may become
   our friend,
and together we may drink the water of life. Amen.

(United Kingdom)

59   One who said I am the eternal water
Dwelt among us
Living with us
Sustaining us.

To receive a cup of the living water
Is not only to cleanse ourselves
But also to cleanse all the waters,
River and well, lake and ocean
And to share them with all.

(Japan)

60   God of life,
God of those who walk miles for water,
God of those whose only supply is contaminated,
bringing death, not life.
May water, clean and life giving,
be available to every living creature.
May that vision be moved forward.
May your will be done.

(Christian Aid)

61   Lord God, spring of living water
give to those who live in dry and barren lands
   the vision needed to see them as they might be
   the skill and resources needed to irrigate them efficiently
   the equipment needed to make them fertile
and, more than these,
   the spiritual insight needed to recognize that
in you alone do our thirsty human souls find true satisfaction.
In Jesus' name. Amen.

(United Kingdom)

62 Jesus Christ: you are the fountain of life
the glistening water lily of the great swamp!
(Ghana: invocation of Jesus of the Deep Forest)

63 God,
the flowing stream of all life,
hear us as we pray for those
who suffer existence as a barren and dried wasteland.
May they know the first drops of gentle and restoring rain
that will revive their spirits,
enliven their hopes,
and quench their dismay.
We ask it in the power of him who is the living water for
thirsting souls, Jesus Christ our Saviour.
(United Kingdom: USPG)

64 Dear saving Lord, make me a bamboo pipe that I may carry
living water to nourish the dry fields of my village.
(Prayer of a Chinese Christian)

65 O Almighty God, I humbly ask you to make me like a tree
planted by the water side, that I may bring forth fruits of
good living in due season. Forgive my past offences, sanctify
me now, and direct all that I should be in the future: for
Christ's sake. Amen.
(Nigeria)

66 O Heavenly Father
open wide the sluice gate into my heart
that I may receive the living water and be fruitful.
(Prayer of a Punjabi Christian)

67 O God, who gives us the water of life through Jesus Christ:
    We pray for those who have an eternal longing to be at one
        with you;
    We pray for those who thirst after peace, those whose lives
        are parched by war, whose hearts are torn by grief;
    We pray for all in our human family who cry out for basic
        necessities for survival, and for those who have given up
        on crying out;
    We pray for those who live in the darkness of fear, guilt,
        doubt, or fearful circumstances within their daily living;
    We pray for your Church, which thirsts after visible unity
        and reconciliation;
    We pray for local congregations and Christian communities
        that long for renewal and deepened commitment and
        service;
    We pray for those who have caught a new vision of the
        community of women and men in the Church;
    We pray for all who have drunk of the living water and yet
        who search for ways to share the water of life.

(From an Indian liturgy)

Encounters with death

*'Then he raised his voice in a great cry: "Lazarus, come out."
The dead man came out, his hands and feet bound with linen
bandages, his face wrapped in a cloth. Jesus said, "Loose
him; let him go."' (John 11:43–44)*

68 Christ
    giver of life
    who raised Lazarus from the dead
    touch the dead, dark places of this world
    with your resurrection.

69 Give them a Lazarus, O Lord; give them a Lazarus!

*(United Kingdom: prayer for a small Methodist
congregation of the 19th-century divine, Samuel Chadwick)*

70 Our Father in heaven, I thank you that you have led me
into the light. I thank you for sending the Saviour to call me
from death to life. I confess that I was dead in sin before I
heard his call, but when I heard him, like Lazarus, I arose.
But, O my Father, the old grave cloths bind me still. Old
habits that I cannot throw off, old customs that are so
much part of my life that I am helpless to live the new life
that Christ calls me to live. Give me strength, O Father, to
break the bonds; give me courage to live a new life in you;
give me faith to believe that with your help I cannot fail.
And this I ask in the name of the Saviour who has taught
me to come to you.

(Prayer from Taiwan)

71 O Christ,
the little girl on her death bed,
the young man on the way to the grave,
and Lazarus three days in the tomb,
could all hear your voice.
May each soul as it passes through death,
hear your friendly voice,
see the look of love in your eyes,
and the smile of welcome in your face,
and be led by you to the Father of all souls.

(Jerusalem: George Appleton)

72 You open and none can shut:
open the gates of your kingdom
to those who have died without hearing your gospel.

(Central Africa: Ukaristia)

73 O God,
    you call us to commitment,
    even at the point of despair.
    Give us the faith of Martha
    to find in our anger and loss
    a true place to proclaim you
    our resurrection and life,
    through Jesus Christ. Amen.

(United Kingdom: Janet Morley)

74 O Lord,
    who cannot fully share my sorrow until I give it to you,
    help me always to turn to you in trouble,
    that I may more truly be one with you.

(USA)

Homeless and at home

'Jesus replied, "Foxes have their holes and birds their roosts; but the Son of Man has nowhere to lay his head."'
(Matthew 8:20)

75 The foxes have holes and the birds have nests,
        but you, Lord, had no place to lay your head.
    Hear our prayers for the homeless:
        couples living with their parents,
        men sleeping away from home,
        whole families herded together in one small room.
    Safeguard the unity of these families.
    Preserve the moral standards of their children.
    And protect those who live in unhealthy conditions.
    We ask it in your name. Amen.

(Prayer from Kenya)

76 O God, bless those who have no homes.
    Bless those who have to live away from home in lodgings
       and boarding-houses and hotels.
    Bless those who have been left alone, and who
       are solitary now.
    Bless those who are searching or waiting for a house.
    Specially bless young couples who have to live in furnished
       rooms, or with relatives, and who have never had the
       chance to be alone together and to have a home of their own.
    Bless those who keep house for other people, and who have
       no house of their own.
    Bless old people who are coming to the end in some institution
       which is very comfortable but which is still not home.
    Help us who have the blessing of a good home to keep an
       open heart and an open door to those less fortunate than
       ourselves.
    This we ask for your love's sake. Amen.

    (United Kingdom: Audenshaw prayers)

77 Jesus, as a baby you were a refugee, as a man you had no
    place to lay your head. Make us aware of the homeless on
    our streets and of families without adequate shelter. Give us
    wisdom to deal with the causes of these problems, that all
    may work together for better living conditions.

    (Brazil)

78 God
    forgive us
    the poverty and homelessness
    that still exist among us.

    Forgive us the conditions
    people are made to endure
    – the overcrowding, insecurity and harassment –
    that deprive them of hope

undermining their confidence and self-respect,
making family life a torment
and giving children small chance
of growing straight and strong
in body, mind and character.

Forgive us the anxiety
and frustrated hopes
of those who set out on marriage
with joy
gladly anticipating the future
but who find the stress and tensions
of searching and waiting for a home
destructive to their delight in each other
and their relationship with relatives and friends.

Forgive us
the deep hurt
of families separated and broken:
the indifference and incompetence
of those who ought to care
and have the power:
our own lack of understanding
and the turning away of our eyes.

(United Kingdom)

'*After some days he returned to Capernaum, and news went round that he was at home; and such a crowd collected that there was no room for them even in the space outside the door.'* (Mark 2:1–2)

79   Give us, O Lord of Capernaum
grace, understanding, compassion and wisdom
in responding to the clamour of good causes demanding
        attention,
and the unexpected interruptions of everyday life.

80   We come to Jesus, whose unfailing gift was to welcome all
      who came to his door and table, and whose grace was such
      that no one had cause to fear overstaying a welcome.
      Aided by his presence and inspired by his example may we
      likewise have the good grace to welcome all who present
      themselves to us, even at the most inconvenient times, or in
      the most unattractive of guises. In all such circumstances,
      good Jesus, give us your verandah grace.

      (Prayer suggested by a message delivered to the cabin of Bishop
      Lesslie Newbigin and his wife on their first embarkation for
      India. The sender asked for them the gift of 'verandah
      grace'; the verandah in India being the meeting place
      between home and the needy world outside.)

81   Pray that our churches may receive all guests
      as they would receive Christ himself.

      (Rwanda)

82   God of intimacy,
      you surround us with friends and family
      to cherish and to challenge.
      May we so give and receive caring
      in the details of our lives
      that we also remain faithful
      to your greater demands,
      through Jesus Christ. Amen.

      (United Kingdom: Janet Morley)

83   O God, our heavenly Father, your son Jesus Christ enjoyed
      rest and refreshment in the home of Martha and Mary of
      Bethany: Give us the will to love you, open our hearts to

hear you, and strengthen our hearts to serve you in others
for his sake; who lives and reigns with you and the Holy
Spirit, one God, now and for ever. Amen.

(USA: Feast of Mary and Martha of Bethany, 29 July)

84   Good Lord,
just as you were pleased to relax
in the home of Martha and Mary,
abide also, we pray, in our homes.

We pray, especially, for those homes of this congregation
where we meet together,
for prayer and Bible study.

Bestow upon them an atmosphere of Christian love,
where your presence can be found,
your Word made known,
your will accepted
and your purpose worked out.
For your great glory. Amen.

(Kenya: prayer for home meetings)

85   Bless our home, Father,
that we cherish the bread before there is none,
discover each other before we leave,
and enjoy each other for what we are,
while we have time.

(Hawaii)

86   O Saviour Christ, who knew the love of an earthly home,
and enjoyed the security of loving parents, and the friendship and affection of fellow men and women, thank you for
our homes, and the homes and lives of others which are
open to us; and make us mindful of all who are excluded in
any way. Amen.

87   Mary, we ask you to bless our house
and keep it safe in your heart.
Make L'Arche our true home.
May it be a refuge for the poor in spirit
and for those who are severely tried.
Give us hearts that are humble and gentle
to welcome all those whom you send to us:
hearts full of mercy to love and to serve them.
Help us to extinguish all discord,
and to see in our suffering brother and sister the living
    presence of Jesus.
Lord, bless us from the hand of the poor.
Lord, smile on us through the eyes of the poor.
Lord, receive us one day in the holy company of the poor.
Amen.

(France: adapted from a prayer used at L'Arche)

88   O Lord, in whose love and reconciliation is our true rest,
save us from taking refuge in any national or ecclesiastical
or cultural satisfaction where you yourself are not at home.
O Son of man, homeless for our human sakes, make our
hearts your dwelling place and our wills your partners.

(Middle East)

*'Here I stand knocking at the door; if anyone hears my voice
and opens the door, I will come in and he and I will eat
together.' (Revelation 3:20)*

89   'Peace be to this house,
             and to all who dwell in it.'

Not a violent entrance, but first a shout or a greeting, and a
quiet knock that calls for an attitude of welcome and active
watchfulness, of confidence and courage. Indifference, the

privileges they have gained, and fear of the new makes
many people spiritually deaf, as a result the Lord passes by
without stopping at their houses. But there are also many in
our countries and in these times who hear the Lord's call
and try to open the doors of their lives. We are living in a
special period of God's saving action, a time when a new
route is being carved out for the following of Jesus

(Peru: Gustavo Gutiérrez)

90   Lord, come to me, my door is open.

(France: Michel Quoist)

91   O God: enlarge my heart that it may be big enough to
   receive the greatness of your love.
Stretch my heart that it may take into it all those who with
   me around the world believe in Jesus Christ.
Stretch it that it may take into it all those who do not know
   him, but who are my responsibility because I know him.
And stretch it that it may take into it all those who are not
   lovely in my eyes, and whose hands I do not want to touch.

(Prayer of an African Christian)

92   Heavenly Father, amid all the perplexities of a changing
   situation, help us to learn the new ways you would have us
   tread; and, along every unknown path, give us the courage to
   follow Jesus, the same Saviour, yesterday, today and forever.

(Uganda)

12

The Shadow of the Cross

'Jesus and his disciples set out for the villages of Caesarea Philippi . . . and he began to teach them that the Son of Man had to endure great suffering, and to be rejected by the elders, chief priests, and scribes; to be put to death, and to rise again three days afterwards. He spoke about it plainly.' (Mark 8:27, 31–32)

1   Tilling the soil
    And counting: how many days
      now
    'Til His Suffering begins?

(Japan: haiku poem based on Luke 9:62)

2   Lord Jesus Christ, who died for us, open the inward ear of our minds to hear your voice speaking of the cross, that we who come after you may travel with you and die daily in your service. Amen.

(United Kingdom)

3   Train us, Lord, to fling ourselves upon the impossible, for behind the impossible is your grace and your presence. We cannot fall into emptiness. The future is an enigma, our road is shrouded in mist, but we want to go on giving ourselves, because you continue hoping in the midst of night, and weeping tears through a thousand human eyes.

(Bolivia: murdered priest Luis Espinal)

4   'O Caesarea Philippi!'
      (Dag Hammarskjöld: Markings*)*

5   Lord, help us to understand the mystery of your cross. Help
     us to love the cross, and, Lord, give me guts to embrace it
     in whatever shape or form it comes.
      (Nicaragua: Miguel D'Escoto, priest and Foreign Minister)

      *'Six days later Jesus took Peter, James, and John with him
      and led them up a high mountain by themselves. And in their
      presence he was transfigured; his clothes became dazzling
      white, with a whiteness no bleacher on earth could equal.'*
      (Mark 9:2–3)

6   God our Father,
     on this day the disciples,
     blinded by the light of his glory,
     had revealed to them the mystery of Jesus.
     With them, let us gaze
     in silence and in wonder,
     at him whose glory we hope one day to see,
     for ever and ever. Amen.
      (France: Cistercian, Praise at Dawn)

7   O Christ, we come into your presence and how beautiful
     it is.
     There is no place so beautiful as the place where you are.
      (Prayer of an Indian Christian)

8   Let the divine spark in me kindle into flame,
     O Christ my Lord,
     that radiance and warmth
     may shine through my whole being,

and show that I have been with you
on the mountain of glory.

(Jerusalem: George Appleton)

9   Take away whatever is opaque in me, O Lord,
and help me to become transparent.

(Brazil: Dom Helder Camara)

10   O Master, teach me to pray, and thus help me to bore a
hole through which I may see you.

(New Guinea)

11   O Lord Jesus Christ, glorified by the Father,
transfigured in holy light on Mount Tabor,
you have opened the gate of glory to the kingdom of
    the Father.
With Peter, James and John, we offer our adoration.

In this day also, O Lord Christ,
were the gates of hell opened
in the skies of Hiroshima
and the unholy light of death unleashed.

O Saviour of the world,
forgive us our blasphemy.
Inflame us by the vision of your divinity
and inspire us by the Holy Spirit
to seek the peace of your kingdom on earth.
By your saving cross and life-giving resurrection,
transfigure your people and your creation,
changing all from glory to glory.

For to you, O Christ, belongs all honour and praise, with
the Father and the Holy Spirit now and ever, unto ages of
ages. Amen.

(United Kingdom)

12   Now there are two ways to walk:
Towards the radiance of the transfigured Christ
Or the radiance of the Bomb.
Towards the radiance that descends to touch,
  to heal, to restore.
Or towards the radiance that descends to defend,
  to murder, and to destroy.
Towards the radiance that glorifies
Or the radiance that vaporizes.
This day I set before you life and death,
  a blessing and a curse:
Choose this day whom you will serve.

(USA)

13   Christ, our only true light, before whose bright cloud your
friends fell to the ground: we bow before your cross that we
might remember in our bodies the dead who fell like
shadows; and that we may refuse to be prostrated before
the false brightness of any other light, looking to your
power alone for hope of resurrection from the dead. Amen.

(United Kingdom: Janet Morley)

14   To you, Creator of nature and humanity,
  in truth and beauty I pray:
Hear my voice, for it is the voice of victims of all wars and
  violence among individuals and nations.
Hear my voice, for it is the voice of all children who suffer and
  will suffer when people put their faith in weapons and war.

Hear my voice when I beg you to instil into the hearts of all
  human beings the wisdom of peace, the strength of justice
  and the joy of fellowship.
Hear my voice, for I speak for the multitudes in every
  country and every period of history who do not want war
  and are ready to walk the road of peace.

Hear my voice, and grant insight and strength so that we
may always respond to hatred with love, to injustice with
total dedication to justice, to need with the sharing of self,
to war with peace.
O God hear my voice, and grant unto the world your
everlasting peace.

(Prayer of Pope John Paul II at Hiroshima)

15   O Lord,
grant people your grace,
that in peace and love they may come to know and love you,
and say like the apostle on Mount Tabor:
Master it is good for us to be with you.

(Greece: Staretz Silovan of Mount Athos)

16   O Christ transfigured, we pray for all those who
acknowledge you as the Beloved Son of the Father, that in
your one Church, united as brothers and sisters they may
witness to your gospel throughout their lives.

O Christ transfigured, we pray for all who seek you, for all
who have not yet acknowledged you as the Son of God.
Draw them to you and reveal to them your light, your
beauty and the love you always offer.

O Christ transfigured, we pray for those in authority
among the nations of the world, that they may establish for
those for whom they are responsible, paths of justice,
freedom and peace.

O Christ transfigured, we pray for all victims of violence
and hatred, for those who suffer in body, mind and spirit,
that your spirit of healing and reconciliation may alleviate
their suffering and restore hope in their hearts.

(Belgium)

17   O transfigured Christ, as our tropical sun radiates its light,
      so let the rays from your face enter every nook of my being
      and drive away all darkness within.
                                            (Adapted from a Filipino prayer)

18   You whose brow is of snow, whose eyes are of fire, whose
      feet are more dazzling than gold poured from the furnace;
      whose hands hold captive the stars, you who are the first
      and the last, the living, the dead and risen again; you who
      gather up in your superabundant oneness every delight,
      every taste, every energy, every phase of existence, to you
      my being cries out with a longing as vast as the universe,
      for you indeed are my Lord and my God.
                                            (Teilhard de Chardin)

'He set his face resolutely towards Jerusalem.' *(Luke 9:51)*

19   Servant Christ,
      help us to follow you on the road to Jerusalem,
      to set our faces firmly against friendly suggestions
      for a safe, expedient life;
      to embrace boldly the way of self-offering,
      the way of life given for others' gain;

      Servant Christ, help us to follow you.
                                  (India: Litany of the Disciples of Christ the Servant)

20   O Christ, as we walk through the land that you loved, in
      the country where you lived and taught, grant us the grace
      and wisdom to see clearly and to understand deeply that all
      you suffered was for the sake of redeeming humanity, and
      how through your life, death and resurrection you have
      made it possible for us to have life and to have it more
      abundantly. Amen.
                                  (Prayer of Palestinian women of Jerusalem)

21   O Lord Jesus Christ, who travelled the roads of Palestine
and made them serve the purposes of your kingdom,
and who finally took the road to Calvary;
extend your sharp eyes, your consideration
and your ready compassion to those of us
who travel today's roads at such greater speeds
and who are so sorely in need of your presence and protection.

22   Thus, with the hope you have given us in your Son, Jesus
Christ our Lord, may we follow him today and forever, that
we may proclaim without fear or favour the gospel of your
suffering, redeeming love.

(Switzerland: Aussbund, *16th-century Anabaptist hymn book)*

It is doubtful whether 'taking a holiday' could ever be an adequate way of
describing the mystery of the resting periods in the life of Jesus – his frequent departures into the hills surrounding the Sea of Galilee; his leisurely
visits to the region of the Ten Towns; his presence as a guest at a family
wedding – and his subsequent return to the relentlessness of his everyday
ministry. But clearly, from Caesarea Philippi onwards, there were to be no
such 'holidays'.

From now on there would be no more respite; no more breaks; no more
lingering in the cornfields; no more looking out over the beloved lake; no
more time for the birds of the air and the flowers of the field; no more pausing in the countryside, sitting by wells, resting up in familiar homes in
Capernaum and Bethany; no more quiet early morning retreats.

It may be that the three companions of Jesus on Mount Tabor were in
holiday mood when they suggested building three tents to retain the glory
of his transfigured presence; but it seems more than possible that, for Jesus,
the 'resplendent miracle' of his transfiguration represented yet another
temptation to take this easy way. Instead he chose the costly route of the
cross as God's way of initiating his Kingdom of enduring glory.

The substance of which flint is formed had already shown itself in the life
of Jesus (Isaiah 50:7); and now, once more, he sets his face 'as a flint' to return
to Jerusalem. The holidays are over; the holy days of the passion have begun.

23   Hard it is, very hard
To travel up the slow and stony road
To Calvary, to redeem humankind; far better
To make but one resplendent miracle,
Lean through the cloud, lift the right hand of power,
And with sudden lightning, smite the world perfect.
Yet this was not God's way,
Who had the power,
Yet set it by, choosing the cross, the thorn,
The sorrowful wounds.

(United Kingdom: Dorothy Sayers)

24   In the blood-drops dripping
along the sorrowful road to the via Dolorosa
will be written the history of human regeneration.
Tracing those blood-stained and staggering footprints
let me go forward.
This day also must my blood flow, following
in that blood-stained pattern.

(Japan: Toyohiko Kagawa)

25   Lord Jesus Christ, Son of the Living God, whose face was
set like a flint to win our full salvation: make us put first
things first and, amid the manifold cries of human need,
bend our wills to seek for every human being that total
wholeness which is your purpose and your gift.

(United Kingdom: CMS)

13

The Mysteries of Christ's Entry into the City

'Crowds of people carpeted the road with their cloaks, and some cut branches from the trees to spread in his path. Then the crowds in front and behind raised the shout: "Hosanna to the Son of David! Blessed is he who comes in the name of the Lord! Hosanna in the heavens!" When he entered Jerusalem the whole city went wild with excitement.' (Matthew 21:8–10)

1   Jesus is passing this way
     This way, this way.
     Jesus is passing this way
     He's passing this way today.

(Sierra Leone: Krio shout)

2   Homage, homage of flowers
     To the Son of God, homage of flowers
     To the flower that blossomed in Jerusalem
     Adoration of the living soul
     Adoration, adoration.

(South India: a Malayalam Bhajan)

3   Seated upon the throne in heaven and upon the colt on earth, O Christ our God, you accepted the praise of angels and the songs of the children who cried out: Blessed are you who comes to recall Adam from the dead.

(Eastern Orthodox Church: Kontakion for our Lord's Entry into Jerusalem)

4 Lord of all creation,
showing your glory in ever changing matter,
who took flesh and blood
to body forth your presence,
may the very stones cry out your life and love. Amen.

(United Kingdom)

5 He is the one for whom
women lay down their cloths on the path,
and pour sweet-smelling oil on his feet.
They run to and fro amid shouts of praise before him:
It is true: Jesus is Chief!

(Ghana: invocation of Jesus of the Deep Forest)

6 Gracious God
as we come together to celebrate
the entry into Jerusalem of the Prince of Peace,
we confess to you
that we are like the people who carpeted the road
and waved their branches,
but who understood so little of this king.
We are tempted to put our trust
in powerful Warrior-Messiahs of our day,
and find it hard to believe
that the way to life
passes through death.
We prefer protection to vulnerability,
control over our destiny rather than faith in God,
who brings life out of self-giving death.
We want our own life to continue,
and find it hard to look beyond our shores
to nations whose ways differ from ours,
but who, like us, need trust, love and life
instead of our mutual defensiveness and fear.
Forgive us and our hostile world,

for we find it hard to follow the Prince of Peace in faith,
or to trust God instead of weapons.
Set us and our world free, we pray. Amen.

(Australia: Confession for Palm Sunday)

7   Jesus, ride again into our cities,
temples, upper rooms and Gethsemanes.
Give us sight so that this time we
might recognize you.

(USA: Prayers for Peace)

8   From a wandering nomad, you created your family;
for a burdened people, you raised up a leader;
for a confused nation, you chose a king;
for a rebellious crowd, you sent your prophets.
In these last days, you have sent us your Son,
your perfect image, bringing your kingdom,
revealing your will, dying, rising, reigning,
redeeming your people for yourself.

(Kenya: Eucharistic Liturgy)

9   When my Saviour was going to Jerusalem riding upon an
ass, the people brought clothes and palm branches and
spread them under his feet. They did not spread them under
the feet of Christ, but under the feet of the ass. Why do that
for an ass? Because the King of Kings is riding upon that
humble animal. When the Christ got down from it nobody
cared about it. The ass was led away and honoured only as
long as the King of Kings was upon it.

Even so, O King of Kings, may something of this weight of
glory rest upon us, not of our own right, but by virtue of
the burden we carry and the path we tread.

(North India: words of a humble Christian evangelist)

10 Lord Jesus
this is your triumphal entry into Jerusalem,
I'll be your donkey.

(Brazil: Dom Helder Camara. Protecting
prayer on occasions when receiving an ovation.)

11 Lord of all creation, you speak to us through your creatures
of your beauty and grace and humour and the loveliness of
your form. So often Lord, we take your gifts for granted, so
often we are blind, so often we are brutal, so often we try
to prove our superiority or make a profit out of your
creatures. In their silence and suffering you rebuke us and
sometimes by riding on a donkey you show us their beauty.
Lord, this day let me not miss the loveliness of flowers or
reject the loveliness of your animals, for if I do that, I fear I
may miss you altogether.

(India: Subir Biswas)

12 The whole creation
was altered by your passion;
for all things suffered
with you,
knowing, O Lord,
that you hold all things in unity.

(Byzantine rite: prayer for compassion for animals)

13 We come to Jerusalem with you, and we see there your
people divided, yet longing to be united in you, as branches
of the one vine. Grant us the courage to go beyond
ourselves, to transcend the burden of history, so that we
may recover our unity in and through you.

We come to Jerusalem, O King, with you seated on the
throne of our hearts, our minds and our lives. We walk the

road to Golgotha with you and partake of your passion. Seeing you nailed to the cross, we bow down before your suffering. Show us the glory of your Resurrection.

(Jerusalem: prayer of church leaders used
on the Palm Sunday walk, 1990)

14 Jesus, King of the universe;
ride on in humble majesty,
ride on through conflict and debate,
ride on through sweaty prayer and betrayal of friends,
ride on through mockery and unjust condemnation,
ride on through cruel suffering and ignoble death,
ride on to the empty tomb and your rising in triumph,
ride on to raise up your Church, a new body for your service,
ride on, King Jesus, to renew the whole earth in your image:
in compassion come to help us.

(India)

'Christianity is about the life and death of Jesus going on day after day in the souls of individual men and women, in the heart of the Church itself, and in the heart of society; and we are all subject to and an essential part of that ongoing process . . .'

The speaker was addressing a group of clergy from a variety of English parishes in town and country on the subject of their role as priests in their differing local communities. 'You yourselves', he concluded, quoting the words of the 17th-century German mystic Jakob Boehme, 'must go through Christ's whole journey, and enter wholly into his process.'

Whether lay or ordained, Christian men and women have always found that part of Christ's whole journey, from the calling of the first disciples through his ministry in Galilee to his final entry into the city of Jerusalem, a particularly fertile ground for personal reflection, prayer and Christian formation. The corporate lives of churches and societies have likewise been profoundly influenced by the healing, teaching and caring activity of Jesus. But in every age and from every continent there have also been those courageous individuals, as well as whole communities and peoples, who have been prepared to follow Christ all the way, and to identify themselves with his passion and death in very concrete circumstances.

'The parish is the passion' is how one vicar identifies the trials and tribulations of his struggling inner city parish with the passion of Jesus. It is a description to which many of us will respond in relation to the changing fortunes of the local congregations to which we belong, turning week by week to that sacrament of salvation, instituted by our Lord on the eve of his own passion, in which all the mysteries of his life and death and resurrection are made available to his followers in all places and at all times, wholly regardless of circumstances.

Certainly the experience of the great mystery of the passion of Jesus going on day after day in the souls of individual men and women, in the heart of the Church, and in the heart of society becomes ever more sharply focused and deeply felt as we enter the city of Jerusalem, and accompany him on that last part of his whole journey which now lies ahead.

> '*When he came in sight of the city, he wept over it and said, "If only you had known this day the way that leads to peace! But no; it is hidden from your sight."*' *(Luke 19:41–42)*

15 O Eternal Lord God, Source of all truth, Lover of all your
children, we thank you for the experience of living in this city.
Grant that we may be humble, grateful people,
worshipping people,
holy people.
Help us to be peace-loving people,
who know the things that belong to peace,
who pray and work for peace,
who try to understand the experiences, the hurts,
the hopes of people from whom we differ.
Let this city be a centre of unity for the churches.
Let it be a place of friendship and understanding for those
of different faiths.
Let it be truly the City of Peace, a joy of the whole earth
and a place of blessing to all nations.
For the sake of him who wept in love over this city
and died in love outside its walls.

Now the Everliving One,
ever present with you to heal and bless,
Jesus Christ our blessed Lord and Saviour.

(Jerusalem: George Appleton)

16 Jesus came to Benares
as he does to Mecca
and to Jerusalem and Rome.
In each place he
raises his hand in peace.
And in each place he
is crucified again.

*(Words of an anonymous Asian poet inspired
by Alphonso's painting 'Christ at Benares')*

17 Lord, I remember how you wept over Jerusalem, your holy
city, because her people did not know how to make peace.
Teach us in our towns and cities the things that belong to
our peace.

*(United Kingdom: prayer of a woman
working in an immigrant area)*

18 Heavenly Father, in your Word you have given us a vision
of that holy City to which the nations of the world bring
their glory; behold and visit, we pray, the cities of the earth.
Renew the ties of mutual regard which form our civic life.
Send us honest and able leaders. Enable us to eliminate
poverty and prejudice and oppression, that peace may
prevail with righteousness, and justice with order, and that
men and women from different cultures and with differing
talents may find with one another the fulfilment of their
humanity; through Jesus Christ our Lord.

(Prayer for Peace at the invitation of Pope John Paul II)

19   Again we pray that God will keep this city, and every city
and country from famine, pestilence, earthquake, flood, fire,
pollution, war and civil strife, that he who loves our
humanity will be gracious and merciful to us.

(Orthodox)

20   Lord Jesus Christ
You once wept over the city of Jerusalem.
Look down, now, we pray, upon the towns and cities of
our country.

Give vision and skill to those who plan their development,
that they may be healthy and beautiful places,
with gardens, parks and open spaces,
with proper amenities for work and recreation.

But in planning for the future,
help us not to lose sight of present needs,
and while building for the prosperity of tomorrow,
make us concerned also for the destitute of today,
and for those who live in slums and shanties. Amen.

(Kenya)

21   God of our daily lives
we pray for the peoples of the cities of this world
working and without work;
homeless or well housed;
fulfilled or frustrated;
confused and cluttered with material goods
or scraping a living from others' leavings;
angrily scrawling on walls,
or reading the writing on the wall;
lonely or living in community; finding their own space
and respecting the space of others.
We pray for our sisters and brothers,
mourning or celebrating –
may we share their suffering and hope. Amen.

(United Kingdom)

22 Lord Jesus Christ,
you looked upon the city of Jerusalem with compassion and
tears. Look with mercy upon our city and surrounding
countryside, and gladden many hearts with the good news
of your transforming love. Amen.

(United Kingdom)

23 May the whole town have health:
May it have to eat
May it have to drink
May the whole town have health.

(Nigeria: a Nupe prayer)

24 This is my city, Lord:
I've flown over it,
driven round it,
walked through it,
and I love it.
Its concrete chasms, its quiet parks,
its massive buildings and its tiny houses,
its suburbs rich and poor.
But most of all, Lord, its people . . .
My city, Lord. Your city.
Remember, Lord, there was one city
over which you stood and wept.
Do you weep over this city?
With its hunger, its greed, its cruelty?
Its foolishness and heartbreak?
Lord, I believe you do.

(Prayer used over Belfast, Ulster)

25   Christ look upon us in this city
And keep our sympathy and pity
Fresh, and our faces heavenward,
Lest we grow hard.

(Found in a clinic in Hong Kong: Thomas Ashe)

26   O Lord soften the stone hearts
of those who preach and practise
intolerance and bigotry;
as the sun's setting glow
softens the stone walls
of your Holy City, Jerusalem.

Lord, the rocky hills, the valleys,
the deserts and the sea shores
are filled with the echoes of centuries of pain.

Lord, bring peace to house and village.
Comfort the mothers who fret
and those who mourn.
Lord, keep strong the twisted old root
of the olive tree,
and protect the young vine.

Lord of water and stone,
of bread and wine,
Lord of the resurrection,
feed hope, and bring peace
to these wracked but beautiful holy lands.

(Jerusalem: Gerald Butt, former BBC correspondent)

'O Jerusalem, Jerusalem, city that murders the prophets and stones the messengers sent to her! How often have I longed to gather your children, as a hen gathers her brood under her wings; but you would not let me.' (Matthew 23:37)

27   Surely, Jesus, good Lord,
you are a mother?
Are you not a mother who,
like a hen, gathers her chicks under her wings?
Indeed, Lord, you are a mother.

(St Anselm, 1033–1109)

28   Of all the names
that we give you,
God
my favourite is:
God of tenderness.

(Germany: evening prayer to be said with children)

29   O Lord Jesus, who would gather up your children in your
arms as a mother hen gathers up her brood under her
wings, hear our prayer:
for young people with no prospect of employment;
older people who see no chance of returning to work;
those dispirited by many years of unemployment;
women seeking jobs to provide their families with the
necessities of life;
for those who suffer disproportionately
from unemployment;
people of other races who experience the vitriol
of racism;
people with disabilities who are so often ignored
and overlooked;
those without skills or schooling who are dismissed out
of hand.

Impress each unemployed person with your loving care of
them, that they may be made newly aware of the proper
value and respect that your love gives them as part of your
Father's creation.

(United Kingdom: Christians Unemployment Group, Sheffield)

30   Dear Jesus,
      as a hen covers her chicks with her wings
      to keep them safe
      protect us this dark night
      under your golden wings.

(India)

'Then he went into the temple and began driving out the traders, with these words: "Scripture says, 'My house shall be a house of prayer'; but you have made it a bandits' cave."'
(Luke 19:45–46)

31   Servant Christ,
      help us to follow you into the temple
      of your chosen people,
      to erase from the worship of your church
      all that hinders the sense of your presence,
      and the free flow of your Word;
      to open up your house
      that it may be a house of prayer for all people.

      Servant Christ, help us to follow you.
(India: Litany of the Disciples of Christ the Servant)

32   O God of justice and joy
      may the goods we bring to the market place
      bring life
      and health
      and well being
      to all who trade there.
      Teach us
      to refuse a bargain
      that leaves others
      without the means of life.

May our world trade
not in human lives
but so that all may live. Amen.

(United Kingdom: Christian Aid)

33   Angry Jesus,
as of old you entered into that temple market
casting out the merchants and money changers;
enter now into the markets of our modern world.
Throw out of them all that is unworthy, unjust and
  self-seeking
and direct the market forces of the world
in the ways of justice, plenty and peace,
for your tender mercy's sake. Amen.

34   Servant Christ,
help us to follow you into the city,
to claim its whole life for God whose image we bear,
to confront the ambitions of those hungry for power,
the inhuman orthodoxy of the legalist,
with the startling message of your present action,
your living power.

Servant Christ, help us to follow you.

(India: Litany of the Disciples of Christ the Servant)

14

Mysteries of the Upper Room

'Now on the first day of Unleavened Bread, when the Passover lambs were being slaughtered, his disciples said to him, "Where would you like us to go and prepare the Passover for you?" So he sent off two of his disciples with these instructions: "Go into the city, and a man will meet you carrying a jar of water. Follow him, and when he enters a house give this message to the householder: 'The Teacher says, "Where is the room in which I am to eat the Passover with my disciples?"' He will show you a large upstairs room, set out in readiness. Make the preparations for us there."' (Mark 14:12–15)

1   Lord,
to those of us who sometimes find your ways of doing things,
and choice of messengers puzzling and perplexing; may that
unnamed water-carrier, who led those first disciples to the
upper room, alert us to the many little-known people who
cross our paths, and who, if followed, lead us through
unexpected doors of welcome and hospitality to
extraordinary revelations of your grace.

(Jordan: from an extempore prayer)

2   Servant Christ,
help us to follow you into the upper room
to share your meal of bread and cup,
to accept our common place in your one body
broken to create a new humanity.

Servant Christ, help us all to follow you.

(India: Litany of the Disciples of Christ the Servant)

'During supper, Jesus . . . rose from the supper table, took off
his outer garment and, taking a towel, tied it round him.
Then he poured water into a basin, and began to wash his
disciples' feet and to wipe them with the towel.'

(John 13:3–5)

3   A chill was in the spring air:
     The disciples watched
     As their feet were washed.

(Japan: haiku poem)

4   In my house there is an indigenous symbol for the Lord
Jesus which I see every day. It is of an ordinary man
emerging from the background of the cross with five
blood-stained wounds, standing in the midst of ordinary
people to serve them.

Our religious ceremonies and rites must, through shared
silence and gestures, especially in small groups, convey the
mystery and majesty of the lowliness of the servant Lord.
Serving food to each other, washing each other's feet in a
natural way in the context of shared worship can convey
the presence of the Lord among us as one who serves.

Nothing good or worthwhile is outside his kingdom, and
nothing evil or painful is outside his power to transform
and make whole. But we must be ready to take risks, suffer
losses and face contradictions. This is where we get stuck
and prefer to remain in our ghettos. We deny like Peter,
betray like Judas, doubt like Thomas, fear like the other
disciples. But the servant Lord is in our midst as One who
serves, and he continues to draw us out of ourselves.

(Sri Lanka: Bishop Lakshman Wickremesinghe)

5   Jesus, servant,
     at supper with your disciples
     you put a towel around your waist.

Like Peter, we protest
and distort your simple parable of love.
Wash us, Lord,
that we may be ready to wash each other's feet
and to serve one another for your sake.

Jesus, servant,
unless your Spirit lives in us,
we will lord it over
the people and institutions in our care.
Come, dwell within us
and within our churches,
that we may learn how to follow you
who came not to be served
but to serve
and to give your life as a ransom for many.

(Korea: 8th Assembly of the Christian Conference of Asia)

6   O Lord, forgive the sins of your servants. May we banish
     from our minds all disunion and strife; may our souls be
     cleansed from all hatred and malice towards others and
     may we receive the fellowship of the Holy Meal in oneness
     of mind and peace with one another.

*(Church of South India. The equivalent of the footwashing
practised in some churches in India on Maundy
Thursday, is for individual members of a congregation
to stoop and touch the shoe of the person beside them,
and to brush their own forehead with the dusty finger,
being in turn blessed and raised to their feet by the
recipient of this ministry. The above prayer is then said.)*

7   May God clean
     my heart as I
     clean my town.

*(Uganda. The social and environmental implications of
the footwashing are explored by Christians in Uganda,
and in this instance the cleaning up of their town is
seen as preparation for a campaign of evangelism
and personal renewal.)*

8   Jesus, Lord and Master,
     as you once washed the feet of your disciples;
     we pray that you will so wash our motives,
     our ambitions and our actions,
     that we may share in your mission to the world
     and serve each other gladly
     for your sake and your glory.

*(United Kingdom: prayer based on some
words of Michael Ramsey)*

9   Let us draw near in fear to the mystical table, and with
     pure souls let us receive the bread; let us remain at the
     Master's side, that we may see how he washes the feet of
     the disciples and wipes them with a towel; and let us do as
     we have seen, subjecting ourselves to each other and
     washing one another's feet. For such is the commandment
     that Christ himself gave to his disciples; but Judas, slave
     and deceiver, paid no heed.

(Orthodox)

*'During supper he took bread, and having said the blessing
he broke it and gave it to them, with the words: "Take this;
this is my body." Then he took a cup, and having offered
thanks to God he gave it to them; and they all drank from it.
And he said to them, "This is my blood, the blood of the
covenant, shed for many."' (Mark 14:22–24)*

10   Be present, be present O Jesus
     our good High Priest
     as you were with your disciples,
     and make yourself known to us
     in the breaking of the bread. Amen.

(Church of South India)

11 In the chill of the spring evening
The blessed Hands seem thin
As they break the bread

(Japan: haiku poem)

12 Jesus celebrated the Eucharist only once, and within
forty-eight hours he was dead, killed at the hands of the
social structure from which he sought to liberate people.
That is the true context for Eucharist.

(Sri Lanka: Father Tissa Balasuriya)

13 Lord, I do so much want to be like you.
Like you, I want to feed human beings
with love and with bread.
I want to bring hope and faith to the world
even if the world crushes me.

(Cameroon)

14 Servant One,
    as you shared your last supper,
    so we share a meal that lasts,
        . . . and lasts
        . . . and lasts

Broken One,
    as your body was broken and
    you shared our suffering,
    so we, the broken and suffering,
    share the stuff of life.

Outpoured Love,
    as you poured out your blood
    in the promise of new life,
    so, as spit and sweat are poured out here,
    we work for renewed lives.

Sharing One,
may the fellowship of your last supper
infuse our lasting meal
with your patience and persistence.

And as, here, we struggle
to suck or chew and swallow,
may we feed on you in our hearts
by faith
and with thanksgiving.

(Portugal: 'The Meal that Lasts'.
In a hall in Lisbon people with cerebral palsy
eat under a mural depicting the Last Supper.)

15   As this bread is broken and this wine poured out
O Seeker and Saviour of the lost,
we remember again the poor and oppressed of the earth.
We recall that your body was broken
that the hungry might be nourished, the oppressed set free
and all replenished with the bread of new hope and new life.

(South India)

16   Where a people is being harshly oppressed, the Eucharist
speaks of the exodus or re-deliverance from bondage.
Where Christians are rejected or imprisoned for their faith,
the bread and wine become the life of the Lord who was
rejected by men but has become 'the chief stone of the
corner'. Where the Church sees a diminishing membership
and its budgets are depressing, the Eucharist declares that
there are no limits to God's giving and no end to hope in
him. Where discrimination by race, sex or class is a danger
for the community, the Eucharist enables people of all sorts
to partake of one food and to be made one people. Where
people are affluent and at ease with life, the Eucharist says:

'As Christ shares his life, share what you have with the hungry.' Where a congregation is isolated by politics or war or geography, the Eucharist unites us with all God's people in all places and all ages. Where a sister or a brother is near death, the Eucharist becomes a doorway into the kingdom of our loving Father.

(Australia: World Conference on Mission and Evangelism, 1980)

17 O Son of God, receive me this day as a guest at your mysterious supper, for I will not reveal your Mysteries to your enemies. I will not give you a kiss like Judas; but like the penitent thief, I will confess you: Remember me, O Lord, in your kingdom.

(Basil of Caesarea, 330–379)

18 I take some comfort in recalling that the Last Supper itself, celebrated by Jesus, was by no means a smooth ritual performance which disturbed no one. In fact I have just read through the accounts given by Matthew, Mark and Luke and can but conclude that the occasion in the upper room was very turbulent indeed.

(Jerusalem: Donald Nicholl)

19 O frequently interrupted Jesus,
when we ourselves are interrupted by the noises of the
    world outside,
and by events occuring in our own midst,
especially during the quiet moments of the Eucharist:
by somebody taken ill;
the cry of a child;
someone in tears;
the interpolation of a handicapped person;
the irritating cough of a 'regular';

help us to realize that these are the ongoing sounds of a
  living community,
and enable us to communicate with you
through the noises and needs of our neighbours.

20   As Jesus Christ remained unknown among men, so his truth
remains among common opinions, without external
difference. Thus the Eucharist among ordinary bread.

(Blaise Pascal, 1623–62)

21   Thank you Lord
for the bread that makes us the same as you,
and the same as others.

(USA: prayer of a 7-year-old child)

22   Dear Lord
we human beings are made in your image;
when we sit at family table eating our daily bread
– whether it be nan or rice, or pitta or noodles or matzos
or tortillas, or puri, or white bread or brown –
we belong to one family
united by similar needs.
Teach us in such company the kind of table manners
that are alert and sensitive to the needs of those
who sit around the table with us here.

(Based on a prayer from Hawaii)

23   Forgive us, O Lord, when we are so clever, so very sure of
ourselves, so bold in speaking out, so ready with answers.
Help us to be shy, Lord. Today two of the servants brought
gifts, a chicken and prawns. They were expensive gifts, but
given quietly, left in the kitchen. Help me this day to give

myself to you in the same quietness and hiddenness as you
give yourself to me in the shyness and hiddenness of bread
and wine.

(India: Subir Biswas)

24   Lord, as I come to the Eucharist today,
I want your touch to be like
that given to a sleeping child.
You can give the wind, fire and earthquake
to those who need it.
Let your presence be like that of a desert breeze.

*(Salford and the Sahara: a parish priest explores the significance
of the mysteries of Christ's presence in city and in desert)*

25   I cannot say I will approach Him
and compel Him to dwell in me.
He Himself comes with yearning for me,
and dwells in my body,
and mingles with my life.
Is it possible for him now to leave me?

(India)

'*Then Jesus looked up to heaven and said . . . "It is not for
these alone that I pray, but for those also who through their
words put their faith in me. May they all be one; as you,
Father, are in me, and I in you, so also may they be in us, that
the world may believe that you sent me."'*

(John 17:1, 20–21)

26 Lord, grant to your Church on earth that peace and unity which were in the mind and purpose of Christ Jesus when, on the eve of his passion, he prayed that all might be one. Amen.

(Canada)

27 Dear Lord,
you wanted all people to live in unity and to love each other.
Help us to break down the walls of separation.
Break down the walls of race, colour, creed and language.
Make us one so that our unity and love for each other
may win many to your fold. Amen.

(Myanmar: Fellowship of the Least Coin)

28 O God forgive us for bringing this stumbling block of disunity to a people who want to belong to one family. The Church for which our Saviour died is broken, and people can scarcely believe that we hold one faith and follow one Lord. O Lord, bring about the unity which you have promised, not tomorrow or the next day, but today.

(Prayer from Africa)

29 Lord, make us realize that our Christian faith is like a rice field; that when it is newly planted, the paddies are prominent; but as the plants take root and grow taller, these dividing paddies gradually vanish, and soon there appears only one vast continuous field. So give us roots of love, and help us to grow in Christian fellowship and service to one another, so that your will may be done in our lives, through our Saviour, your Son, Jesus Christ. Amen.

(Philippines)

30 O Lord, you have brought all your faithful people into a single, universal family, stretching across heaven and earth.

Bind us together with a spiritual love which is stronger than any human love, that in serving one another we may neither count the cost nor seek reward, but think only of the common good. Amen.

(Spain: Mozarabic Sacramentary, 3rd century)

31 Lord Jesus Christ, you blessed five loaves of bread and fed the five thousand. Bless this bread too, and make us holy, as we now share it among us. Just as this bread was scattered over the fields and, gathered up, became one, so may your Church be gathered from the ends of the earth. Grant that she may overcome all her divisions so that all who believe in you can share in the meal of your love. May we all meet as guests at the eternal meal in the kingdom of your Father and there glorify, adore and praise you, together with the Father and the life-creating Spirit for all eternity.

(Orthodox: blessing of the bread)

'Peace is my parting gift to you, my own peace, such as the world cannot give.' (John 14:27)

32 O Lord, you have said to us 'Peace I leave with you.'
This peace that you give is not that of this world:
    it is not the peace of order, when order oppresses;
    it is not the peace of silence, when silence is born of
        supression;
    it is not the peace of resignation, when such resignation is
        unworthy.
Your peace is love for all people,
    is justice for all people,
    is truth for all people,
the truth that liberates and stimulates growth.

Lord, it is this peace we believe in because of your promise.
Grant us peace, and we will give this peace to others.

(Italy: the Waldensian Liturgy)

33   Our heavenly Father, may the rulers of the earth come
      together and settle the world's quarrels. Teach the people of
      the earth to live in peace and to love one another, following
      the example of Jesus Christ.

                         (Zaire, now the Democratic Republic of Congo)

34   Come, Prince of Peace,
      enter the silo of the heart
      and disarm each warhead
      before we start
      the fire of the dead.

                                                             (USA)

35   God, you are the God of life.
          Transform us in the depths of our hearts
              into people, through whom your peace
                  is carried out into your world.

      Send your Spirit into the hearts of those
          who are captured in the net of violence
              be it as perpetrators or as victims
                  and let us never give up the search
                      for the chance to talk to them.

                                                          (Croatia)

36   Almighty God, our great Elder, we have sat at your feet,
      learnt from your word, and eaten at your table. We give
      you thanks and praise for accepting us into your family.
      Send us out with your blessing, to live and witness to you in
      the power of your Spirit, through Jesus Christ, your First
      Born. Amen.

                         (Kenya. Echoing Colossians 1:18, this post-communion
                         prayer conveys to its African users the image of children
                         leaving an elder's hut.)

37   The God of Peace will be with you
     and grant you his peace at all times,
     peace beyond our understanding,
     that purifies the heart, mind and body,
     until his Kingdom comes.
     Having shared the Feast of God's love,
     go into the world to share his love in your life,
     in the name of Christ.

                                        (South India)

15

Gethsemane

'Then he went out and made his way as usual to the mount of Olives, accompanied by the disciples. When he reached the place he said to them, "Pray that you may be spared the test." He himself withdrew from them about a stone's throw, knelt down, and began to pray: "Father, if it be your will, take this cup from me. Yet not my will but yours be done."

And now there appeared to him an angel from heaven bringing him strength, and in anguish of spirit he prayed the more urgently; and his sweat was like drops of blood falling to the ground.

When he rose from prayer and came to the disciples he found them asleep, worn out by grief. "Why are you sleeping?" he said. "Rise and pray that you may be spared the test."' (Luke 22:39–46)

1   If you are coming to look for a couch for a soft occasion
do not trouble to enter where the most beautiful flower
   is found.
This is a place disposed only for sacrifice.
Here you have to be
   the last to eat
   the last to have
   the last to sleep
   the first to die.

(El Salvador)

2   O Saviour Christ,
in whose way of life lies the secret of all life,
and the hopes of all the people,

we pray for quiet courage to meet this hour.
We did not choose to be born or to live in such an age;
but let its problems challenge us,
its discoveries exhilarate us,
its injustice anger us,
its possibilities inspire us,
and its vigour renew us,
for your kingdom's sake. Amen.

(Bangladesh)

3   It is perhaps significant that the disciples sleep through this
momentous struggle of Jesus Christ. It is as if the gospel
writer wanted to say: When you pray 'Your will be done'
you should not think that God depends only on you, for
you were asleep when the petitition 'Your will be done' was
prayed in the most decisive manner. And yet we are invited
to pray as he prayed . . .

*(Australia: Bible study preparatory to
WCC World Mission Conference, Melbourne, 1980)*

4   Come Holy Spirit
and utter within me
and within each of our hearts
the total 'Yes' of Jesus to the Father.

(United Kingdom)

5   Lord, I am not yet ready for you to have your way with me
– but I am willing to be made willing.

(Spain: St Teresa of Avila, 1515–82)

6   You asked for my hands
       that you might use them for your purpose.
    I gave them for a moment
       then withdrew them for the work was hard.

    You asked for my mouth
       to speak out against injustice.
    I gave you a whisper that I might not be accused.

    You asked for my eyes
       to see the pain of poverty.
    I closed them for I did not want to see.

    You asked for my life
       that you might work through me.
    I gave a small part that I might not get 'too involved'.

    Lord, forgive me for my calculated efforts to serve you
       only when it is convenient for me to do so,
       only in those places where it is safe to do so,
       and only with those who make it easy to do so.

    Father, forgive me
       renew me
       send me out as a useable instrument
       that I might take seriously the meaning of your cross.

(South Africa)

7   In an address given some time ago to the bishops of the
Mar Thoma Church and the Churches of North and South
India, Dr C. S. Song of Taiwan made the point that the
disciples, in addition to sleeping at the Transfiguration, also
went to sleep in Gethsemane. In their defence he said that
the journey and the excitement of the previous days must
have exhausted them. That the tremendous intensity that
surrounded them at the Last Supper must have made great
demands on their physical and emotional reserves. 'But',
said Dr Song, 'when Jesus is praying "with sweat like clots

of blood falling to the ground" there was no excuse for the
disciples falling asleep. But sleep they did. That was why
they failed to grasp the messianic meaning of the cross, and
therefore deserted their Messiah.'

Dr Song concluded 'Fighting back drowsiness must be
part of our Christian discipleship.'

(India: editorial in the Church of South India Churchman*)*

8   O wide-awake Jesus,
we thank you that even as
the mystery of our redemption
was being completed
while your disciples slept;
so we, for our part,
may be roused from the many occasions of sleep –
whether the sleep of sin,
sloth and indifference,
or of sheer physical and mental weariness –
to find you up and ever active on our behalf
O wide-awake Jesus of Gethsemane.

9   Dear God,
I pray for my friend
and for those like him,
for the invisible community of suffering people
who feel themselves to be unknown and unloved by
    the Church.

*(USA: prayer inspired by the agony portrayed
in Vincent Van Gogh's 'Olive Orchard')*

10 Lord Jesus, you knew the agony of depression
    when you were in the garden before your death.
  Reach into the depths of the souls of those who
    suffer depression.
  Comfort and care for all depressives
    and make them realize that always in the soul's darkness
    you are there beside them always.

(United Kingdom)

11 Good Lord, give me the grace,
    in all my fear and agony,
  To have recourse to that great fear
    and wonderful agony, that you, my Saviour,
  Had at the Mount of Olives before your
    most bitter passion;
  And meditating thereon,
    to conceive spiritual comfort
    and consolation, profitable to my soul.

(England: Thomas More, 1478–1535)

12 Jesus
  we would enter Gethsemane with you
  on behalf of all who are frightened and anxious
  all who are prone to panic;
  those wounded and hurt in life
  all who suffer loneliness
  all little children afraid of the dark
  all elderly people who are prey to irrational fears
    and fantasies.
  Jesus, by your presence in Gethsemane
  and by your presence in that other garden of resurrection,
  we thank you that you remain alive and present to us
  in the midst of all our fears and anxieties.

13   Of your goodness, O Lord,
we have this oil to offer,
fruit of the olive and of human hands,
and that which through many centuries has lit the lamps
and served the needs of many people;
may the life of your son crushed in agony
under the olive trees of Gethsemane
likewise serve the everlasting comfort and light and joy
of your people everywhere.

*(Middle East: prayer based on some words
of Bishop Kenneth Cragg)*

'While he was still speaking a crowd appeared with the man called Judas, one of the Twelve, at their head. He came up to Jesus to kiss him; but Jesus said, "Judas, would you betray the Son of Man with a kiss?"
When his followers saw what was coming, they said, "Lord, shall we use our swords?" And one of them struck at the high priest's servant, cutting off his right ear. But Jesus answered, "Stop! No more of that!" Then he touched the man's ear and healed him.
Turning to the chief priests, the temple guards, and the elders, who had come to seize him, he said, "Do you take me for a robber, that you have come out with swords and cudgels? Day after day, I have been with you in the temple, and you did not raise a hand against me. But this is your hour – when darkness reigns."' (Luke 22:47–53)

14   Cold the winter night:
Somewhere in it,
One there was named Judas.

(Japan: haiku poem)

15 O Jesus
watch over me always,
especially today
or I shall betray you
like Judas. Amen.

(Italy: St Philip Neri, 16th-century founder of the Oratory)

16 Lord, in penitence
I offer you my own mixed up anger,
that it, with theirs, may be taken up into your redemptive will
in which the clash between anger and fear,
oppressed and oppressor,
can give way,
to the incomprehensible action of love
bringing about the reconciliation and healing
the embrace of the other
the alien
the enemy
creating the festival of shalom
in which the wolf shall lie down with the lamb
and the whole of life on earth shall rejoice
in the splendour of your glory.

(South Africa)

17 No 'saviour mentality' arrogance can stand in the face of
this insanity. My soul aches, my reason is nauseated, my
mind refuses to rest before the magnitude of gross
inhumanity and insists on understanding, yet without
success. My body, my strength, wants to be heroic, active,
fling itself down or climb to the heights for the sake of
peace and justice, but instead I continue in my little corner
– fretting instead of praying.

And my spirit. My spirit is deeply disturbed although my
faith is unshaken. Somehow God is big enough to encompass
the reality that I want to deny. I don't need to help him be
God just because Rwanda doesn't fit my theology.

Lord, accept this inner turmoil as a prayer offering on your altar. Guide me through the struggle and help me to use the tools and weapons you are offering to meet my needs. Don't allow me to add an imported anger, hatred and bitterness to a situation already seething putrid with such evil. When you call may I be ready to respond, but don't let me stray outside your will just to indulge myself or impress my neighbour.

(Rwanda: diary of an aid worker)

18 Lord
remind me when
I need to know,
you did not
ask me to
defend your Church
but to lay
down my life
for people.

(Namibia: prayer of Bishop Colin Winter)

19 O Christ, who bound your apostles in a union of love, and has bound us, your believing servants to you with the same bond, grant us without dissimulation to do your commands and to love one another, O you who alone love your people everywhere.

(Orthodox: Troparion for the Increase of Love and the Eradication of Anger)

20 Lord, you placed me in the world
to be its light.
I was afraid of the shadows;
afraid of the poverty.
I did not want to know other people.
And my light slowly faded away.
Forgive me, Jesus.

(Uruguay: prayer inspired by the words 'This is your hour – when darkness reigns')

21   Receive, Lord God, the worship we raise this day;
      make us living torches for your Christ;
      since your grace delivers us from the works of darkness,
      may we hold firmly to your Word of life
      through Jesus Christ, your Son, our Lord. Amen.
                          (Canada: prayer echoing the words of John 18:3)

      *'Then they arrested him and led him away. They brought him
      to the high priest's house, and Peter followed at a distance.'*
                                                      (Luke 22:54)

22   Jesus
      who yourself underwent the experience of being arrested
      and of being deserted by friends and followers
      be with all who today are arrested.
                                              (United Kingdom)

23   Lord, I am afraid of my fear,
      I am afraid of deserting you.
      Lord, I am afraid of my fear.
      I am afraid of not holding out right to the end.
      Lord, I suffer and I pray to you;
      You are glorious, forget me not.
      Give to me the courage to give my life for you
      And the love which will make me one with you.
                          *(China: a Christian student, after one
                          of his companions had apostasized)*

24   The three evangelists testify that when Jesus was led to the
      High Priest, Peter followed 'at a distance'. He who had been
      an intimate companion of the Master, and a member of the
      so called inner circle, present on the Mount of
      Transfiguration and in the Garden of Gethsemane had now
      become a 'distant disciple'. But the trouble with that kind of
      discipleship is that it loses its value altogether.

In the face of moral and spiritual crisis, distant disciples will not say a word. They have no word of comfort for the victims of injustice like political detainees and their families. They will even deny whatever relationship they may have with someone out of favour with the ruling powers. They may talk about heaven and prayer, love and faith and hope; and about mission and evangelism, but not about something that may spark off their own persecution. And most certainly they will not talk about violation of human rights, and cases of injustice, and suppression of the truth, and the death of freedom. Such distant discipleship is a dishonour not only to our Lord, but to ourselves.

(Philippines)

25 Lord, grant that we may follow closely, whatever the cost.

26 I stepped aside
While you stood, silent and sorrowful,
Like the spurned lover who sees his loved one carried off by
his rival.
I'm so ashamed that I feel like crawling to avoid being seen,
I'm afraid of being looked upon by my friend,
I'm ashamed of being seen by you, Lord,
for you loved me, and I forgot you.

I forgot you because I was thinking of myself.
And one can't think of several persons at once.
A person must choose, and I chose.

(Sri Lanka: Confession from a Liturgy of Liberation)

27   Loving Father, we are humbled when we hear of those who through trial and tribulation, stand firm in the truth of the Gospel and place their loyalty higher than material or physical gain. We pray that in the hour of testing, we too may draw on your limitless resources, through Christ.

(Zambia)

28   From resignation and despair, from cynicism and sarcasm, Good Lord, deliver us.

From violence in the night, from false arrest,
Good Lord, deliver us.

From starvation and propaganda,
Good Lord, deliver us.

From pride of intellect, from arrogance of mind,
Good Lord, deliver us.

Grant that we do not give you a kiss like Judas,
but confess your love like the thief,
Grant this, O Lord.

Grant that we may enter with the sinner in the new age,
Grant this, O Lord.

(United Kingdom: Oscar Romero Memorial Service)

29   Servant Christ,
help us to follow you into the garden to watch with you
ever vigilant for signs of the dawning of your day
to struggle unsparingly to understand and to be obedient
to your perfect will.

Servant Christ, help us to follow you.

(India: Litany of the Disciples of Christ the Servant)

16

The Stations of the Cross

'It is your vocation because Christ himself suffered on your behalf, and left you an example in order that you should follow in his steps.' (1 Peter 2:21)

Tradition has it that after the death of Jesus, his mother Mary would often walk the way her son had walked on his last journey to the cross, pausing here and there to recall some happening on that never-to-be-forgotten journey.

It was from walks such as these that there grew the early Christian practice of walking the Via Dolorosa in Jerusalem. In earlier days many stops were made. 'Stations' they were called, after the Roman stopping-places. These have now been reduced in number, and, due to the changing shape of the inner city of Jerusalem over the centuries, now follow a slightly different route. The intention, however, remains the same: to journey with Jesus to the cross and empty tomb.

Nowadays, thousands of people of every nationality, language and tradition walk that way, and the very name 'Via Dolorosa' has entered the emotional and devotional language of the entire world. Of course, many people will never visit the Holy City itself, but Friday by Friday, in many different ways and in countless different places, Christian people commemorate the passion of Christ, and join their prayers with those of pilgrims walking the way of the cross in Jerusalem.

For most ordinary Christians – members, say, of poor but vibrant Christian communities in Central America; of rapidly growing churches in Africa; of hard-pressed minority churches in Asia – there seems litle prospect of ever being able to walk the actual Via Dolorosa in Jerusalem. However, walking the way of the cross in their own circumstances, and mostly in situations of great privation, hardship and danger, they are bringing to the passion story a sharp relevance and a fervour of devotion often lacking in those of us who come from older and more staid traditions.

'I think my people understand that figure hanging on the cross between two thieves better than your people', said the Afro-American writer James Baldwin. And although some may wish to extend that claim to embrace a wider circle of people around the world, who can deny that much of the quickening and the real red-blooded life in the Church today is to be found in countries of the two-thirds world, some of whose voices and prayers we have been hearing on this journey?

'For to carry the cross and follow Jesus', declared East Asian Christians at one of their gatherings, 'means to carry it in blood and sweat and tears, and not to transport it around in an automobile appealed for from the west.' Hard words no doubt, but ones that are being echoed and lived out in many different parts of the world.

'For me', affirmed Subir Biswas of Calcutta, shortly before his own untimely death, 'the crucifixion of Christ is to be found these days, not in churches amidst the singing of hymns and the saying of prayers, but outside in the world, and attended by unlikely people and in unexpected circumstances. It is here that we find him. It is here that Christians, by their involvement, discover new things. It is here that the Church is renewed.'

In taking the Stations of the Cross out of their familiar devotional setting, and by locating the Via Dolorosa within that world of 'unlikely people and unexpected circumstances' – as has also been attempted with regard to the other Mysteries of Christ – the hope is that those of us who are willing to get involved in this way, may also 'discover new things', and be renewed in faith for the journey ahead.

O loving Father, make me like Jesus:

> the Jesus who went about doing good;
> the Jesus who made time to talk to Nicodemus;
> the Jesus who could not bear to hear the mother cry
>   at Nain;
> the Jesus who would not let the marriage at Cana be
>   spoilt for lack of wine;
> the Jesus who would not condemn the woman taken
>   in adultery;
> the Jesus who could sleep peacefully in gale and storm;
> the Jesus who spent nights in prayer;
> the Jesus who took a towel and knelt and washed the feet
>   of the men who were going to deny, betray and forsake
>   him;

the Jesus who could give a patient word when smitten on
  the face;
the Jesus who could pray for those who nailed him to
  the cross;
the Jesus who was strong enough not to answer back
  when accused unjustly;
the Jesus who could shrink from the cup of suffering, yet
  drink it to the last dregs.

O loving Father, make me like Jesus who came to the world
to show what you are like.

(South India: prayer of Bishop C. K. Jacob
of Central Travancore)

I: Jesus is tried and condemned

'As soon as morning came, the whole Council, chief priests, elders, and scribes, made their plans. They bound Jesus and led him away to hand him over to Pilate. "Are you the king of the Jews?" Pilate asked him. "The words are yours," he replied. And the chief priests brought many charges against him. Pilate questioned him again: "Have you nothing to say in your defence? You see how many charges they are bringing against you." But, to Pilate's astonishment, Jesus made no further reply.' (Mark 15:1–5)

1   Almighty God,
your Son is at all times assailed by false witnesses,
and while wickedness remains in the world
is ever exposed to calumny and accusation;
grant that even now,
while he continues silent before his detractors,
his defence may be undertaken by genuine disciples,
in the power of the Holy Spirit. Amen.

(Prayer based on some words in Contra Celsum, *by Origen of Alexandria, 185–254)*

2   Just that
just that to say
very quiet, very soft
very gentle
in loneliness and pain, in agony
in terror, in fright
just that remains, in sleep and in dreams
in sorrow and in joy
one thing sweet remains
Christ never denying himself.

(Uganda: a Christian woman's meditation)

3   O God,
     mindful of the presence of your Son
     arraigned before his accusers
     yet maintaining absolute integrity;
     we ask that,
     in thought and in deed,
     in speech and in silence,
     at work or at leisure,
     in public and in private,
     our lives also may embody
     the perfect consistency
     of his life and death;
     to his glory. Amen.

*(United Kingdom: based on an extempore
prayer heard in a small house group)*

4   The day was Friday.
     But it was quite unlike any other day.
     It was a day when men went very grievously astray, so far
     astray in fact that they involved themselves in the utmost
     iniquity. Evil overwhelmed them and they were blind to the
     truth, though it was as clear as the morning sky. Yet for all
     that they were people of religion and character and the most
     careful of men about following the right. They were endeared
     to the good and none were given to profounder meditation.
     They were of all people most meticulous, tenderly affected
     towards their nation and their fatherland, sincere in their
     religious practice and characterized by fervour, courage and
     integrity. Yet this thorough competence in their religion did
     not save them from wrongdoing, nor immunize their minds
     from error. Their sincerity did not guide them to the good.
     They were a people who took counsel among themselves, yet
     their counsels led them astray. Their Roman overlords, too,
     were masters of law and order, yet these proved their
     undoing. The people of Jerusalem were caught that day in a

vortex of seducing factors and, taken unawares amid them,
they faltered. Lacking sound and valid criteria of action, they
foundered utterly, as if they had been a people with neither
reason nor religion.

They considered that reason and religion alike laid upon
them obligations that transcended the dictates of
conscience. They did not realize that when men suffer the
loss of conscience there is nothing that can replace it. For
human conscience is a torch of the light of God, and
without it there is no guidance for mankind. When
humanity has no conscience to guide, every virtue collapses,
every good turns to evil and all intelligence is crazed.

On that day men willed to murder their conscience and
that decision constitutes the supreme tragedy of humanity.
The events of that day do not simply belong to the annals
of early centuries. They are disasters renewed daily in the life
of every individual. Men to the end of time will be
contemporaries of that memorable day, perpetually in danger
of the same sin and wrongdoing into which the inhabitants of
Jerusalem then fell. The same darkness will be theirs until
they are resolute not to transgress the bounds of conscience.

(Egypt: a Muslim reflects on the meaning of the crucifixion)

5   Deliver us, O God,
from politics without principles,
from wealth without work,
from pleasure without conscience,
from knowledge without character,
from commerce without morality,
from worship without sacrifice,
and from science without humanity. Amen.

(India: prayer based on some words of
Mahatma Gandhi, 1868–1948)

6   Have mercy, O Lord,
on all who bear high office and abuse its authority;
all who plot courses of political action for the sole purpose
of protecting their own positions;
all who persecute prophets because of the evil they expose;
all who manufacture a lie for public consumption;
all who treat prophets and public alike as pawns and puppets:
on all such, everywhere, O Lord, have mercy.

(United Kingdom)

7   God of love and strength
Your Son forgave his enemies and accusers
Even while suffering shame and death.
Strengthen those who suffer for the sake of conscience;
When they are accused
Save them from speaking in hatred or anger
When they are rejected
Save them from bitterness
When they are imprisoned
Save them from despair;
Give them grace to discern your truth
That our society may be cleansed and made new
In the name of our merciful and righteous judge
Jesus Christ our Lord.

(South Africa)

8   In the trial of twenty-two farmers indiscriminately arrested
and accused as rebels, I saw Jesus' face reflected in their
own faces. From our fact-finding mission I knew that there
was no basis for the accusations. Looking on the farmers'
pale faces, dirty and trembling, especially that of one
half-blind youth, the image of Jesus' own trial before the
high priest flashed before my mind. The word of Jesus rang
in my ears 'Stay with me'.

(Philippines: words of a nun)

9   Jesus, you were unjustly condemned by Pontius Pilate: strengthen our brothers and sisters who are suffering injustice and persecution.

(Central Africa: Ukaristia)

10   O Christ, Lord of life, deliver us from the dungeons of indifference, that we may not cease to plead on behalf of all who are wrongly accused, knowing that in their sufferings you are crucified again.

(United Kingdom: Amnesty International)

11   Lord, I know that if I try to live a little like you, I shall be condemned,
I am afraid.
They are already singling me out,
Some smile at me, others laugh, some are shocked,
and several of my friends are about to drop me.
I am afraid to stop,
I am afraid to listen to men's wisdom,
It whispers: you must go forward little by little, everything can't be taken literally, it's better to come to terms with the adversary . . .
And yet, Lord, I know that you are right.
Help me to fight,
Help me to speak,
Help me to live your Gospel,
To the end,
To the folly of the Cross.

(France: Michel Quoist)

'Now in the presence of God . . . and of Jesus Christ, who himself made that noble confession in his testimony before Pontius Pilate, I charge you to obey your orders without fault or failure until the appearance of our Lord Jesus Christ . . .'
(1 Timothy 6:13–14)

12 One thing that became clearer than ever to me was that we Christians would have to remain true to our faith no matter what the cost . . .

Not for us the policy of 'tactical dissimulation' which . . . has had the most unfortunate effect on our people over the centuries . . . so much so that often among so-called friends, you can never be sure where you are with them. The art of hiding your real intentions, and sometimes pretending to the contrary, has thus become part of Iranian life, affecting the relationships between people and government . . . These vices of hypocrisy and pretence, prevalent among all peoples on earth must be combated in order to have healthy and happy societies.

I realize that it is here that the Christian Church has something very positive to offer. There is no doctrine of tactical dissimulation in Christianity. Christ was almost ruthless about being and showing what you are. 'Then he called the people to him, as well as his disciples, and said to them "Anyone who wishes to be a follower of mine must leave self behind; he must take up his cross and come with me."' Thus I saw that we, the Church, must go on as usual, not heeding the threatening signs. We had to be true to what we had discovered to be our true selves. 'What does a man gain by winning the whole world at the cost of his true self?' In this matter, Robert Bolt's play *A Man for All Seasons,* and the manner in which Thomas More stood up for what his true self believed, has been a great inspiration to me.

(Iran: Bishop Hassan Dehqani-Tafti writing at the time of sustained attempts by the revolutionary government to destroy the small Christian Church in Iran)

13 Grant, O God, that we your followers
may seek the truth
hear the truth

learn the truth
love the truth
tell the truth
hold the truth
and defend the truth to the death;
for it is by the truth
that we will be saved from sin,
from the power of the Evil One,
and from the death of the soul.
We pray in the name of our blessed Lord,
who for truth's sake
died and rose again.

(Based on some words of Jan Huss, died 1415)

14   Almighty God, have mercy on all that bear me evil will, and
would do me harm, and their faults and mine together, by
such easy, tender, merciful means, as thine infinite wisdom
best can devise, vouchsafe to amend and redress, and make
us saved souls in heaven together where we may ever live and
love together with thee and thy blessed saints, O glorious
Trinity, for the bitter passion of our sweet Saviour Christ.

(St Thomas More, 1478–1535)

*'When Pilate saw that he was getting nowhere, and that there
was danger of a riot, he took water and washed his hands in
full view of the crowd. "My hands are clean of this man's
blood," he declared . . . He then released Barabbas to them;
but he had Jesus flogged, and then handed him over to be crucified.' (Matthew 27:24, 26)*

15   Have mercy, O Lord, on all those whose judgement of truth
is rooted in the opinion of others; all who are swayed by
pressure groups, to do deeds which they themselves would
never think of doing; all whose lack of purpose, lack of

conviction, lack of stability, or lack of employment, makes them available to the purpose of others and delivers them as a weapon into the hands of evil men. Give to all people everywhere, O Lord, a spirit of responsibility and discernment, and make them more ready to seek for the truth, and less ready to believe a lie; through Jesus Christ our Lord.

(United Kingdom)

16   O Lord, how can I even hope to listen to the chaplain when he talks of God's love and the compassion of Jesus in this bedlam of bluster and brutality; help me, at least, to keep a picture in my mind, if not in my cell, of Christ at the scourging pillar.

17   Servant Christ, help us to follow you into the Judgement Hall, to stand mocked and condemned for daring to speak clearly of divine forgiveness, daring to claim God's personal commissioning, daring to disrupt the plans of unscrupulous leaders for the control of the masses to stand for those whose own right to stand has been usurped.

Servant Christ, help us to follow you.

(India: Litany of the Disciples of Christ the Servant)

18   One Passion Sunday, members of the congregation of St Paul's Cathedral, Calcutta were invited to meditate on small crosses made from the wood of shacks of pavement dwellers forcibly evicted from their homes.

Lord, they were very poor things, just pieces of broken plywood held together with string. Yet, Lord, once upon a time they represented a man's home, his identity, the place from which he set out to work, the place to which he returned for love and comfort and rest. It gave him a sense of belonging. It is more than shelter. His wife and children and you lived with him. After twenty years, Lord, his dreams were shattered, he was rudely told that he didn't belong, that he was illegal, but no alternative was given. He was of no consequence, his poverty made that clear. He was a marginal citizen of little value, easily dispensed with.

Lord, you also suffered rejection, you also were marginal to both church and state, of little consequence; it was expedient that you should be crucified that a nation and city may be saved. Open our eyes, Lord, to see your continued crucifixion in Calcutta. How can we love you if we cannot even see when you suffer in our streets? Forgive our blindness. Forgive us when we are part of the forces that reject you yet again in this city, and crucify you and choose Barabbas.

(India: Subir Biswas)

19 O God, you know our weakness: have mercy on us and on all Christian people when we are tempted to cast away our confidence in Christ. When the high and mighty are against him and when the crowd cries for his blood, help us to cling to his cross and behold his face. And as you saved and delivered the first disciples, so, by the power of the resurrection, save and deliver us too, we pray, through the same Jesus Christ our Lord. Amen.

(United Kingdom)

II: Jesus takes his cross

'Then the soldiers of the governor took Jesus into his resi-dence, the Praetorium, where they collected the whole com-pany round him. They stripped him and dressed him in a scarlet cloak; and plaiting a crown of thorns they placed it on his head, and a stick in his right hand. Falling on their knees before him they jeered at him: "Hail, king of the Jews!" They spat on him, and used the stick to beat him about the head. When they had finished mocking him, they stripped off the cloak and dressed him in his own clothes. Then they led him away to be crucified.' (Matthew 27:27–31)

1   Good Jesus, patient as a lamb in the presence of your
captors, keep us silent and still with love for you.
(United Kingdom: Edward Bouverie Pusey, 1800–82)

'Aha! aha! . . .' In Pilate's courthouse, stripped naked, crowned with thorns, clothed in scarlet, and exposed to derisive laughter, Jesus is commemor-ated at Station II as a figure of fun, a buffoon, and the laughing-stock of his fellows. Together with that earlier event in which he himself takes the ini-tiative and chooses to enter Jerusalem riding on an animal traditionally associated with fools and country yokels, this is often referred to as belong-ing among the 'Comic Mysteries' of Jesus.

Beloved of actors in mediaeval mystery plays and by God's clowns and story-tellers of every age, this and the many other indecorous episodes in the life of Jesus – the manner of his birth, his liking for parties, his submission to baptism, to perfumed massage at the hands of a woman of questionable char-acter, his insistence on washing the feet of his followers; not to mention the stories he told on those occasions, exalting the qualities of childlikeness and simplicity, and questioning the preoccupation of people with their own self-importance and privilege – all give substance to his claim that he and his fol-lowers have given men and women a new tune to which to sing and to dance. Because of their pomposity and false piety, it is an invitation to which they have signally failed to respond (Matthew 11:16–19).

Taking Jesus as his model in this matter, it was the strong conviction of St Paul that these foolish – some may say comic – aspects of Christ's life, must also take their rightful place alongside the joyous and sorrowful and glorious mysteries in the life of the believer (1 Corinthians 4.10).

2   O Holy Saviour Jesus,
hustled mercilessly
from Annas to Caiaphas,
from Pilate to Herod,
the object of jokes and jeers;
yourself the original and quintessential April Fool:
have mercy on all today
whose convictions or physical appearance
make them the laughing stock of others,
and give them quiet dignity and courage
in following in your footsteps. Amen.

3   Oh Jesus!
You have made a fool of yourself – through love!
(Italy: St Mary Magdalene of Pazzi)

4   Christ once accursed, lover of the world,
give us courage to be foolish with our love,
and not give in to hate or apathy.
May we be the kind of fools who would rather heal wounds
than exact revenge.
May we be the kind of fools who would strive against injustice
rather than let it be.
May we be the kind of fools to band together in the name
of Christ
who was broken to heal the world;
and never mind if they burn our bibles
and break our bones.
God in Christ, we are with you:
be with us.

(United Kingdom)

5 The spring breeze
   A crown of thorns
   And a reed.

(Japan: haiku poem)

6 Our Father who are in heaven
   (and here in the police headquarters, amongst us, the
   detained. We who meet in your name day after day.)

Hallowed be your name
(despite all the jeers and roughness with which they treat
us when we name you.)

Your kingdom come
(where there is no degrading treatment, no infringements
of liberty, nor roving salesmen dressed in rags, nor
humiliated prostitutes, nor police obeying unjust laws.)

Your will be done on earth
(and on this part of the earth in particular.)

As it is in heaven

Give us this day our daily bread
(the bread which takes away hunger and the bread which
maintains within us the hunger and thirst for justice.)

And forgive us our sins
(those that we have done to the police when we refuse to
treat them as brothers, or when we refuse to accept that
they also live with great tensions and contradictions.)

As we forgive those that sin against us
(or rather, as we try with all our being to forgive those
that sin against us, even the commissioner of police.)

Don't allow us to fall into temptation
(by responding to a curse with a curse, to hatred with
hatred, to maltreatment with maltreatment.)

Free us from evil
(from grovelling and fawning, from humiliation, from
despair and desperation, and from our sense of loneliness
and isolation.) Amen.

*(Chile: 'Our Father' as prayed by ten people
detained in the Central Police Station, Santiago)*

7   You are the Untiring Porter
troubled hearts are your headload!
You are the Mighty One who is our friend
who carries thorny sticks and canes.
You stand amid the briars
and make a head-pad from the thorns.

(Ghana: invocation of Jesus of the Deep Forest)

8   Lord God,
whose blessed Son our Saviour
gave his back to the smiters
and did not hide his face from shame:
give us grace to endure the sufferings of this present time
with sure confidence in the glory that shall be revealed;
through Jesus Christ our Lord. Amen,

(England: The Alternative Service Book)

*'Jesus then said to his disciples, "Anyone who wishes to be a
follower of mine must renounce self; he must take up his
cross and follow me."' (Matthew 16:24)*

9   Servant Christ,
help us to follow you unto the cross
to recognize the true way of life in your death
to see our hope in your self-spending love
to die to all within us not born of your love.

Servant Christ, help us to follow you.

(India: Litany of the Disciples of Christ the Servant)

10 When many Christians from the west talk about taking
up the cross and following the Lord, they convey the
impression that it is like an executive briefcase, easily
picked up and carried by a convenient handle. But the cross
that Jesus took up and carried was awkward and clumsy,
ungainly and unwieldy. It had to be slowly dragged, pulled
up steps, hoisted along by a man staggering under its
weight, walking almost blind with exhaustion by the time
he got to the end of the road. There was no handle to the
cross. If this was God's way of solving the human problem
it certainly went counter to all human ways of problem-
solving we may devise. It was the slowest, most inefficient,
unsuccesful method that could possibly have been devised.
But the peasants of Africa or Latin America, crouched
under their load of poverty, the Bantu of Southern Africa,
stumbling over the clumsy mass of discrimination at every
step, can recognize and understand the God that is bound
under that weight of wood. They don't mind that this
solution to the problems takes longer than the plans and
panaceas in our efficient briefcases, for they have seen in
him a saviour who is not only for them, but with them.

(Japan/USA: Kosuke Koyama)

11 Jesus you take your heavy cross
It gives you pain
Help all who suffer
Forgive us for the pain we give you and others.

(Australia: an Aboriginal woman)

12 I was afraid to take up your cross, Lord,
for it meant a foolishness
I could not accept.
I could not take up your cross, Lord,
for it spoke of Christ's foolishness;

for in many ways his acts
were the acts of a clown – a clown
who knows the seriousness of life.
In lowering himself
he helped people up.

He was laughed at
scorned and mocked.
He did not mind – for he knew
the laughter of children
is the gift of God.
And that is why I am afraid
to take up your cross.
Lord, I am afraid
of appearing silly and stupid.
Help me not to be afraid,
not to hide behind false ideas
and notions of prestige and power;
but to see and speak for you –
of your kingdom,
the good news of love, hope and justice,
of liberation and freedom.
Help me not to be afraid
to be a clown!

(India)

13 Lord Jesus, let us not recoil before the weight of your love;
To follow the foxes to their dens, the birds of the air to
  their nests.
Let us not seek the warm of their quiet nights
And the softness of their pillows
On which to rest our heads.
On! we are not worthy to hear your heart beating through
  the life of the world,
Give us only, wrapped in your love,
The rugged angles of your cross.

(Cameroon)

14   O God,
We do not protest even if our life is destined to lead to
   the cross
or if the way leads to losing our lives.
Teach us how to dispense with unnecessary things.

(Japan: Toyohiko Kagawa)

15   O Jesus, poor and abject, unknown and despised, have
mercy upon me and let me not be ashamed to follow you.

O Jesus, hated, calumniated, and persecuted, have mercy
upon me, and let me not be afraid to come after you.

O Jesus, betrayed and sold at a vile price, have mercy upon
me, and make me content to be as my Master.

O Jesus, blasphemed, accused, and wrongfully condemned,
have mercy upon me and teach me to endure the
contradiction of sinners.

O Jesus, clothed with a habit of reproach and shame, have
mercy upon me, and let me not seek my own glory.

O Jesus, insulted, mocked, and spat upon, have mercy upon
me and let me run with patience the race set before me.

O Jesus, dragged to the pillar, scourged and bathed in blood,
have mercy upon me, and let me not faint in the fiery trial.

O Jesus, crowned with thorns and hailed in derision;

O Jesus, burdened with our sins and the curses of the people;

O Jesus, affronted, outraged, buffeted, overwhelmed with
injuries, griefs and humiliations, have mercy upon me, and
conform my whole soul to your holy, humble, suffering
Spirit.

(United Kingdom: John Wesley, 1703–91)

III: Jesus falls

'Ours is not a high priest unable to sympathize with our weaknesses, but one who has been tested in every way as we are, only without sinning. Let us therefore boldly approach the throne of grace, in order that we may receive mercy and find grace to give us timely help.' (Hebrews 4:15–16)

1   I will come to you, Lord,
with the heavy day on my shoulders.
I have done my simple duty;
I could not continue on my knees,
but I was walking and working.
I call to you
from the depths of tiredness
that surrounds me now
and at the end of each day.
I offer you
all the simple tasks
that I must daily repeat.
I offer you too
all that my neighbour does.
I offer you my transient life,
my sorrows and my joys.
I offer you my weary feet and my tired hands.

(Poland)

In keeping with the spiritual expectations of early European Christendom, from which most pilgrims to the Holy Land once came, devotion along the Via Dolorosa and to the cross tended to be intensely individualistic, and laid great emphasis on the physical sufferings of Christ.

Thus it was that the observance of as many as seven 'falls' on the part of Jesus between his trial and crucifixion focused on his extreme exhaustion and weariness, and on his need of many periods of rest to enable him to keep going.

In seeming contrast, many Christians living today in parts of Latin America, Africa and Asia, tend to dwell on the more corporate implications of Jesus walking the way of the cross and bearing on his shoulders the sins of the world. Even so, this wider social concern is combined with an intense and personal devotion to the human aspects of the passion of Christ.

In the following prayers, relating to his first 'fall', Jesus is portrayed as the one who addresses our human experience of weariness, while walking a route destined to lead to justice, freedom and salvation for all God's creatures.

2   The cross drags heavily
        Tearing the earth
        And its young grasses
                                    (Japan: haiku poem)

3   Lord, I'm tired and afraid. Yet, Lord, I know my charge is
     simple: to love and serve you, to keep the faith, to spread
     your loving kindness. Lord, give me strength to continue in
     your service.
                (United Kingdom: Sybil Phoenix, a black lay preacher,
                and a spiritual mother of the freedom movement among
                black Christians in Britain)

4   Dead-tired Jesus
     help me and my dear ones
     to endure patiently
     the helpless weakness
     of our souls and bodies.
                (Lithuania: from the prayer book of four Catholic girls)

5   O God,
     you have told me that without you I can do nothing,
     but with you I can do anything.
     Life has taught me that I am helpless by myself.

Give me strength to do my day's work,
  even when it is difficult and hard.
Give me strength to conquer my temptations
  even when they are very strong.
Give me strength to bear my own sorrows and
  disappointments
  and not to bore other people by talking about them.
Give me strength to bear my own burden
  and to give others a hand with theirs.
Give me strength to say yes to the right thing
  and not to the wrong thing.
Give me strength to walk with you and not to fall from you
  until I reach your greater presence.
This I ask for Jesus' sake. Amen.

(United Kingdom: Audenshaw prayers)

6   Lord Jesus,
      You who have marked seventy times seven our falls each day,
      And who know the dull frenzy of our eyes, darkened with
        fever and rancid wine,
      You who know the snares of the fowler,
      And his net that circles our steps in the bush, and our paths
        to the villages
      Here we are given over to the horn of the rhinoceros
      And here are hovering the vultures and goshawks.

      But you who know the frailty of our two feet of clay,
      And the place of our weakness and that of our rousing again,
      Lord, let us not yield to temptation,
      But deliver us from evil.

(Cameroon)

7   O Lord, in times of weariness and discouragement we pray
      that you will continue to nudge your people along in the
      ways of justice and peace.

(Latin America)

8   Take the burden, Lord.
I am exhausted with this heavy load.
And I stumble, stumble
Along the way.
Oh, lead with your unfailing arm
Again today.

Unless you lead me, Lord,
The road I journey on is all too hard.
Through trust in you alone
Can I go on.

Yet not for self alone
Thus do I groan.
My people's sorrows are the load I bear
Lord, hear my prayer –
May your strong hand
Strike off all chains
That load my well-loved land.
God, draw her close to you.

(Japan: Toyohiki Kagawa)

9   How vulnerable and exposed and helpless human beings are
when lying down. How easily it happens, and how terrible
the fate of those who fall and are stumbled over and
trampled underfoot in situations of panic in a football
stadium; in an underground; at a mass meeting, or wherever.

Lord Jesus, by your falling to the ground, lift up all who
stumble and fall in situations of blind panic and fear and
alarm, and give to all an eye and a concern for the fallen in
our midst. Amen.

10   He fell.
For a moment he staggered, then fell prostrate,
God in the dust.

(France: Michel Quoist)

11   O Lord, when I feel myself sliding into the pit, stay close; sit with me in my silence and confusion and give me your shoulder to lean on. Prevent me from falling too far, and in your good time help me to rise to my feet again. In Jesus' name. Amen.

(United Kingdom)

12   Of all men,
Of all friends,
You are the one able to understand me, Lord Jesus,
The one who will never jeer at my staggering steps,
The one who will never shake the head in despair when I fall;
On the way from Jerusalem to Jericho,
You are the one who will not pass by on the other side of me . . .

But you – you know what it is to sleep in an old canoe
    tossed by the waves
Because one is so weary –
And at midday to sit exhausted by the Wells of Sychar
In the sun,
And you know the language of hearts come out from all the
    bush villages
To hear you at evening, when hunger makes the feet drag
And the hill paths too difficult.
And you say to us: 'On your paths, of serpents, of ravines,
    and of flints,
I will send my angel to cradle you in his arms,
For I would not have you trip against a stone,
I would not have your feet suffer hurt.'

Of all men,
Of all friends,
You are the one able to understand us, Lord Jesus,
The one who never laughs at our stumbling steps.

(Cameroon)

13 As the banyan spreads her branches to give shelter to the weary traveller, so be a shelter to me, O God, and when my journey is completed, take me home to my native place with you in heaven.

(India)

14 Marked as our lives are by risings and fallings,
by hatreds and reconciliations,
by fears and deliverances,
in which the greater joy is often preceded by the greater fear;
even so, O God our Creator,
it is your Son, who died and rose,
who came down and ascended,
who shares our great sorrow,
and leads us to the greatest joy.

(North Africa: prayer based on words
of St Augustine of Hippo)

IV: Jesus meets his mother on the way

'This child is destined to be a sign that will be rejected; and you too will be pierced to the heart.' (Luke 2:34–35)

The story of the encounter between Jesus and his mother Mary, standing on a bend of the road on the Via Dolorosa, is legendary. It reflects the way lovers of Mary feel she would have ministered to him on his way to the cross; and indeed the way in which they themselves would wish to minister to him in the world today.

Certainly all human experiences of women waiting; waiting for their children to emerge from school; waiting by hospital beds; waiting outside police stations or prisons; waiting for a birth; waiting for family members to return from war; waiting at pitheads after a mining disaster, or at airports after news of an accident, all suggest that Mary would have been standing on the Via Dolorosa that day. To some observers, the very muteness of this encounter, as indeed of Mary's later, silent standing by the cross, is regarded as specially significant. 'We read', comments St Augustine, 'that Mary stood, we do not read that she wept.' (John 19:25)

1   O wait meekly and murmur not
     O wait meekly and murmur not
     O wait, O wait
     Meekly wait and murmur not.

(Sierra Leone: a Krio shout commonly used by Christian women in their gatherings)

2   Lord, at this hour of crucifixion look upon the women of the world, relieve their distress, and accept their patient watchfulness and prayer on behalf of all those whose lives are most vulnerable at this time. Amen.

3   My own heart's blood,
     My Christ on the cross,

Where are you, where have they laid you?
Are you under arrest or under the soil?
God let you be in my womb
and I carried you nine long months;
they snatched you from my womb
and me they abandoned maimed.
The way of the cross,
of Herod or Pilate
is the way of cruelty
and the washing of hands.
But the way they thought
to be ending in Calvary
dissolved in resurrection,
in a shroud and an empty tomb.

The way of my cross
through prisons and processes
takes me nowhere
except to the Plaza de Mayo.

Passer-by, unheeding
and silently unaware:
tell me if there be any grief
as great as a bodiless burial.
Tell me and do not pass by –
Nor wash your hands!
Do not forget there are other Christs,
the victims of new crucifixions!
And Mary, his mother, is present again
in the Plaza de Mayo.

(Argentina: anonymous poem)

4   Seeing her own Lamb led to the slaughter, Mary, his
mother, followed him with the other women and in her grief
she cried: 'Where are you going, my child? Why are you
running so swiftly?

'Is there another wedding in Cana, and are you hastening there to turn the water into wine? Shall I go with you, my child, or shall I wait for you? Speak some word to me, O Word; do not pass me by in silence. Preserver of my virginity, You are my Son and my God.'

(Eastern Orthodox: hymn from the
Little Compline of Holy Friday)

5   Mother and Son,
You see them both:
She leans on you;
You lean on her;
And behind you, the unseen procession of humanity that
    cries 'To death!'
And in your sobbing, Mother,
I hear the voice of all the mothers of Africa,
The sobbing of those whose children have gone away
Without goodbye,
To venture into a darkness where the old customs are no more,
From which they return no more.
And I read in your features, O Son most beautiful of the
    children of men,
The shame of the prodigal sons, the weariness of the deceived,
And the despair of those who have never known the manly
    joy of giving oneself,
That virile joy as at feasts of great initiations,
Of those whom suffering has consecrated.

Mother and Son,
Here we are together, all around You.
We from Africa:
Orphans in search of the mother;
Mothers weeping over the tracks of their sons.

(Cameroon: meditation on the IVth Station in the
form of a traditional African funeral lament)

6   I thank you for pain
the sister of joy.

I thank you for sorrow
the twin of happiness.

Pain, joy, sorrow, happiness
Four angels at work on the well of love.

Pain and sorrow dig it deep with ashes
Joy and happiness fill it with tears that come with smiles.
For the seasons of emotion in my heart
I thank you, O Lord.

(India)

7   Then a woman said, Speak to us of joy and sorrow. And he
answered: Your joy is your sorrow unmasked. And the
self-same well from which your laughter rises was oftentimes
filled with your tears. And how else can it be? The deeper
that sorrow carves into your being, the more joy you can
contain. Is not the cup that holds your wine the very cup that
was burned in the potter's oven? And is not the lute that
soothes your spirit the very wood that was hollowed with
knives? When you are joyous, look deep into your heart and
you shall find that it is only that which has given you sorrow
that is giving you joy. When you are sorrowful, look again in
your heart, and you shall see that in truth you are weeping
for that which has been your delight.

(Lebanon: Kahlil Gibran, 1883–1931)

8   Give us, O God,
like Mary,
the gift of patience;
patience with others;
patience with thirst while travelling;

patience with weariness;
patience with children;
and so to accept everything with patience,
both happiness and suffering.

(Nigeria: prayer based on words of a nomadic Fulani woman)

9   At the entrance to the maternity ward a little waiting area
is heaped with flowers and there is a small white statue of
the Madonna. One gets to rely on her after a while; that
simple passivity, absorbing all, at crossroads, hospital
wards, cemeteries. Although somehow, through her very
ubiquitousness, the quiescent figure becomes not so much a
protecting presence as a reminder that, whatever happens,
all will go on as before. Without her and her crucified son,
usually much smaller and hidden away by some dusty
central-heating pipe near the ceiling, you might imagine that
what was happening to you here and now was unique, and
desperately important.

(Italy)

10   She walks in the crowd, unknown, but she doesn't take her
         eyes from you.
    Every gesture of yours, every sigh, every blow, every wound,
         enters her heart.
    She knows your sufferings,
    She suffers your sufferings,
    And without coming near you,
         without touching you,
         without speaking to you,
    Lord, with you she saves the world.

    Lord, show me your Mother, Mary,
    The useless one, the ineffectual one in the sight of
         human beings.
    But the co-redemptrice in the sight of God.

Help me to walk among men and women, eager to know
their miseries and their sins.
May I never avert my eyes.
May I never close my heart, that in welcoming the sufferings
of the world, with Mary, your mother, I may suffer and
redeem.

(France: Michel Quoist)

11 O God, show me, with Mary, the deep importance of being
useless and insignificant in the eyes of those who pass me
by; for the sake of Jesus. Amen.

12 When I was arrested under the Nazis, I saw prisoners being
taken out to exercise in the prison yard. Each one was
handcuffed behind his back, and they were chained one to
another so that they had to walk in a circle. A fellow
prisoner, a Catholic priest, noticing this, exclaimed: 'A human
rosary!' And as he had no beads, he said his 'Hail Marys',
seeing every man chained to him as a knot in the rosary.

(Germany: Pastor Richard Wurmbrand)

13 Let us ask Mary, whose son suffered imprisonment and
torture and death for our sake, to join her prayers to ours:

Holy Mary, as a mother you shared the sorrow and
suffering, the loss and loneliness of so many families who
have seen their loved ones taken from them, tortured and
put to death. Join your prayers with ours for the oppressed
and their families. Stand at the foot of their cross now as
once you stood by the cross of your Son. Commend them in
suffering and distress into the loving arms of our Father,
that he may bring consolation, comfort and peace to all.

*(United Kingdom: prayer used in meditating
on the Sorrowful Mysteries)*

V: Simon of Cyrene helps Jesus carry the cross

'A man called Simon, from Cyrene, the father of Alexander and Rufus, was passing by on his way in from the country, and they pressed him into service to carry his cross.'

(Mark 15:21)

1   Servant Christ,
help us to follow you even unto the Cross,
to share in carrying your cross like Simon the African;
to recognize our life in your death,
our hope in your self-spending love,
to die to all within us that is not born of your love.

Servant Christ, help us to follow you.

(India: Litany of the Disciples of Christ the Servant)

2   A poor weary man, he comes from the country, a man
of Africa!
And in his head, the fatigue of the day weaves
a long-drawn refrain,
The burden of the day drags like a fireball on his
stumbling steps,
On his moving lips,
On his heaving heart that can do no more.

A poor African, with his chechia and his big boubou;
He is no deputy, no councillor, nor an important person
listened to in the centres of tradition,
And the soldiers before him do not spring to attention!
And the passers-by do not greet him: 'Good evening, Sir!'

Here is a poor African who walks timidly,
And who bears upon himself a sky of mystery,
Like a big boubou all starred with mystery,
One of those men who do not understand, who do not even
understand themselves,

Who bear within them a great coil of silence where God
   sings melodies unknown to other men,
A great seal of silence where God signs a call to love in the
   depths of his bleeding heart.

See – they have laid hands on him, jostling him, dragging
   him in
To make him carry the cross of the condemned . . .
And Jesus
Stands awaiting him like a brother . . .
This poor African for whom all this is not clear,
Who is weary, and does not want the cross of a convict.
Jesus waits for him like a brother,
And in his heart bleeding from fatigue and love
His hand signs the great compact of the call at the
   crossroads of their two lives . . .

There, on the sky-line, in front of Simon,
Man of Cyrene, man of Africa,
The dawn rises on the redemption of the world.

My Jesus, you wait for me also;
With Simon, the man of Cyrene, see – I come.

(Cameroon: from a meditation on the Vth Station)

3   Simon's day ought perhaps to be for us the Festival of the
       Passer-by, the Feast of the Unexpected. Imagine 'coming out
       of the country' and being caught up in the redemption of the
       world! A parable in the time field of the truth of sainthood in
       the person, the claim of the divine in the ordinary, the critical
       in the trivial, the eternal moment which is always now.

Lord of Simon's calling-to-aid,
hallow our every day with your need of us.
Make us to understand its meaning
wherever it meets us,
and give us readiness of heart and hand and mind.

(Middle East: Bishop Kenneth Cragg)

4   Simon of Cyrene, did you have any idea of the grandeur and price of your work, and did your heart quicken the rough effort of your body already tired by the day's work? O God, it is so hard and difficult for us to understand that it is just the most despised and least spectacular part of our lives which is the most capable of being associated with the redemption of the world. For we have a tendency to reject from our lives that which makes us poor and abject, whereas in reality it is just that which renders us fit to be requisitioned by your love in the train of the Saviour. No one requisitioned a rich, welldressed man standing in front of his own house, but on the contrary it is the poor man that is picked upon.

(Jerusalem: meditation on the Vth Station
by a member of Jyotiniketan)

5   Almighty God, whose Son our Saviour Jesus Christ taught us that to serve the least of his brethren is to serve him; we give you thanks that Simon from Africa was there to help Jesus our Lord carry his cross, and we beseech you to grant us compassion like his and a ready willingness to serve the weak and helpless as though we were serving Jesus.

(Middle East)

6   Jesus Christ,
who in death as in life reached across the ethnic boundaries
between Samaritan, Roman, Syro-Phoenician and Jew,
who offered fresh sight to the blind,
and freedom to the captives;
help us to break down the barriers in our community,
enable us to see the reality of racism and bigotry,
and free us to challenge and uproot them
from ourselves, our society
and our world. Amen.

(United Kingdom: The Churches Commission for Racial Justice)

7 We offer our thanks to you for sending your only Son to die for us. In a world suffocated with colour bars, how sweet a thing it is to know that in you we all belong to one family. There are times when we, unprivileged people, weep tears that are not loud but deep, when we think of the suffering we experience. We come to you our only hope and refuge. Help us, O God, to refuse to be embittered against those who handle us with harshness. We are grateful to you for the gift of laughter and song at all times. Save us from hatred of those who oppress us. May we follow the Spirit of your Son Jesus Christ.

(South Africa: prayer of a Bantu pastor)

8 Oh, nobody knows the trouble I've seen
Nobody knows but Jesus
Nobody knows the trouble I've seen
Glory Hallelujah!

Sometimes I'm up, sometimes I'm down,
Oh, yes, Lord;
Sometimes I'm almost to the ground,
Oh, yes, Lord;
Although you see me going along so,
Oh, yes, Lord;
I have my trials here below,
Oh, yes, Lord.

One day when I was walking along,
Oh, yes, Lord;
The element opened, and the Love came down,
Oh, yes, Lord;
I never shall forget that day,
Oh, yes, Lord;
When Jesus washed my sins away,
Oh, yes, Lord.

(USA: Negro spiritual)

9   I was on my way to the fields when I saw him carrying his cross; and multitudes were following him.

Then I too walked beside him.

His burden stopped him many a time, for his body was exhausted. Then a Roman soldier approached me saying, 'Come, you are strong and firmly built; carry the cross of this man.'

When I heard those words my heart swelled within me and I was grateful.

And I carried his cross.

He asked me if I was able to drink his cup, and so saying he placed his hand on my free shoulder. And we walked together towards the hill of the skull.

But now I felt not the weight of the cross. I felt only his hand. And it was like the wing of a bird upon my shoulder.

Then we reached the hilltop, and there they were to crucify him.

And then I felt the weight of the tree . . .

Should they say to me again, 'Carry the cross of this man', I would carry it till my road ended at the grave . . .

This happened many years ago; and still whenever I follow that furrow in the field, and in that drowsy moment before I sleep, I think always of that Beloved Man. And I feel his winged hand, here, on my left shoulder.

(Lebanon: Kahlil Gibran)

10   And now
when I fall down
under the burden of my cross
Lord Jesus
be my Cyreneo.

(Nicaragua)

11   The cross is the hope of Christians
      The cross is the resurrection of the dead
      The cross is the way of the lost
      The cross is the saviour of the lost
      The cross is the staff of the lame
      The cross is the guide of the blind
      The cross is the strength of the weak
      The cross is the doctor of the sick
      The cross is the aim of the priests
      The cross is the hope of the hopeless
      The cross is the freedom of the slaves
      The cross is the power of the kings
      The cross is the water of the seeds
      The cross is the consolation of the bondmen
      The cross is the source of those who seek water
      The cross is the cloth of the naked
      We thank you, Father, for the cross.

                              (A 10th-century African hymn)

12   O God you who are from generation to generation the
      Creator of the ends of the earth and all that it contains. We
      of the continent of Africa bow our heads to you in humble
      thanks for the work that you have wrought in our lands
      and communities over the years.

      We remember with joy the refuge which your only begotten
      Son our Saviour and his earthly parents took in Africa. We
      rejoice when we remember the journey of the Ethiopian
      eunuch, and his Christian fellowship with your disciple
      Philip in the Gaza desert.

      It is a wonderful tribute to Africa that Simon of Cyrene
      helped to bear the heavy wooden cross upon which you
      hung and suffered for us sinners here in Africa and all over
      the world.

We can never forget the countless men and women of other lands who spread throughout Africa the gospel news of the saving grace of Christ, and now that same call comes to us to do the same.

When we think of these things our gratitude knows no bounds.

(Nigeria)

VI: Veronica wipes the face of Jesus

'He had no beauty, no majesty to catch our eyes, no grace to attract us to him. He was despised, shunned by all, pain-wracked and afflicted by disease; we despised him, we held him of no account, an object from which people turn away their eyes . . . But he was pierced for our transgressions, crushed for our iniquities; the chastisement he bore restored us to health and by his wounds we are healed.'

(Isaiah 53:2–3, 5)

1   Pray that our congregations
       may see the face of Christ
       in all they serve.

(Bidding from Nigeria)

2   One of the most special 'stations' for me on the Via Dolorosa, the Way of the Cross, in Jerusalem, is the Sixth Station where we remember Veronica. This Station is one of the 'non-historical' ones never mentioned in scripture. Yet tradition marks the benevolence and human kindness of Veronica as she simply wipes the face of Jesus on his way to Calvary for his crucifixion.

Today the Little Sisters of Jesus minister at the Sixth Station. To support their ministry the Sisters paint icons, especially appropriate as the word Veronica means icon or image.

The humanness expressed at this Station brings to light the fact that we are created in the image – in the icon – of God. As Veronica wiped the face of the rejected and forsaken Jesus, so the sisters reach out with their loving hands to the rejected – the poorest of the poor, the homeless, the hungry and dispossessed – of today's society. This is indeed the challenge that we all have as we attempt to live as Christians in this fast-changing world. To live in the image of God is to help wipe the faces of those who carry their own crosses.

(Jerusalem: Canon John Peterson, former
Dean of St George's College)

3   Lord God, source of cleansing and author of real life, remember those who work in your name among the outcast and unwanted men and women of our world. Give them the faith to believe that you alone can cleanse filthy souls stained by sin and degradation, and can remake shattered lives, broken by disobedience, to your glory and their joy. For Jesus' sake. Amen.

(United Kingdom)

4   Do not let your Church close its eyes, O Lord, to the plight of the poor and neglected, the homeless and destitute, the old and the sick, the lonely and those who have none to care for them. Give us the vision and compassion to labour tirelessly to heal those who are broken in body or spirit, and to turn their sorrow into joy; through Jesus Christ our Lord, who lives and reigns with you and the Holy Spirit, one God, for ever and ever. Amen.

(USA)

5   Jesus is the Word – to be spoken
Jesus is the Truth – to be told
Jesus is the Light – to be lit
Jesus is the Life – to be lived
Jesus is the Love – to be loved
Jesus is the Joy – to be shared
Jesus is the Peace – to be given
Jesus is the Bread of Life – to be eaten
Jesus is the hungry – to be fed
Jesus is the thirsty – whose thirst is to be quenched
Jesus is the naked – to be clothed
Jesus is the homeless – to be taken in
Jesus is the sick – to be healed
Jesus is the lonely – to be loved
Jesus is the unwanted – to be valued

Jesus is the leper – whose wounds are to be washed
Jesus is the beggar – to be given a smile
Jesus is the drunkard – to be listened to
Jesus is the mentally ill – to be protected
Jesus is the little one – to be embraced
Jesus is the blind – to be led
Jesus is the dumb – to be spoken for
Jesus is the crippled – to be walked alongside
Jesus is the drug addict – to be befriended
Jesus is the prostitute – to be removed from danger
Jesus is the prisoner – to be visited
Jesus is the elderly – to be served.

(India: Mother Teresa's meditation)

6   O God, in all human beings, however coarse, rude, ugly, repulsive, wicked, marred by blood, dust, spittle, whatever, help us to see the countenance of your Son, waiting for a Veronica.

(India: after the words of Abhishiktananda)

7   Lord God,
help us to see your image in others,
that we may learn to love those we find it hard to like.

(United Kingdom)

8   According to the ancient traditions of the Church, when our Lord was carrying his cross his face could not be recognized because of the blood and sweat mixed with dust and dirt on it. Then a woman by the name of Veronica went forward, and with her handkerchief cleansed the face and made it possible once more for the real countenance to be seen.

Men and women are made in God's image. His face in them is so often unrecognized because of all kinds of dirt on them. But she of whom I speak was a Veronica who cleansed many a face in Iran; one of them being my own. That is why I thank God for her and people like her, and, far from asking for their repentance, my prayer is that their like may be increased.

(Bangkok: Bishop Hassan Dehqani-Tafti of Iran, rejecting demands that western missionaries repent of their influence and even their presence in their adoptive countries, at the 1973 Conference of World Mission and Evangelism)

9   Loving God,
we know that in many of our sisters and brothers
your image has been scarred and tarnished.
They have been drained by exploitation.
Your image has been destroyed
by people subjugating one another.
The female part of your image
has been conveniently forgotten.
But you mean your creation to be good,
your image to be whole.

Restore it, good Lord.

(Hong Kong: prayer of Asian women for the restoration of the divine image)

10   Whenever I feel God near me in this solitary cell I always have the impression that there is also a female presence. St John in conditions similar to mine, alone, exiled on Patmos, saw God sitting 'as a man'. But there also appeared to him as a great wonder, 'a woman'. (Revelation 4:2–3; 12:1.)

(Germany: Pastor Richard Wurmbrand)

11   Creator God, since with such a wonderful delicacy of touch
      you have translated yourself in human terms; give us also
      sensitivity to recognize that each person made in your
      image, being unique and different from us, has something to
      tell us about yourself that no one else can tell.
                                      (United Kingdom: prayer based on some
                                      words of Cardinal Basil Hume)

12   This is your face, Lord,
      Your divine face that we seek . . .
      And our hearts have always leapt to the challenge
          of your face,
      Behind the anguish of our nights before we were Christians,
      When all things murmured to us of the approach
          of your face . . .

      All things spoke to us of your face;
      Every man's smile was a hint of your smile;
      All tears, every wrinkle on the brow of suffering man
      Outlined for us your likeness.
      Indeed, it is your face, Lord,
      Your divine face that we seek!

      On the blank cloth of yesterday's hopes,
      On the loin-cloth whiter than all the cotton of Kaele,
      That we have woven out of dreams, of sufferings, of the
          hopes of men and women,
      On the threshold of your great day,
      Lord Jesus, print on us your likeness,
      Your divine likeness,
      For it is your face,
      Your divine face that we long for.
                                      (Cameroon: meditation on the VIth Station)

13 Lord, we marvel, hold our breath, dazzled, as we see
you there.

We look at the famished families of Dacca, we see you there.
We meet dissidents in the prisons of China, we go to the
camps of Palestinian refugees, we see you there.
We see war in the Sudan, we visit the night clubs in Tokyo,
we go into the gambling houses in Paris, we see you there.
In the smoking chimneys of Dusseldorf, in the oil fields of
Kuwait, we look, we see you there.
We look at the maddening motorists on the parkways of
New York,
at the gathering crowds on the streets of Manila,
in the bye-lanes of Shanghai, in the favelas of Buenos Aires,
we see you there.
On Sri Lankan plantations, among the workers of Eastern
Europe, amid the tribal conflict in Rwanda, with the
Aboriginal people of Australia, with Singapore's highrise
dwellers, with Aids victims in Uganda and amputees in
Cambodia, we see you there.

Lord, we marvel, hold our breath, are dazzled, as we
see you there.
And we pray, Lord, abide there.

(India)

14 To drink from the same cup
and to be broken for justice and truth
not in a symbolic way
but in flesh and blood as you did
yes, to be broken and to bleed
for love and forgiveness.

To be betrayed and yet triumphant
and walk with the cross
to the bleeding horizon
reaching out to your face
eternal face . . . I come . . .

(India)

15 Lord Jesus,
take away the veil from our eyes
that we may contemplate the beauty of your perfect humanity.
Grant to us your power,
to the end that we may be faithful partakers
of the joys and sufferings of your kingdom.

(Brazil)

16 O God, who before the passion of your only-begotten Son
revealed his glory upon the holy mountain: Grant to us that
we, beholding by faith the light of his countenance, may be
strengthened to bear our cross, and be changed into his
likeness from glory to glory; through Jesus Christ our Lord.
Amen.

(USA: prayer at the VIth station)

VII: Jesus falls again

*'Therefore he had to be made like his brothers in every way,
so that he might be merciful and faithful as their high priest
before God, to make expiation for the sins of the people.
Because he himself has passed through the test of suffering,
he is able to help those who are in the midst of their test.'*
(Hebrews 2:17–18)

Located in close proximity to the Gate of Judgement on the Via Dolorosa, where sentences of death were once posted, the VIIth Station of the Cross commemorates the second 'fall' of Jesus, and is the place where the imprisonment of Christ, and the fate of prisoners everywhere, is traditionally remembered.

The small chapel known as 'The Prison of Christ' in the Church of the Resurrection, in which local women are frequently encountered at prayer for their imprisoned male relatives, and the dark and claustrophobic cisterns deep below the Church of St Peter Gallicantu, both lay claim on the imagination as places in which to contemplate the overnight imprisonment of Jesus; nevertheless, the VIIth Station on the Via Dolorosa in present-day old Jerusalem, with its passing policemen, and the frequent sight of some prisoner handcuffed and in chains being escorted to the nearest police post, provides a very immediate flashback to the indignity of Jesus' own arrest and imprisonment, and a spur to prayer and concern on behalf of the fate of prisoners everywhere, whatever the circumstances surrounding their imprisonment.

1 Jesus my Lord, you are depth,
Indeed my Lord, you are depth:
Having no sin, yielding to no evil.
Your hands sweet and clean,
Yet you became the friend of sinners,
Your love freely shared among them.

Jesus my Lord, you are depth,
Indeed my Lord, you are depth:
Loosing the chains of those who were bound
In body or in spirit,

Yet you yourself, in chains, went the dolorous way
From Gethsemane to Calvary.

(Nigeria: leprosy sufferer Harcourt Whyte,
father of Igbo choral music)

2   Lord, please go before us, to lead:
walk beside us, to befriend;
be above us, to protect
stay behind us, to direct;
be beneath us, to support;
abide with us, to love.

(South Africa: prayer written in prison)

3   When my soul sheds its tears,
when my heart languishes in longing,
when my whole being shivers in fatigue,
come, O Jesus, I beg you to come.
Draw near, Reviver and Consoler!
What is it you wish to tell me
by means of these people,
by these circumstances,
by this stretch of time?
Jesus, I implore you to shorten
the time of trial for us,
for my dear ones, for my exhausted nation.
Jesus, I ask you, help those
who laid down their lives for our well-being:
assist those for whom you wish me to pray.

(Prayer of Lithuanian prisoners)

4   If the Lord is in prison with me,
    what do I fear?
Lonely and solitary though I am,

I believe
I praise
I give thanks

If the Lord is in prison with me,
    why do I grieve?
The Lord knows my trouble and pain,
with him I entrust my heart and my all,
    I believe
    I rejoice
    I sing.

(Taiwan: prayer of an imprisoned pastor)

5   I thank you, Lord and Master,
        that you have deemed to honour me
    by making complete my love for you
        in that you have bound me with chains
    of iron to your apostle Paul.

(Prayer of Ignatius of Antioch, 35–107)

6   Almighty Father, whose Son sent word of comfort to his
    cousin John in prison, enabled Paul and Silas to rejoice and
    sing your praises in a cell, and through your angels led Peter
    from captivity to freedom; comfort, encourage and deliver
    those for whom we pray today; give compassion to their
    captors, wisdom to those who seek their release, and bring
    glory to your name through Christ Jesus our Lord. Amen.

(Beirut: prayer for hostages)

7   Eternal God, no suffering is hidden from you, no pain is
    beyond the reach of your compassion. Give to all hostages a
    sense of your abiding presence and an assurance that fellow
    believers are one with them in spirit; encourage them to face
    each new day in confidence and hope; and grant that they

may soon be restored to those whom they love, through
Jesus Christ our Lord. Amen.

(United Kingdom: prayer for hostages, adapted)

8 '*Without protection, without justice, he was taken away.*'
(Isaiah 53:8, NEB)

We have read these words often, Lord;
but we have not really felt their awful burden –
the agony, the tears, the heartbreak behind them.

They speak of God's Suffering Servant, and of Jesus
     our Saviour.
They speak too of others who have walked the Via Dolorosa,
who have dragged their cross its full length – and then
     have disappeared.
Theirs is a hidden Calvary, unseen, but not forgotten.

We pray then for them now, wherever they are.
Give them strength to endure, faith to overcome
and a love that triumphs over all.

For those who wait, bewildered and weak with anxiety
     and fear,
we also pray.
Give them grace to trust and not be afraid,
and a peace that passes understanding.

For their persecutors we pray.
Melt their hearts with your compassion.
Turn them from wickedness to righteousness and rid the
     world of evil,
not tomorrow, but today.

(Latin American federation of relatives of disappeared prisoners)

9   Lord Jesus,
     you experienced in person
     the sufferings and the death of a prisoner of conscience.
     You were plotted against, betrayed by a friend,
     and arrested under cover of darkness
     by men who came with clubs and swords.
     You were tortured, beaten and humiliated,
     and sentenced to an agonizing death
     though you had done no wrong.
     Be now with prisoners of conscience throughout the world.
     Be with them in the darkness of the dungeon,
     in the loneliness of separation from those they love;
     be with them in the fear of what may come to them,
     in the agony of their torture
     and in the face of execution and death.
     Stretch out your hands in power
     to break their chains and to open the gates of freedom,
     so that your kingdom of justice
     may be established now among them.

     *(United Kingdom: prayer suggested by the Catholic Truth
     Society for use on behalf of all prisoners of conscience)*

10   Lord,
     we pray for those all over the world
     who are mistakenly accused and unjustly convicted,
     and for those who are imprisoned, tortured and killed
     for their beliefs. Amen.

     *(China: prayer after the events of Tiananmen Square,
     3 June 1989)*

11   Lord Jesus Christ,
     you suffered all the indignities of a prisoner;
     hear our prayer for all who suffer similarly today.
     Give us the wisdom to see you

in prisoners of conscience all over the world
who are harassed and hurt each day.
Give us the wisdom to know what to do
to bring peace and justice to the world,
and the courage to do it.

(Pax Christi)

12   Lord Jesus, you are the scapegoat of the human race, taking
away the sins of the world by your death as a criminal
'outside the city'. Make us more sensitive to those of our
brothers and sisters who are treated as scapegoats,
especially prisoners and their families. Give us generous
hearts, ready to offer them what practical help we can, and
also, give us humble hearts, aware that we are sinners
whose only hope is in your loving mercy, Jesus, Saviour of
us all. Amen.

(United Kingdom: Prisoners' Week)

13   God of justice and compassion, you alone can truly judge your
creation. Help us to pray for all prisoners, no matter what
their crimes may be, that they may find mercy in your sight.

(United Kingdom: Prisoners' Week)

14   In her account of journeys in Latin America, the German
woman theologian Dorothee Soelle writes of a Presbyterian
minister who found himself in prison because he had
distributed food among hungry people in Chile. In prison he
held daily prayers and bible readings for his fellow-
prisoners, who were mostly socialists. Later he confessed
that he had never had such a receptive congregation! Prior
to his release, fellow prisoners wrote their names on his
back with burned matches. It was a warm day in
November. He got out of prison without a body search, but

he was afraid lest he should sweat, so he took his release
very coolly. Once out of prison, he went straight to the
peace committee, and most of the names of the men, who
were regarded as missing, were still legible on his back.

*(Celebrating Resistance: The Way of
the Cross in Latin America)*

15 Lord Jesus, in the prisons of our land hundreds of people
are hurting. Some of them are your followers. Show them
how they may help others to know you as their Saviour.

Reveal to them that you never waste your people's sorrows.
You are just as real in a prison cell as on the outside. You
can enable them to grow, and guide them to useful ways of
spending their time. You can increase their faith to trust you
for the opening of the prison doors, and prepare their hearts
to use their freedom as a precious gift from yourself.

Comfort their hearts concerning their loved ones; where they
have been wrong give them repentance; where there has
arisen bitterness and a hard spirit, replace them with your
peace which passes all understanding, for your glory. Amen.

(South Africa)

16 Now, God, will you please open all prison doors.

(South Africa: arrow prayer of Bishop Desmond Tutu)

17 Peter-in-prison
for whom the Church offered prayer without ceasing
and who was wonderfully released:
come to our aid.

Paul-in-prison
whose every experience of captivity was turned to
  good purpose
and who held himself never to be a prisoner of men
  or of circumstances,
but always 'the prisoner of the Lord':
come to our aid.

Blessed Jesus-in-prison
even unto death,
who visited spirits in prison, preached liberty to captives
and through your resurrection burst open every prison:
come to our aid.

VIII: Jesus speaks to the women of Jerusalem

'Great numbers of people followed, among them many women who mourned and lamented over him. Jesus turned to them and said, "Daughters of Jerusalem, do not weep for me; weep for yourselves and your children. For the days are surely coming when people will say 'Happy are the barren, the wombs that never bore a child, the breasts that never fed one.' Then they will begin to say to the mountains 'Fall on us', and to the hills, 'Cover us.' For if these things are done when the wood is green, what will happen when it is dry?"'
(Luke 23:27–31)

1   No single teardrop lies hidden from you,
my God, my Creator, my Deliverer,
no, nor any part thereof.

(Syria: Orthodox, St Simeon the Graceful)

At Yad Vashem, the Memorial of the Holocaust, in west Jerusalem, is the sculptured figure of a grieving Jewish mother holding the limp body of a child; and in distant Nazareth the almost identical figure, this time of Hagar from the Old Testament, head lifted, mouth stretched wide open almost to the limits of her face, in the act of giving vent to an awful lament, representing the grief of Palestinian women for the lost children of the intifada. Together they provide their own most up-to-date and poignant commentary on the New Testament incident commemorated at the VIIIth Station: Jesus speaking to, and in some interpretations of the event consoling, the mourning women of Jerusalem.

Another interpretation suggests that the weeping women were professional mourners who were weeping, not out of their own genuine grief, but to fulfil the formal expectations of the time.

Here, at this stopping-place on an uphill street in the old city of Jerusalem, Jesus responds to the weeping of the women. But he bids them mourn, not for him, nor merely out of custom, but on account of those forces of evil which have brought him to this point on his road, and which, unless recognized and repented of, will continue to bedevil the lives of successive generations of human beings.

2   Lord Jesus Christ,
you told the women of Jerusalem not to weep for you
but to weep for themselves.

Be with women who suffer violence in their homes:
as they weep for their sons caught up in the violence.

Be with women and children trapped in prostitution
and poverty.

Be with the women who live in domestic violence,
who have learnt not to weep for their own pains,
who have suffered so long they are numb.

Strengthen your Church in its care and support
of all who are in pain.

Help us all to be sensitive and caring,
for you are the Lord who suffers and serves.

(Papua New Guinea)

3   Jesus, you hid your own suffering to comfort the women.
Be close to those who are suffering now,
especially women and children.

(Australia: prayer of an Aboriginal woman)

4   Jesus, who did console the women of Jerusalem, console
today our sisters, daughters, brides, wives and mothers
who are oppressed by sorrow because of the suffering of
their beloved.

*(Lithuania: prayer book of four women
exiled to camps in Siberia)*

5   My Jesus is a woman on welfare and getting a foodstamp
outback.
My Jesus is pregnant and thirteen and doesn't know where
she's going to sleep tonight.

My Jesus lies in the bloody dust of El Salvador with Maura
and Dorothy and Ita and Jean.
My Jesus is called drunk, junky, bum, crazy, nigger, honky,
gook, boy.
And I come to you, God, today, as your angry, outraged,
infuriated daughter, sister, friend, lover, comrade . . . with
my psalm of rage and songs of fury . . .

My Jesus is in the supermarket with the elderly, buying dog
food for dinner tonight.
My Jesus stumbles into the dark and lonely night with all
the named and nameless victims and Galileans of the
universe . . . the unloved, the unwanted, the unnecessary . . .
And I turn to you, Jesus, and lift up my life and clenched fist
and joyously pray, Come Jesus!

> *(USA: prayer of the founder of 'Rosie's Place',*
> *a shelter for women)*

6   Blessed One, you know our fears. You always release us
from them by your love, and give us courage to act:
  against rejection – for love;
  against oppression – for justice;
  against poverty – for life abundant;
  against sickness – for wholeness;
  against loneliness – for companionship;
  against violence – for peace;
  against death – for life.
We thank you. We ask you to show us each day the part we are
to take in your work as living witnesses of your Holy Spirit.

> *(Brazil: a group of women respond to the story in John 8:3–11)*

7   Teach your Church, O Lord,
to mourn the sins of which it is guilty,
and to repent and forsake them;
that, by your pardoning grace,

the results of our iniquities may not be visited
upon our children and our children's children;
through Jesus Christ our Lord. Amen.

(USA)

8   We own our sorrow – and let it connect us with all those
who suffer in this assault upon life. With the herders and
farmers and townspeople now under our bombs. With the
animals and birds of the desert, with the very stones of that
ancient land, cradle of our civilization.

We own our shame – and let it reveal our connections with the
weapon-makers and generals and politicians whose appetite
for profits and power led our people into this dark way.

We own our anger – and let it link us with all who are
betrayed. All from whom the war-makers would divert
our gaze. The hungry and homeless in our cities, and the
children whose future we prepare.

We own our dread of what lies in store for us – and let it
remind us of the fear that walks the streets of Baghdad and
hides in the hearts of our warriors.

We own our weariness – and let it connect us with our
ancestors, who were tired too, as they struggled forward
through countless ordeals, in oppression and exile and long
marches through the ages of ice. And so we connect with
their endurance also. They did not give up.

Though hard to bear, the sorrow and shame, the anger and
fear and fatigue – each is a gift. For each can bring into
focus our deep, invisible interconnections in the web of life.
And lift us out of our narrow selves, and bring us into
community across space and time. Each can open us to the
boundless heart. Though found through pain, that
boundless heart is real – and the ground of all healing.

(USA: meditation during the Gulf War)

9   One day in a town in the Far East a column of prisoners
was being marched from a transit prison to the goods
station for embarkation. After the column ran weeping
women seeing off their fathers, husbands, sons . . .

    A young Orthodox priest was marching in the column
beside my father. His wife was hurrying alongside after the
column. As she took leave of him, she cried, 'Vasya! Don't
lose heart! The darker the night, the brighter the stars!' The
priest's heartening reply rang out above the column of
prisoners: 'The deeper the sorrow, the nearer is God.'

(USSR)

10   Women, you are the voice that rose from Ramah,
You are the voice of Rachel;
Women, do not weep for me!
You daughters of Africa, I have called you daughters of my
    Jerusalem,
And you are the palings of peace along this way of suffering;
You are the palm trees shading this sad pilgrimage;
I say to you: 'Wrap me in your silence, daughters of my
    Africa,
Clothe me with your compassion.'

Weep not over me,
But sum up for me the milky ways of your sleepless nights,
The deserts, the savannahs, the pools and the forests of
    your thousand streams,
And the factories by the rivers of the South where you were
    sold for copper rings, for ivory, pepper, pearls and coconuts.
Women, tell over for me the names of your dead sons,
And your ceaseless tears that rained down in the warm
    night on the body of the first-born
Dead on the threshold of the season, after the first rains, in
    the supreme hour of the marsh-fevers.
Tell me their names

That on my fingers I may tell them like a long rosary of
   suffering and pity.
Do you go to shout your despair to the Mountains of
   the Moon?
Do you say to Kilimanjaro: 'Lend us the shining loin-cloth
   of your eternal snows'?
To the Cameroons: 'Open to us your noose of sunlight, O
   Mountain of God'?
Women, do you cry to the Crystal Mountains: 'Cover us'?
And I stand here in tempest like virgin forest which dies not:
But you, women of Africa, and your children whose heads
   gleam like the sun at midday,
You are the savannahs scorched by the harmattan, prey to
   the greed of the first fires of the dry season.
I say to you: 'Come to me:
I am the evergreen tree, the living tree that shall never die.'

   (Cameroon: meditation on the VIIIth Station)

Anticipating the day when the sorrow of mourning womenfolk will be
turned into joy, and a new era of hope ushered in by his resurrection from
the dead, Jesus in an earlier promise made to women, has signalled a new
unfolding of God's plan for humanity:

*'It happened that as Jesus was speaking, a woman in the
crowd raised her voice and said, "Blessed the womb that
bore you and the breasts that fed you!" But he replied,
"More blessed still are those who hear the word of God and
keep it."' (Luke 11:27–28, New Jerusalem Bible)*

11   'Jesus' concern for full female personhood arises when a
woman shouts his praises' says Louise Tappa, a Baptist
theologian from Cameroon. She makes the point that in
these words the mother of Jesus appears to be 'reduced to
one womb and two breasts'. This, she says, was exactly

how first-century women did think of themselves and their function in life, 'But in contrast', she goes on, 'Jesus says "Blessed are those who hear the word of God and keep it." Jesus does not deny that his mother is blessed. He says she is blessed because she responded positively to the word of God, not simply because she became a mother, even *his* mother. This statement implies that for males as well as females, biology is not destiny. Our spiritual commitment is our destiny. Consequently, blessedness is open to all: single women, childless women, mothers; it is open to men and children as well as women. It is open to all of us, whether male or female, healthy or crippled. The only thing that really matters is our willingness or unwillingness to adhere to the plan of God for humanity.'

(Cameroon)

12 O Christ, as we follow you down the road to Calvary
guide us to become active participants, not curious bystanders.
O Christ, as we stand with the mourners at the cross
give us the love that can forgive those who trespass against us.
O Christ, as we witness the new life given to us through
  your resurrection
empower us with faith to act and spread the good news.

(Jerusalem: prayer of Palestinian women)

IX: Jesus falls a third time

1   Ask my pardon
    And get up quickly
    You see, it is not falling that is wrong.
    But staying on the ground.

(France: Michel Quoist)

Not just once, but three times, according to the ongoing tradition of the Via Dolorosa, Christ stumbles and falls. And each time he gets up and goes on again. For Christians all down the ages, repeatedly to fall, to repent and to get up again has been a familiar experience. Members of the Eastern churches have a long tradition of this constant faithful following which goes back to early centuries. One of them, a present-day monk, when asked what was the secret of their survival, replied: 'We fall and get up, fall and get up, fall and get up again.'

For a group of pilgrims, recently walking the Via Dolorosa through Jerusalem streets lashed by winter rains, it was the thought of Christ stumbling and falling, and picking himself up and going on, not once, but three times, that stiffened the resolve of the walkers to continue to the end, in spite of the weather.

On the part of the Gospel writers there is a tendency to use images from the external environment: day and night; wind and rain; cloud, darkness, storms and earthquake; and to use them not only as descriptions of outward circumstances, but as expressions of their own inner feelings. In spite of all such changing feelings the journey continues.

'There was', writes the 17th-century Scottish divine, Samuel Rutherford, 'a bitter cold wind blowing on the day they crucified my Lord, which bloweth even yet in the hearts of those who love him.' Similarly, many contemporary poets, and haiku and hymn writers, especially those from Asia and Africa, also make use of climatic images, particularly those of the harsh and unpleasant realities experienced in their own environment, to suggest ways in which Christian believers are called to enter into the loneliness, isolation and rejection of Jesus during the last hours of his life. And so, for instance, a modern Korean hymn writer sings plaintively of the sky being grey and chilly, and the plain 'frozen hard' at the time of the crucifixion; and the prayer of an African Christian speaks of a 'sun-scorched saviour' hanging on the cross. Instances of this kind of imagery have already appeared in earlier stopping places along our route, and more will follow as pilgrims from many lands and cultures continue to draw nearer to the cross.

For their part, Christians coming from other traditions with a long experience of Christ as the 'man for all seasons' have, over countless years, known many springs, summers, autumns and harsh winters of the human spirit, and over the course of time, to their cost, have had much experience of stumbling and fumbling, of falling and constantly picking themselves up again. This faithful and dogged perseverance has found expression in the prayers of all generations, and continues to do so today.

2   O Almighty God, from whom to be turned is to fall,
       to whom to be turned is to rise,
       and in whom to stand is to abide forever,
       grant us, in all our duties, your help,
       in all our perplexities, your guidance,
       in all our dangers, your protection
       and in all our sorrows, your peace,
       through Jesus Christ, our Lord. Amen.

(North Africa: St Augustine of Hippo, 354–430)

3   I have no other helper than you, no other friend to whom I
          may pray.
       Only you can help me. My present misery is too great.
       Despair grips me, and I am at my wit's end.
       O Lord, Creator, Ruler of the World, Father,
       I thank you that you have brought me through.
       How strong the pain was – but you were stronger.
       How deep the fall was – but you were even deeper.
       How dark the night was – but you were the noonday sun in it.
       You are our father, our mother, our brother and our friend.

(Africa)

4   O God, my heart lies open before you as the earth lies open
          to the seasons of the year.

(Prayer of an early English mystic)

5   We thank you, O God, for the equations of life
      joy and pain,
      work and recreation,
      sun and rain,
      victory and defeat
    that, having experience of the one,
    we may understand the other also.

(Hawaii)

6   We see ourselves, O God,
    people of faith and faithlessness –
    dancing in the sun one day
    and overwhelmed by our realities the next,
    joyfully announcing the gospel sometimes
    and then trembling in our uncertainty.
    We see the hope that lies among us –
    and hope that we might care
    and live in community with each other
    and the world.

(Australia)

7   Pray for us, brothers and sisters,
    that we fail not in offering the oil of comfort,
    the wine of justice,
    the involvement of the patient mule,
    and the generosity which, having given,
    promised still more, until rehabilitation was complete.

(Hong Kong: prayer based on the story of the Good Samaritan)

8   O Lord God, when you give to your servants to endeavour
    any great matter, grant us also to know that it is not the
    beginning, but the continuing of the same unto the end,
    until it be thoroughly finished, which yields the true glory;

through him who, for the finishing of your work, laid down
his life, our Redeemer, Jesus Christ. Amen.

(Prayer based on a phrase of Sir Francis Drake, 1540–96)

9   O Christ Jesus,
     we know that you are alive and present in all of us.
     You strengthen us by your own journey to Calvary.
     We shall not give up!

(Sierra Leone)

10   Thank God for struggling churches.
     Struggling to mend broken windows
         and clear up after the break-in.
     Struggling to pay their way
         in spite of diminishing resources.
     Struggling to remain involved with the rest of the Church
         in spite of fewer people to represent them.
     Struggling to care for the local community
         in spite of indifference or hostility.
     Struggling to keep their confidence
         when they hear the 'success stories' of other Christians.

     Thank God for struggling churches:
         reminding us of the cost of being faithful
         shining as a light in the darkness
         and a sign of hope to us all.

(United Kingdom, 1996)

11   We pray not, O Lord, that our path may be smooth, but
     that you would give us faith to tread it without fear; not
     that we might always behold the heights and measure the
     depths on either side but that your lamp may light up the
     way before our feet, so that we do not falter; through Jesus
     Christ our Lord. Amen.

(United Kingdom)

12 Lord, help me to mean
every 'Amen' I pray. Amen.

(Uganda)

13 O Lord God, who has called your followers to steadfastness
in perplexity and to courage in the face of evil, renew in us
in this our day the strength of will and patience of soul
whereby your servants before us fulfilled their calling in
your will.

Let no discouragement deflect us from the straight path and
no dismay deter us from our avowed intent to follow it. Give
us boldness that we may defy all that – your grace apart –
would daunt our spirits and beset our ways with fears.

Give us a sure confidence in the issue of our lives that no
powers of earth or hell may hold us in the thrall of false
anxiety. Rather let us labour night and day to make good a
pilgrim's constancy, come wind, come weather. By your aid
and goodness, hear our prayer.

(Prayer adapted from 'The Pilgrim Song'
by John Bunyan, 1628–88)

14 Lawd, You pick 'em up, and I'll put 'em down
You pick 'em up, and I'll let 'em down . . .

(USA: Negro prayer of faithful following)

15 Keep a-inch-in' along, keep a-inch-in' along,
Mas-sa Jesus com-in' by an' by;
Keep a-inch-in' along, like a po' inch worm;
Mas-sa Jesus com-in' by an' by;
I died one time, guine di no mo'
Mas-sa Jesus com-in' by an' by;
O you in de word an' de word in you

Mas-sa Jesus com-in' by an' by;
How can I die when I'm in de word?
Mas-sa Jesus com-in' by an' by.

(USA: Negro folk song)

16 O God of pilgrimage and covenant, grant us the faith to stay with you as you travel on; that amid changes that leave the mind bewildered, anxieties that wear away our strength, and hopes deferred which make the heart sick, we may never doubt the triumph of your love, while he who is the way, the truth and the life is shining before us, even Jesus Christ our Lord.

(United Kingdom)

17 O God, grant that we may wait, long, meekly,
in the wind and the wet, in the thunder and the lightning,
in the cold and the dark, until you come,
knowing that you never come to those who do not wait;
and never take their road.
And when you come, grant that we may go with you,
slowly, falling a little behind;
quickening our pace only if you quicken yours,
slackening our pace as you slacken yours,
going not only slowly, but also in silence,
for you are God.

(United Kingdom: prayer based on words
of F. W. Faber, 1814–63)

18 Lord, it is Holy Week, when the liturgy of your Church takes us in companionship with you through to Jerusalem and beyond. It is very hard for a priest to be without his people at this time. It is hard to know, as you stay awake through the long nights, of all the unfinished work you have left for others. But in the middle of the night you come, Lord, with your peace. All our work is your work and we place it back into your hands. I do not ask for forgiveness for the unfinished work, for you will finish it through your other children whom you have given me as my brothers and sisters. When on the cross you said 'It is finished', you included not only your work but my unfinished work as well.

Help me not to be anxious but to rest in you; for always, all through life, you share the load as you have promised and if I cannot continue the journey you are there to finish it.

(India: Subir Biswas, during his last illness)

19   Nothing that is worth doing is completed in our lifetime; therefore we must be saved by hope.

Nothing which is true or beautiful or good makes complete sense in any immediate context of history; therefore we must be saved by faith.

Nothing we do, however virtuous, can be accomplished alone; therefore we must be saved by love.

No virtuous act is quite as virtuous from the standpoint of our friend and foe, as from our own standpoint; therefore we must be saved by that final form of love which is forgiveness.

(South Africa: words of Reinhold Niebuhr quoted by Joost de Blank, Archbishop of Cape Town)

X: Jesus is stripped

'They took his clothes and, leaving aside the tunic, divided them into four parts, one for each soldier. The tunic was seamless, woven in one piece throughout; so they said to one another, "We must not tear this; let us toss for it." Thus the text of scripture came true: "They shared my garments among them, and cast lots for my clothing."'

(John 19:23–24)

1   Every part of your body suffers, Jesus,
as they pull off your clothing.
You give up everything for us.
Thank you, Jesus.

(Australia: prayer of an Aboriginal woman)

2   His face looks bashed in, God,
His clothes is all torn and taken away from him,
His body is stuck.
How come, God?
Don't seem like you had to rough him up like that.

(USA: prayer of a delinquent teenager)

3   In the nuclear holocaust Jesus Christ is the central victim.
Even as he hungers with the hungry, thirsts with the thirsty,
is estranged with the stranger, is stripped with the naked,
suffers with the tortured, ails with the sick and is
imprisoned with the prisoner; so his skin is peeled back in
the heat of nuclear explosion, his hands develop blisters and
burns, as the bloody flesh beneath is exposed, his body set
alight. He is disfigured as are all the nuclear victims, born
or unborn. He is crucified afresh.

(Franciscan reflection, referring to Matthew 25:35, 36)

4   On a ruined wall in Hiroshima is dimly etched the figure of a human being, who was standing next to it when the flash came. The body, though instantaneously vaporized, stopped enough of the awful light to leave that abiding epitaph. When German theologian Heinrich Vogel gazed at that dim silhouette, the thought gripped him: Jesus Christ was there in that inferno with that person; what was done to him was done to Christ; the horror he had no time to experience, Jesus felt. The light of the world stood uncomprehended, comprehending, and undone by the hideous splendour of man's stolen fire.

(USA)

5   For three days she was silent. Culture shock? You could put it that way. She was stripped naked and examined internally just to make sure she was a virgin. Just to ensure that she was not an 'illegal immigrant'.

Lord Jesus, you must understand.
You remained silent.
You were stripped, mocked, humiliated.
Forgive us, Lord, that we go on crucifying you.
(United Kingdom: a woman working in a multi-racial community)

6   It happened in South Africa. Children stoned a delivery van and the army was called. They opened fire and a 10-year-old girl was killed.

One of the soldiers was set to guard the body as it lay in the dust. The child's dress was torn and her body exposed. The soldier took off his army shirt and covered the little corpse. He remained on guard wearing only his trousers.

The other soldiers in the armoured vehicle jeered at him. He replied quietly: 'She also is made in the image of God.'

(South Africa)

7   Jesus, stripped and humiliated in the hour of your death, we
      give thanks for all who reverence your living presence in
      those who suffer in the world today, and we ask your
      blessing upon them.

8   Lord Jesus,
      as in our churches during Holy Week we strip our altars of all
      forms of decoration, mindful of the words:
          'They divide my garments among them:
          they cast lots for my clothing';
      make us ever mindful of your command that if we, your
      followers, would honour you aright, we must clothe our
      fellow human beings with dignity and honour.

      We remember the poor and destitute in many countries,
      against whom the lottery of life is so heavily loaded;
      and we pray for all those who bring pressure to bear upon
      national and international institutions to ensure a fairer
      distribution of the fabric and finance of the world;

      we pray for those who live rough and cold on the streets of
      our cities;

      we remember rag-pickers on the rubbish tips of the world,
      living off the rags and tatters of other people;

      we think of small children who are dressed permanently
      and often unsuitably in the cast-offs of others;

      we pray for all women whose bodies have been abused by
      rape or domestic violence, in their need of the kind of
      clothing that will fit gently over bruised bodies and spirits;

      we think of refugees, rendered homeless and without
      adequate clothing, by reason of their precipitate flight;

      and we pray for all who give, collect and distribute clothing
      to those in need of it.

May all such garments, sensitively given and shared,
betoken that precious garment bestowed upon each one of
us in the gospel. Amen.

> *(In a number of churches of different traditions in*
> *various countries, the occurrence of a disaster or*
> *the emergence of some special need has prompted*
> *congregations to make the connection between the*
> *stripping of Jesus, that of the altar on Maundy*
> *Thursday, and the nakedness of fellow human*
> *beings; and to make this an occasion for the*
> *collection of blankets and clothing.)*

9   Man of peace
       Son of God
         Give us your robe.

We are not men of war,
    we do not cast lots,
       but we would share your robe.

Hold it out to us men and women,
    offer it as a garment to the poor,
       a blanket for the ill,
       a mantle for the world.

Man of peace
    the robe wanted by those ancient men of war,
       give to us,
         an expression of love,
         to share with love.

(Egypt)

10   Great God, you are the blanket that covers us:
as the sea and the land give birth to life,
so you swaddle us with your care.

Great God, you are the cloak we put on
you give us dignity as a garment
and, like the stars, adorn us with your glory.

Great God, our fleeced Lamb:
marked for slaughter and bearing our pain,
your wounds bleed like ours.

Great God, the blanket with which we are clothed,
you hunt to save us and bring us home:
as we enter your kraal, welcome us warmly.

(South Africa: a Xhosa hymn)

11   Your robe without seam,
It was your mother who wove it for you with her slim fingers,
According to the art and skill and tradition of the ancestors.

Weaving, she sang the songs of Judah,
The song of Deborah, the song of Anna the Prophetess,
And the hymn of Miriam, sister of Moses.

Your robe without seam – look!
Along your arms, along your body it slips, wrenched off by
    the executioners.
And you are the naked palm tree, the palm tree shorn by
    the tempest;
You are the lone trunk without leaves, without branches,
    without bark to shield you from the biting wind.

And you would die free and naked of the robe without seam,
Naked of the tribal robe woven by your mother's fingers,
Naked of the clan fervours that weave about the heart like
    a nest of sympathy and pity.
And your mother is alone, and alone the beloved disciple
    who trembles and feigns among the mob run riot,
And you are alone, and you are wholly love,
And you surrender yourself.

Lord Jesus, grant us to be Africa naked and free to
  give ourselves
To your love,
That all men who have become lonely through the hate of man
Find again in you the brotherly meeting-place of all hearts.

Then your robe without seam
That your mother has woven with her slim fingers
Shall become the gathering of all men about you.

(Cameroon)

12 This garment which impedes us from being freely yours,
O Jesus; it is not easy to cast it off like a coat which one
puts on in the morning and takes off at night, for it is stuck
to our skin by all the wounds caused by our sin. That is
why it was necessary, O Jesus, before you died, for your
garments to be seized from you, tearing away your flesh and
causing your wounds to bleed once more.

(Jerusalem: meditation on the Xth Station
by a member of Jyotiniketan)

13 Help us, naked, to follow the naked Christ.

14 There is nothing more exhilarating than to walk through
the world unencumbered. Stripped to the skin! Stripped to
the skin! That is the way to follow Christ.

(Japan: Toyohiko Kagawa)

15 O God, we thank you for our stripping.
Help us not to be afraid of change.
Guide us into new ways of serving you
and keep us steadfast in perfect freedom. Amen.

(Sri Lanka: Fellowship of the Least Coin)

XI: Jesus is crucified

'They brought Jesus to the place called Golgotha, which means "Place of a Skull", and they offered him drugged wine, but he did not take it. Then they fastened him to the cross . . .
It was nine in the morning when they crucified him; and the inscription giving the charge against him read, "The King of the Jews". Two robbers were crucified with him, one on his right and the other on his left.' (Mark 15:22–27)

1   O God,
      nails would not have held your Son to the cross
      had not love held him there.
      Make us truly thankful for his great love
      shown on the cross;
      and grant that it may fix and steady us
      in those situations and places
      which we might most happily desert.
                (Prayer based on some words of Catherine of Siena, 1347–80)

2   With their nails and their hammers
      They have opened your two hands which were always open,
      Your hands of compassion, of mercy, of pity,
      Your hands of healing, which opened our eyes and our ears,
      That gave back to our dead limbs the spring of youth,
      That washed our leprosy, closed up our sores, and from
            pieces of bread and of fish
      Satisfied a crowd starving and numberless.

      Your hands which blessed, which blessed always
      And cursed never,
      Your hands which forgave, which forgave always
      And never condemned;
      Your hands always opened, from the abundance of death
            unfurling
      The super-abundance of life,
      We have opened them, with great hammer blows

So that your blood spurting on our brows
Imprints there the seal of your-love-that-saves.

And we have opened your two pilgrim feet
Which knew by their names all the villages of Africa,
Which have never, from anger or discouragement, shaken
  off the dust of our desolate tracks;
And your two feet walk still, to call to the hamlets, to call
  to the tatas, to call to the Sares of Diamare,
Whenever in Africa there remains a lost sheep caught in the
  nets of evil,
Your two feet go walking to fill up your sheep-fold,
Your feet that we have dug into with great hammer-blows,
Lord Jesus, so that on the dust of African trackways;
Your blood shall trace for us the way,
For it is in your footsteps that we shall walk.

(Cameroon: meditation on the XIth Station)

3   I hear
The grinding,
Grinding,
As they take my leg;
I see
The Christ upon His cross!

(Japan: leprosy patient Shinja)

4   Our Father, we bow in humility as we remember the sacred
day of Christ's suffering and death. We still cannot
comprehend the depth of human cruelty to which he was
subjected. And yet we know that people are still being
tortured and killed for their beliefs. Help us to bring your
divine word of love and justice into every crisis situation, as
we seek liberty for the oppressed.

(USA)

5   O Christ,
     who in the interests of our redemption refused the
          drugged wine;
     deal deeply and redemptively, we pray,
     with the circumstances that make for the exploitation and
          misuse of drugs;
     and in the midst of many temptations and pressures
     give men and women and young people everywhere
     the courage to refuse;
     and the ability to perceive your presence,
     and to enjoy your peace. Amen.

*(Via Dolorosa: which today is reputed to
be a centre for drug dealing)*

6   For ages you eluded us, Jesus of Bethlehem, Son of Man,
     Going first to Asia and Europe and the Western sphere,
     Some say you tried to come to us,
     Sending your messengers of old . . . But . . .
     They were cut off by the desert and the great mountains of
          Ethiopia! . . .

     Later on, you came, O Son of Man:
     Like a child delayed you came to us.
     The white man brought you.
     You were pale and not the sunburnt son of the desert.
     As a child you came –
     A wee little babe wrapped in swaddling clothes.
     Ah, if only you had been like little Moses, lying
     Sun-scorched on the banks of the river of God
     We would have recognized you . . .

     And yet for us it is when you are on the cross,
     O Jesus of Nazareth, with holed hands and open side, like a
          beast at sacrifice:
     When you are stripped, naked like us,
     Browned and sweating water and blood in the heat of the sun,
     Yet silent,
     That we cannot resist you.

*(South Africa: composed in the style of African
praise songs recited before a chief on important occasions)*

7 Jesus, by your wounded hands; teach us diligence
      and generosity.
   Jesus, by your wounded feet; teach us steadfastness
      and perseverance.
   Jesus, by your wounded and insulted head; teach us
      patience, clarity and self-mastery.
   Jesus, by your wounded heart; teach us love, teach us love,
      teach us love.

8 Love demands everything, Jesus. It touches the very centre
   of our being. Thinking of us you gave up what we cherish
   most. You breathed out your life in love, that we might live.
                         (Australia: prayer of an Aboriginal woman)

9 If I had not suffered
   I would not have known the love of God.

   If many people had not suffered
   God's love would not have been passed on.

   If Jesus had not suffered
   God's love would not have been made visible.

                                                          (Japan)

10 I sometimes think, Creator,
    that you must be a fool:
    a fool to make this crazy beautiful world;
    a fool to enter it in Christ crucified.

    Had you no idea?
        – No appreciation of power or propriety?
    You were well out of order,
        dying like that.
    Now we trace in it some kind of plan,
        some necessity,
        some orderliness.

But that day on Golgotha you were well out of order,
like someone dressed as a clown
in church on the wrong day.

A fool can tell the truth,
but you told too much.
Is your life beyond foolishness?

(United Kingdom)

11   So the Master of the garden took Bamboo and cut down
and hacked off his branches and stripped off his leaves and
cleaved him in twain and cut out his heart. And lifting him
gently, carried him to where there was a spring of fresh,
sparkling water in the midst of the dry fields. Then putting
one end of broken Bamboo in the spring and the other end
into the water channel in his field, the Master laid down
gently his beloved Bamboo. And the spring sang welcome
and the clear sparkling waters raced joyously down the
channel of Bamboo's torn body into the waiting fields. The
rice was planted, and the days went by, and the shoots
grew, and the harvest came. In that day was Bamboo, once
so glorious in stately beauty, yet more glorious in his
brokeness and humility. For in his beauty was life abundant,
but in his brokeness he became a channel of abundant life
to his Master's world.

(Parable from Hong Kong)

12   Take one moment of my life, Lord,
on to your cross.
Draw it into the dark forge of your love;
So that, broken,
healed,
transfigured,
cleansed,
reborn,

it may be lived,
even yet,
in praise.

(United Kingdom)

'Jesus said, *"Father, forgive them; they do not know what they are doing."'* (Luke 23:34)

13   This has always been your method, Lord . . . and ever shall be. We must bear the suffering without any hatred. Those who killed . . . really did not know what they were doing, therefore we must pray for them from the bottom of our hearts.

(Bishop Hassan Dehqani-Tafti of Iran writing after the
murder of Aristoo Sayyah, a senior priest in the diocese,
and that of his own son, Bahram)

O God
We remember not only our son but also his murderers;
Not because they killed him in the prime of his youth and
    made our hearts bleed and our tears flow,
Not because with this savage act they have brought further
    disgrace on the name of our country among the civilized
    nations of the world;
But because through their crime we now follow thy
    footsteps more closely in the way of sacrifice.

O God
Our son's blood has multiplied the fruit of the Spirit in the
    soil of our souls;
So when his murderers stand before thee on the day
    of judgement
Remember the fruit of the Spirit by which they have
    enriched our lives.
And forgive.

(Prayer arising out of events in Iran)

14 Father, forgive
   the covetous desires of men and nations to possess what
   is not their own.
   Father, forgive
   the greed which exploits the labours of other men and
   women and lays waste the earth.
   Father, forgive
   our envy of the welfare and happiness of others.
   Father, forgive
   our indifference to the plight of the homeless and the
   refugee.
   Father forgive
   the lust which uses for ignoble ends the bodies of men
   and women and of children.
   Father, forgive
   the pride which leads to trust in ourselves and not in God.

   (United Kingdom: Coventry Cathedral)

15 In my contemplation I recognized that it was no easy thing
   to call that figure on the Cross 'Lord'. I heard again his
   words, 'Father, forgive them, for they know not what they
   do.' This he said for his enemies; and what was I to say for
   mine? I could not say what he had said, for he was
   innocent, whereas I was not. Humbly, I had to ask:

   Father, forgive me *and* my enemies,
   for we know not what we do.

   (River Kwai, Thai-Burmese border)

16 Father, forgive me,
   renew me,
   send me out
   as a usable instrument
   that I might take seriously
   the meaning of your cross.

   (South Africa)

'And he said, "Jesus, remember me when you come to your throne." Jesus answered, "Truly, I tell you: today you will be with me in Paradise."' (Luke 23:43)

17   Remember me Lord
      Remember me Lord
      Remember me Lord
      When you come into your kingdom.

(Sierra Leone: Krio shout)

18   Christ,
      who saved the thief on the cross,
      save us from robbing and exploiting
      our fellow human beings.

19   Jesus, you forgave the thief on the cross:
      bring all men and women to penitence and reconciliation.

(Central Africa: Ukaristia)

'And at three Jesus cried aloud, "Eloi, Eloi, lema sabachthani?" which means, "My God, my God, why have you forsaken me?"' (Mark 15:34)

20   From Holy Scripture
         One word, one phrase recalled,
         And all his agony reappears.

(Japan: haiku poem)

21   Eloi, Eloi, lema sabachthani?
      My God, my God, why hast thou forsaken me?
      Yet three days later he rose from the ashes.
      But the dispossessed coming from those ashes

will one day have their Easter.
For their God will never forsake them.

(Beirut: prayer poem by Francis Khoo, whose wife was working in Sabra camp when the atrocities occurred)

22 How meaningful is that cry of yours in the language of your mother! . . . When suffering reaches the limit where life itself is suspended . . . then if a shred of voice remains, we call our mother, because our mother is love.

But you, being the Son of God, had all your love in God, and to God you called out. And, as man you also had love in your blessed mother; so that, in the impossibility of calling upon both, you called to the Father with the voice of your mother.

How beautiful you are in that infinite suffering, Jesus forsaken!

I wish to bear witness before the world that Jesus forsaken has filled every void, illuminated every darkness, accompanied every solitude, annulled every suffering, cancelled every sin.

(Italy: meditations of Chiara Lubich)

'Then Jesus uttered a loud cry and said, "Father, into your hands I commit my spirit."' (Luke 23:46)

23 Lord, on the cross you taught us so much and you taught us also to pray. The word 'Father' said from a cross is so different from the word said by the coasts of Galilee. In the dead of night, in the middle of emptiness and fear, I thank you for the gift of your spirit which moved me to pray for my fellow-patients, for the nurses and doctors. It was so cleansing an experience that in your Son we are all in relationship; that the suffering of Jesus is sufficient to encompass the pain of all your children.

(India: Subir Biswas at dead of night in a hospital ward)

'Jesus said, "It is accomplished!" Then he bowed his head and gave up his spirit.' (John 19:30)

24 He uttered a triumphant cry: 'It is accomplished!'
    and it was as though he had said: 'Everything has begun!'
    (Nikos Kazantzakis: The Last Temptation*)*

25 Today in the left-hand aisle of the church of Sant' Egidio,
    you can see a wooden cross. We found it sometime ago,
    thrown away by the roadside. One can hardly call it a cross
    because it lacks the transversal branch, the arms. Today,
    only the central body, the trunk, of the cross remains. It
    even conveys an expression of suffering. We call it 'the
    Christ without arms', 'the powerless Christ', 'the Christ of
    weakness'. For us it symbolizes the call to transform the
    world through the weakness of the cross, without resorting
    to powerful means.
    (Italy. The Sant' Egidio community works for peace,
    with both adults and children, in various
    countries in Africa and Latin America.)

26 O Christ, whose body was broken for the peace of the
    world, give your patient and compassionate Spirit to all
    who pray and work for peace; and the courage to reject all
    symbols and semblances of power in the pursuit of unity
    and reconciliation, following in the way of your own
    suffering and weakness. Amen.

27 O Cross, how is it that I shall sing your praise?
    You are like precious warmth on winter days!
    (Japan: leprosy sufferer, Nagata)

28   O Tree of Calvary,
send your roots deep down
into my heart.
Gather together the soil of my heart,
the sands of my fickleness,
the mud of my desires.
Bind them all together,
O Tree of Calvary,
interlace them with your strong roots,
entwine them with the network
of your love.

(India)

29   O Lord, let me rest the ladder of gratitude against your
cross, and mounting, kiss your feet.

(Prayer of an Indian Christian)

30   The Cross of our Lord protect those who belong to Jesus
and strengthen your hearts in faith to Christ
in hardship and in ease, in life and in death,
now and for ever.

*(Iran: blessing given by Simon, a bishop,
at the time of his martyrdom in* AD *339)*

XII: Jesus dies

'Jesus again cried aloud and breathed his last . . . And when the centurion and his men who were keeping watch over Jesus saw the earthquake and all that was happening, they were filled with awe and said, "This must have been a son of God."' (Matthew 27:50,54)

1   There! Didn't I always tell you there must be a God like that?

(Old Chinese scholar, hearing for the first time the story of the cross)

2   Let my heart always think of him
Let my head always bow down to him
Let my lips always sing his praise
Let my hands always worship him
Let my body always serve him with love
O Lord of grace, immense like a mountain peak full
   of goodness!
Do thou forgive my sins!
When my spirit leaves my body
Let me behold thy divine face,
Radiant like the lotus, even on the cross
On which thine enemies nailed thee
And let my heart rejoice in thy sacred name
Grant this boon to me, O Lord!

(India)

'The soldiers accordingly came to the men crucified with Jesus and broke the legs of each in turn, but when they came to Jesus and found he was already dead, they did not break his legs. But one of the soldiers thrust a lance into his side, and at once there was a flow of blood and water . . . this happened in fulfilment of the text of Scripture: "No bone of his shall be broken." And another text says, "They shall look on him whom they pierced."' (John 19:32–24, 36–37)

3   A Holy Rood
     I see the five wounds –
     And a piercing cold besets me.

                              (Japan: haiku poem)

4   With his task done on the cross
     His blood forms itself into a streamlet
     Grace flows from West Heaven in long patience:
          Trials in four courts
          Long walks at midnight
     Thrice denied by friend before the cock crew twice
     Six-footed hanging at the same height as two thieves
     It is a suffering that moves the whole world and all ranks
     Hearing his seven words make all souls cry.

                         (China: The Emperor Kangxi)

5   My mind is forever splintered
     on the anvil of Time
     and my spirit wanders restlessly
     through the caverns of Eternity.
     You ask me why?
     I was an ordinary legionary in Jerusalem
     nigh two thousand years ago.
     One chill, windy morning
     we nailed a Man to a cross.
     (It was a routine job.)
     He died rather soon.
     I remember throwing down a dice
     (we were gambling for his clothes),
     and, picking up my spear, a trusty weapon
     that had seen me through many a skirmish
     in Gaul and Libya,
     I thrust it into his side
     to make certain before telling the centurion.

I saw water and blood trickle down the haft
gripped in my hands.
I saw more – though, by the bird of Jupiter,
I wish I hadn't.
Looking into his deathless eyes
I saw his heart was broken
for me.

(India)

6   Sacred Heart o' Jesus, take away our hearts of stone and
give us hearts o' flesh!
Take away murdherin' hate an'
give us thine own eternal love!

> *(Eire. The bereaved Juno's climactic angry prayer from Sean
> O'Casey's* Juno and the Paycock, *delivered in a
> performance in Jerusalem in the very auditorium in
> which Adolf Eichmann had been tried, was an experience
> that no one in that audience is likely to forget.)*

7   O Christ, as the spear opened a passage to your heart: I pray
that you would ever keep open a way to my heart. Amen.

*'This child is destined to be a sign that will be rejected; and
you too will be pierced to the heart.' (Luke 2:34)*

8   Hail, Mary, full of grace,
the Lord is with you.
Blessed are you among women,
and blessed is the fruit of your womb, Jesus.

And in him are blessed:
all those who look to him at the point of death;
hospices, homes, and hospitals, and all who care for the
    terminally ill;

those who die suddenly or violently;
all who mourn the death of a loved one;
and those for whom the process of dying is fearful . . .

Holy Mary, Mother of God,
pray for us sinners, now and at the hour of our death.

9   O Lord Jesus Christ, whose perfect love met death by
violence and was not extinguished; so enter the hearts and
minds of those affected by violence, that frailty may give
way to your strength, loss to your gain, bitterness to your
total and victorious love; for your name's sake. Amen.

(United Kingdom: prayer used at the place
where a young woman was murdered)

10   What was Hiroshima like, Jesus, when the bomb fell? What
went through the minds of mothers, what happened to the
lives of children, what stabbed at the hearts of men when
they were caught up in the sea of flames?

What was Auschwitz like, Jesus, when the crematoriums
belched the stinking smoke of the burned bodies of people?
When families were separated, the weak perished, the
strong faced inhuman tortures of the spirit and the body?
What was the concentration camp like, Jesus?

What was it like?

(USA)

11   The Japanese novelist Rinzo Shiina was attracted in his
youth to the Communist Party, but was so overwhelmed by
a fear of death that he lacked the courage to face up to the
kind of struggle that the party might demand of him. In this
state of mind he went one day to visit a friend in hospital.
On a wall in the entrance hall was a painting of Christ on a

cross; a painting of a death so complete that it was to liberate him from his fear of death. He describes how it happened:

'The painting was that of the body of a man on the cross. There was nothing more than a white cloth wrapped around his loins. The brown body was stiff with death. The torso, the arms, the legs looked like a withered tree that had been cut and felled. The sight of it all pierced my heart. There wasn't a single spot of live tissue left in that dried out tree. It gave me the feeling that every cell in the body was so dead that it had become like a rock; even worms couldn't have lived in that dead tree. I even felt envious of that dead body. I'd never before seen such a complete death.'

(Japan)

12 O Lord God, our heavenly Father, regard we beseech you, with your divine pity the pains of all your children; and grant that the Passion of our Lord and his infinite love may make fruitful for good the tribulations of the innocent, the sufferings of the sick, and the sorrows of the bereaved; through him who suffered in our flesh and died for our sake, the same your Son our Saviour Jesus Christ. Amen.

(France: 1915)

XIII: Jesus is taken down from the cross

'When evening fell, a wealthy man from Arimathaea, Joseph by name, who had himself become a disciple of Jesus, approached Pilate and asked for the body of Jesus; and Pilate gave orders that he should have it. Joseph took the body, wrapped it in a clean linen sheet, and laid it in his own unused tomb, which he had cut out of the rock. He then rolled a large stone against the entrance, and went away.'
(Matthew 27:57–60)

1   O my God, Jesus,
I am in every way unworthy of you.
Yet, like Joseph of Arimathaea,
I want to offer a space for you.
He offered his own tomb;
I offer my heart.

Enter the darkness of my heart,
as your body entered the darkness of Joseph's tomb.
And make me worthy to receive you,
driving out all sin and darkness
that I might be filled with your light.
(Italy: St Bonaventura, 1217–74)

2   Mother of Sorrows,
What cradle-song have you crooned to your child so still
    and stiff,
As in the days of his first slumber
When your voice lulled him, and behind his closed lids
He smiled at you in his sleep,
His still lips smiled to your singing lips?

But today your Son keeps silence,
The silence of his quiet heart and body;
But today your Son is a corpse,
And you no more than a mourner begging pity
    of passers-by;

And in your arms, see – the sorrow of all mothers
  without children,
With your tears, the tears of those whose life is a desert,
And your silence is poignant as the crying of the widows
  of Bamileke
Over the graves that swallowed their only sons in the night;
And your face is grave and meek like the face of
  a young mother
Leaning over the empty cradle where rang her babe's
  first crying.

Mother, what cradle-song have you sung to your Son in
  his slumber,
To waken him from the night of the tomb?
You know we have fear of that night.
Give us the aid of your arms, the help of the voice of
  your faith so wholly resigned;
Sing us your cradle-song, Mother
Your own cradle-song, Mother of Jesus Christ.

(Cameroon)

3   Mary's body and your body are one, Jesus.
     Your life lives on in her body.
     She carries on your life in herself.

(Australia: prayer of an Aboriginal woman)

4   I often think of Mary: I suffered so much when they arrested
     my son. When I went to ask where he was, they said they
     didn't know. I searched and searched, but couldn't find him.
     Finally his corpse appeared, his head in one place and his
     body in another. I fainted when I saw him. I thought of how
     the Blessed Virgin also suffered when they told her that her
     son had been arrested. Surely she went searching for him and
     later saw him die and buried him. That is why she
     understands my sorrow and helps me to carry on.

Mary, you suffered
so much misery and repression on earth,
and even now, though safe in heaven,
still remain our compañera,
and suffer with us.

> (El Salvador: a testimony and prayer typical of the way in which
> Salvadoran women express their sufferings caused by the
> torture or murder of their husbands and children)

5   Weep not for me, but for my Father's Asian family
in whose pain, whose poverty and dignity, you see my face.

They may not suffer violence so visibly,
but many meet indifference, injustice and abandonment
to hunger, prison, sickness, humiliation, debt;
to discrimination against caste, religion, faction, race;
to prostitution and the selling of their children;
to life and death in teeming public street and tenement.
The Tiananmen Square's deaths;
Jaffna's, Dacca's,
    Hiroshima's and Kuwait's rape
which sent the migrant unemployed home –
a million empty pockets, a hundred hands to every broom –
were caused by human beings, powerful, losing control,
like those whose pride, resentment, hatred, fear
nailed you to the cross.

Perhaps the sculptor sees you lying thus,
released from suffering, desire and rebirth;
some, believing you a prophet, may say
you were not crucified.
But we believe that in your very human birth
and death, God laid you naked in a mother's arms,
and raised you up, unique, Saviour and Son,
whose pulse beats still in all of Asia's pain.

Inspire new will and vision, Lord,
opening the way to reconciliation,
peace and justice, love and healing,
succour and salvation.

> *(Meditation in response to a sculpture by a Sri Lankan*
> *Buddhist of the figure of Mary cradling the dead Christ*
> *in her arms, and described as 'an image of suffering here*
> *and now, throughout Asia')*

6   O Lord,
who within the family of your Church
has conferred honour and dignity
upon those who touched and handled your body
at the beginning and ending of your earthly life;
look now with your mercy
upon those women and men
who care for the young and aged in our society,
especially those ravaged by disease and injured in accident,
whose bodies are not easy to handle,
and give them proper reward
and the respect appropriate to their calling.

> *(South Africa: prayer inspired by concern for inadequately*
> *paid black servants who have traditionally given so much*
> *of their time and energy to caring for children and the*
> *elderly in white households)*

John, in his Gospel, associates Nicodemus, 'the man who visited Jesus by night', with Joseph of Arimathaea, in the quiet task of anointing the body of Jesus for burial (John 19:39). Apart from brief but important appearances, these two men, appear to have remained largely unknown in the ongoing life of the early Christian community, as recorded in the New Testament; but the nocturnal setting of Nicodemus's enquiry, and the unobtrusive activity of the two men, have long made them a model for many anonymous and otherwise hidden aspects of Christian life and ministry.

7   Almighty God, whose blessed Son Jesus Christ ministered to the spiritual needs of Nicodemus under cover of darkness, and was himself, in turn, cared for quietly on the dark night of his death; we thank you that the reverberation of such actions continues until this present time, and offers impetus and encouragement to all who seek to meet the 'night' needs of people everywhere. Amen.

8   Where today
ministers and priests,
social workers and counsellors,
Samaritans and sensitive listeners
hear of the secret of malevolence
which ruins the lives of others;
sit with them, Lord.
And through them
open paths to repentance and change
at whatever cost honesty and love demand.

(Scotland)

9   Bless all, O Lord, who worship you in secret; all whose hearts are growing round an undeclared allegiance; all whose life is laden with a treasure they would pour out at your feet; all who know with greater certainty each day that they have found the pearl of greatest price; then by the power of the cross, O Christ, claim your victory in their hearts, and lead them to the liberty of being seen by others to be yours, for your dear name's sake. Amen.

(United Kingdom: prayer for secret believers)

10 Merciful God, whose servant Joseph of Arimathaea with reverence and godly fear prepared the body of our Lord and Saviour for burial, and laid it in his own tomb; Grant to us, your faithful people, grace and courage to love and serve Jesus with sincere devotion all the days of our life; through Jesus Christ our Lord, who lives and reigns with you and the Holy Spirit, one God, for ever and ever. Amen.

(USA: Feast of Joseph of Arimathaea, 31 July)

XIV: Jesus is buried

'It was the day of preparation, and the sabbath was about to begin. The women who had accompanied Jesus from Galilee followed; they took note of the tomb and saw his body laid in it. Then they went home and prepared spices and perfumes; and on the sabbath they rested in obedience to the commandment.' (Luke 23:54–56)

1   You Holy Women who crushed sweet ointment to embalm our Lord, crush some sweetness from this work of mine; crush me too that I might spread a sweet fragrance before the feet of our Lord.

(North Africa: Charles de Foucauld)

2   You, the Life, were laid in the grave, O Christ, and the hosts of the angels shuddered, praising your humility.

(Orthodox)

3   O blessed Lord, your body is as cold as the stone around you, your skin as white as the shroud that covers you.

O blessed Lord, you are all alone in the tomb, your friends too frightened to come near you.

O blessed Lord, my heart is cold, my soul is white with fear; I feel lonely, I have no friends at my side.

I wait for your glory, when the bright sun of God's love will warm all humankind, and everyone will be at peace with his neighbour.

(Celtic song to Jesus)

For many pilgrims to the Church of the Holy Sepulchre in Jerusalem, no object evokes the sense of the stark reality of death so poignantly as the huge slab of the anointing stone just inside the main door. Nor is anything more expressive of the sense of continuity with the mourning women of Holy Saturday than the single flower so often to be found laid upon it. A small gesture of love and faith offered by the hands of unknown, present-day women of Jerusalem.

4   From the land of the Resurrection and the cradle of the
    promise of salvation to all humankind through Jesus Christ
    our Lord, and with a candle of hope, we pray to you, God
    our Father, that the action of peace seekers and peace
    makers may bear fruit, so that
        Hope will take the place of despair,
        Justice will prevail over oppression,
        Peace will turn strife into love.
                        (Jerusalem: prayer of Palestinian women)

5   To look at the promised land from afar
    And not to set foot on its soil,
    To dream of milk and honey
    And not to taste the mixture –
    This was the lot of Israel's greatest prophet.
        There are many prophets in the wilderness
        Who die outside the promised land.

    Squeezed between Good Friday and Easter,
    Ignored by preachers and painters and poets,
    Saturday lies cold and dark and silent –
    An unbearable pause between death and life.
        There are many Saturday people
        To whom Easter does not come.
        There are no angels to roll the stones away.

    There are many Saturday people in the world today:
        children dying for want
        of food and affection
        brides who bring little or no dowry

mothers who break stones and carry bricks
boat-people waiting for the end
of the right-to-asylum debate
prisoners who die in custody
and those killed while trying to escape
hostages who do not see the light of day
and detainees who do not see a courtroom
tribals evicted from forests
and fisherfolk separated from the sea
generations without nations and peoples
and tribes doomed to die without hope...

The prophets who lead the Saturday people
Die with them outside the promised land.

There is a Cross in every resurrection.
Is there a Resurrection in every cross?

> *(India: written in response to the account of a service
> in the cemetery of the former Nazi concentration
> camp of Bergen-Belsen. Weakened by long and
> harsh imprisonment many died after the camp
> had been liberated; for them freedom came too
> late. Hence the final question of the meditation.)*

6   There is something between us now;
The cry you did not raise.

You have washed your hands again.
Put down the pitcher,
This water will flow between us.

Give me back Jesus;
He is my brother.
He will walk with me
Behind the grey ghetto wall
Into the slaughter-house.
I will lead him into the lethal chambers
He will lie down upon the poisoned stone;
The little children pricked with the death bubble

Will come unto him.

Return to him the yellow badge
Give me back Jesus;
He is not yours.

(Words of a Jewish woman, addressing a Christian friend)

7   Time is an unfathomable secret to the one who is always in
a rush. Time is a strange solver of the problems that afflict
heart and mind. Time is a comforter. Time is a friend . . .
Time transforms the child into an adult. Time buries
tyrants. In tune with time, the sick are healed, the broken-
hearted recover, and the seeds of wheat that lie buried under
the snow prepare for future growth . . . in the day of your
distress, meditate on the way in which time deals with you
– and wait.

(Japan: Toyohiko Kagawa, meditating on John 16:16–18)

8   Not straight away. Not at once. Not
in the moment of time in which the veil was torn in two.
Not immediately in order to comfort and promptly to
assure
His stricken friends, His ravaged mother.
No.
He did not rise at once. But
on the third day. It was only
when the fact of death had arrived at successively deeper
levels into the disciples' mind; when information had
become knowledge;
when knowledge had become truth;
when all were quite sure He was dead:
it was only then that
He rose again.

Lord, when we wait for your promises to come true,

give us patience, give us faith, give us hope,
give us obedience
to wait for
the
'third day'.

(United Kingdom)

9 Let's forget it now,
And all go home.
He is buried and the stone is in place.
His family is in tears, his friends are lost.
This time it is really over.

Lord, it is not over.
'You are in agony till the end of time', I know.
People tread the Way of the Cross in relays.
The resurrection will only be completed when they have
    reached the end of the way.
I am on the road; I have a small share of your suffering and
    the others have theirs . . .

Lord, help me to travel along my road faithfully, at my
    proper place in the vast procession of humanity.
Help me above all to recognize you and to help you in all
    my fellow pilgrims.
For it would be a lie to weep before your lifeless image, if I
    did not follow you, living, on the road that men and
    women travel.

(France: Michel Quoist, meditation on the XIVth Station)

10 Bent into the body of Christ
laid out under glass
like some enshrined wino
sleeping off a draught of death
in the corner of the shrouded cathedral,

an old Indian woman
swayed under musty skirts,
her cracked lips
skipping over words
in whispers not meant
for me to hear.

What is she asking Him for?
Supper?
The soul of a son?
Forgiveness for a suddenly
remembered sin?
To be taken into His
bosom tomorrow?

I stand in the shadows
under the chipped angel
with a lurid neon halo,
a gringo adrift here
at the top of the world,
praying with her lips
that we each get
what we need.

(La Paz, Bolivia)

11   How fair and lovely is the hope which the Lord gave to the
dead when He laid down like them beside them.
Rise up and come forth and sing praise to Him who has
raised you from destruction.

(Syrian Orthodox Liturgy)

*'Christ too suffered for our sins once and for all, the just for
the unjust, that he might bring us to God; put to death in the
body, he was brought to life in the spirit. In the spirit also he
went and made his proclamation to the imprisoned spirits . . .'*

(1 Peter 3:18–19)

12 God, Father of the living,
on this day your Son went down to visit
the spirits who were in prison.
Look with kindness on all who wait in hope
for their liberation from the corruption of sin and death,
and give them a share
in the glory of the children of God,
through Jesus, your Son, our Lord.

(France: Cistercian, Lauds for Holy Saturday)

13 O God of Abraham, Isaac and Jacob,
we ask you to hear the prayers of all your children whose
forefathers did not know you in this life. You know them
all. Consecrate the bond of kinship which binds us to them,
and mercifully make us all partakers in him who died on
the cross for the sins of the whole world, who preached to
the spirits in prison, and rose again to be ruler over all of
your creation, your Son, our Saviour Jesus Christ. To him,
with you and the Holy Spirit, be all praise and all glory, for
ever and ever, world without end. Amen.

(Japan)

14 Eternal Father, God of our ancestors,
before your power all things tremble,
but through your Son, we approach your throne.
We have done wrong, and neglected to do right
our sins – and those of our fathers –
   weigh heavily on our hearts;
Lord, have mercy, count them not against us.
Grant us the joy of forgiveness,
and lighten our hearts with the glory of Christ,
who died and rose again for us. Amen.

(Kenya)

15   O God, you go deep down.
From far above where the sun and the stars are to be found,
you come down to earth and enter completely into
the life of humankind; penetrating all living things.
And, not content to remain on the surface,
but going deep down into the dust from which we come,
you restore the land itself to life.

(Australia: the God who goes deep down
is a recurring theme in Aboriginal art and prayer)

'*You died; and now your life lies hidden with Christ in God.*'
(Colossians 3:3)

16   Accept, our Lord, from us – at this hour and all hours – our
supplications; make our life easy; direct us to behave in
accordance with your commandments. Sanctify our spirits;
purify our bodies; straighten our thoughts; cleanse our
desires; heal our sicknesses; forgive our sins; and save us
from all evil, sorrow, and heartache. Surround us by your
holy angels that we may be kept in their camp, and guided
so as to arrive at the unity of faith and the knowledge of
your glory, imperceptible and boundless.

(Egypt. Each Egyptian day is punctuated seven times by the
Horologion, commemorating, among other mysteries,
the crucifixion, death, and burial of Jesus. Each
recollection concludes with this prayer.)

17   O living God, in Jesus Christ you were laid in the tomb at
this evening hour, and so sanctified the grave to be a bed of
hope to your people. Give us courage and faith to die daily
to our sin and pride, that even as this flesh and blood
decays, our lives still may grow in you, that at our last day
our dying may be done so well that we live in you for ever.

(Prayer at Night)

18   Lord, in you we live and have our being.
You are he who brings to birth and brings to death.
You do not weary of humankind,
But give day by day the gift of life,
Making men and women the creators
In the tireless procession of the generations,
Fearfully and wonderfully made.
Grant us in our time the hallowing of the womb
And reverence for the mystery of life.
Teach us, in the teeming world, the due trust of birth,
To keep faith with the newly born, the yet unborn,
Lest the crowded earth shall not suffice them.
And in the midst of life, we pray for those in death,
In the ceaseless exodus of the departing.
Yours it is to summon, yours to have mercy and to save.
Amen.

(Prayers for Christian and Muslim use: Bishop Kenneth Cragg)

19   Blessed be your name, O Jesus, Son of the living God:
blessed be the sorrow you suffered when your holy hands
and feet were nailed to the tree; and blessed your love
when, the fullness of pain accomplished, you gave your soul
into the hands of the Father; so by your Cross and precious
Blood redeeming all the world, all longing souls departed
and the numberless unborn; who is alive and reigns in the
glory of the eternal Trinity, God for ever and ever.

(Orthodox)

20   Gracious Lord,
in this season of fullness and completion,
we praise you for all living and all dying.
We thank you for that great circle
in which we are united with all who have gone before us.
Bring us all, good Lord, to the day

when you will free our eyes from tears,
our feet from stumbling,
when we shall walk before you in the land of the living.

(USA: All Saints' Day)

21   On the seventh day of creation, Almighty God,
you rested from your work;
but by our sin death came into the world.
Now on this day Jesus rests in the tomb,
having finished the work you gave him to do.
In him new life springs up and overflows;
may all the living give you thanks
in every time and place,
through Jesus the Christ, our Lord.

(France: Cistercian, Vespers for Holy Saturday)

22   And now, O Father, we commit
our struggles and sufferings into your Son's wounded hands,
our hopes and aspirations into his praying hands,
our poor and exploited into his just hands,
and our living and departed into the hands of him
who holds the key of the world of death.
Blessed be the Lord, for ever. Amen and Amen.

(Church of South India: Recalling and Offering)

17
The Resurrection Mystery

1   Ah, the fragrance of new grass!
    I hear His footsteps coming –
    The Lord of the Resurrection!

(Japan)

'*So the disciples went home again; but Mary stood outside the tomb weeping. And as she wept, she peered into the tomb, and saw two angels in white sitting there, one at the head, and one at the feet, where the body of Jesus had lain. They asked her, "Why are you weeping?" She answered, "They have taken my Lord away, and I do not know where they have laid him." With these words she turned round and saw Jesus standing there, but she did not recognize him. Jesus asked her, "Why are you weeping? Who are you looking for?" Thinking it was the gardener, she said, "If it is you, sir, who removed him, tell me where you have laid him, and I will take him away." Jesus said, "Mary!" She turned and said to him, "Rabbuni!" (which is Hebrew for "Teacher"). "Do not cling to me," said Jesus, "for I have not yet ascended to the Father."' (John 20:10–17)*

2   In the sky
    The song of the skylark
    Greets the dawn
    In the fields wet with dew
    The scent of the violets
    Fills the air
    On such a lovely morning as this

Surely on such a lovely morning as this
Lord Jesus
Came forth
From the tomb.

(Japan: leprosy sufferer Misuno Genzo)

3   Blessed be you, O Living One
to whose tomb came women
spice-bearing, to embalm your body
and found you risen
adding spice to all our lives.
Blessed be you, O Fragrant One.

4   O God, who has implanted in the hearts of men and
women a great love of gardens; grant that in barren and
clamorous days the men and women of Iran (and every
land) may once again enjoy the fruitful and life-affirming
aspects of their rich heritage, and so by this route enter the
garden in which your Son reveals himself alive as master
gardener and fructifier of all your creation, even Jesus
Christ our Lord.

*(Jerusalem: prayer offered in the Garden Tomb at a time when
the small Christian church in Iran was facing great difficulties)*

5   It was raining outside.
I was alone in a foreign city.
Beside the hotel window I stood
and reflected on my country.
What is the destiny of my people?

The people of Korea:
In each of them I see
the mysterious presence of our Lord.

Through the wet glass of the window
His face is seen dimly.
He is being crucified.
There are spots of blood and
his body is bruised.
And even in his sufferings his is
the glory of the Risen Lord.

Scattered small flowers
surround him with graceful dew.

(Korea)

6   The stone put there by the military
    by the systems which bind; the stone of violence.
The stone that guards the entrance to ourselves,
    that keeps us from one another.

The stone against our voices
    against our stories, our heroines.
The stone against our education
    against our bread.

The stone against our God.

Women roll back the stone
    in Chile and elsewhere
Sharing stories, organizing around needs,
    gathering at women's centres, recognizing, deepening
    celebrating a transforming lifeforce.

It's the resurrection message
    after all.
God's spirit resists containment in tombs
    and walks among us.

(Chile)

7   O Wisdom, let me see with new eyes so that I may not pass
by the women in these Bible passages as women have been
'passed by' unheeded so often before. Open my ears to hear
their voices in fresh and perhaps surprising ways. Let the
power of their lives become a grace in my own. Amen.

*(A woman's prayer, reflecting on some of
the largely overlooked women of the Bible)*

8   Jesus,
we believe that you are living.
The steps that you took before, we are taking now.
Your resurrection is present in each sister and brother who
   rises up.
Help us so that all people may be resurrected in a
   new Guatemala,
where peace, justice and equality will reign, so that nobody
   is hungry.

(Guatemala: prayer of an Indian woman)

9   Lord, in these times when we are about to lose hope and
our efforts seem futile, grant that we may perceive in our
hearts and minds the image of your resurrection which
remains our only source of courage and strength, so that we
may continue to face the challenges, and struggle against
hardship and oppression born of injustice.

(Philippines: from a liturgy used by the poor)

10   Lord, you are the giver of life,
in the midst of suffering we celebrate the promise
   of your peace;
in the midst of oppression, we celebrate the promise of freedom;
in the midst of doubt and despair, we celebrate the promise
   of faith and hope;

in the midst of fear, we celebrate the promise of joy;
in the midst of sin and decay, we celebrate the promise of
   salvation and renewal;
in the midst of death we celebrate the promise of eternal life.
   (World Council of Churches, 1983 Assembly, Vancouver)

11   Living God, who came to your world and entered human
      pain
      Come and be in every painful place in our lives,
      in every painful place in our world, today.

   Living God, who worked in the secret darkness to raise
      Christ from the grave
      Come and work in every secret, dark place in our lives,
      in every secret, dark place of our world, today.

   Living God, who sent women out to proclaim the
      resurrection to the frightened, imprisoned disciples
      Come and empower us in every frightened, imprisoned
         place in our lives,
      in every frightened, imprisoned place in our world, today.

   Living God, Risen Son, Easter God:
      Come and make us your living Church
         your risen Church
         your Easter Church
      Today and every day.

            *(Ecumenical Forum of European
            Christian Women, 1990 Assembly)*

12   Christ is risen from the dead: trampling down death by
      death; and upon those in the tombs bestowing life.

   Though you went down into the grave, O Immortal
   One, yet you put down the power of Hades and rose a
   conqueror, O Christ our God: you spoke clearly to the

myrrh-bearing women: Rejoice; upon the apostles you
bestowed peace, and to the fallen you brought resurrection.

(Orthodox)

13   Sun, moon, sky, stars, mountains, valleys, heights, plains,
fountains, pools, rivers, seas, whatever flies, crawls or
swims, lift up your voices to the glory of Christ.

Today the world's Redeemer returns victorious from the
inferno.

*(Ancient prayer depicting the whole of
creation worshipping the risen Christ)*

*'Late that same day, the first day of the week, when the dis-
ciples were together behind locked doors for fear of the Jews,
Jesus came and stood among them. "Peace be with you!" he
said.' (John 20:19)*

14   Christ is in the midst of us!
He is, and ever shall be!

(Russian Orthodox acclamation)

15   Christ who appeared to your disciples
when the doors were shut;
appear unto all of those in the world today who live their
lives behind closed doors.

(United Kingdom)

16   You come through thick stone walls, armed guards and bars.
You bring me a starry night and ask about this and that.
You are the Redeemer. I recognize you.
You are my way, my truth and my life.
Even my cellar blooms with stars, and peace and light pour
forth.

You sprinkle beautiful words on me like flowers:
'Son, what are you afraid of? I am with you.'

(Lithuania)

17   Lord, help us and the peoples of the world to accept the gift
of peace that Jesus came to bring.

(USA)

18   Lord God, in the service of your kingdom
grant us the peace we may have,
show us the peace we should seek,
and give us the strength to do without
the peace we must forgo for Jesus' sake.

(Scotland)

'*A week later his disciples were once again in the room, and
Thomas was with them . . . Then he said to Thomas, "Reach
your finger here; look at my hands. Reach your hand here and
put it into my side. Be unbelieving no longer, but believe."
Thomas said, "My Lord and my God!" Jesus said to him,
"Because you have seen me you have found faith. Happy are
they who find faith without seeing me."*' *(John 20:26–29)*

19   Almighty God, who to your holy Apostle Saint Thomas our
Patron revealed your incarnate Son in his risen glory; draw,
we pray, the peoples of our land to know and confess him
as their Lord and God, that coming to you by him they may
believe and have life in his name; through the same your
Son Jesus Christ our Lord and Saviour. Amen.

(India: Feast of St Thomas the Apostle, Patron of India)

20   How glad we are to know and feel the touch of the risen
Lord Jesus.

(Nepal)

21 Lord, as we remember Job,
    stripped of all that he held most dear,
    and maintaining his faith
    on the rubbish-tip of his native town;
    and Paul affirming that all things
    are to be counted as garbage
    for the sake of following Christ;
    we thank you for those who even today
    in many different parts of the world
    are maintaining their integrity and discovering faith
    in situations of unbelievable privation and need.
    May we who have so much and suffer so little
    be more worthy of their company.

    (Jordan: on seeing village rubbish tips)

22 Almighty Father, remove our despair and renew our faith.
    Grant us a vision of your Son, victorious over suffering and
    death, so that we too may be filled with his faith in the
    infinite power of self-emptying love. Grant that we too may
    share your cross and inherit your kingdom.

    (India: M. M. Thomas)

23 Lord, when our success and comfort make us
    forget those who suffer:
    Show us your hands and your side.
    Lord, when we are confused, lost and bewildered:
    Grant us your peace, and send us out in confidence
    to do your will in the world.

    (Australia)

24 Remembering St Thomas, we invoke the blessing promised
    to those who have not seen the nailmarks of your hands,
    and the spear thrust into your heart, and yet believe; that

leading others to confess you as their Lord and God, they
may together find life in you. Amen.

(Sri Lanka)

'*That same day two of them were on their way to a village called
Emmaus, about seven miles from Jerusalem, talking together
about all that had happened. As they talked and argued,
Jesus himself came up and walked with them; but something
prevented them from recognizing him.*' *(Luke 24:13–16)*

25 God of all life, all worlds,
you draw near to us in many forms,
we confess that through our dimness of vision,
our dullness of mind and our coldness of heart,
we so often fail to recognize you on life's road.
Break through all the barriers we set up
that obscure the light of your presence in the world.

Lord of life, draw near to us
break through to us this day.

(India)

26 O Saviour, who journeyed with Luke and Cleopas to
Emmaus; journey with your servants who now prepare to
travel, defending them from every evil happening, for you
alone love all your creatures, and you alone are almighty.

(Orthodox)

27 Father, we pray for all lonely people, especially those who,
coming home to an empty house, stand at the door hesitant
and afraid to enter. May all who stand in any doorway with
fear in their hearts, like the two on the Emmaus road, ask
the living One in. Then, by his grace, may they find that in
loneliness they are never alone, and that he peoples all
empty rooms with his presence.

(New Zealand)

28   Stay with us, Lord
for the day is far spent
and we have not yet recognized your face
in each of our brothers and sisters.

Stay with us, Lord
for the day is far spent
and we have not yet shared your bread
in grace with our brothers and sisters.

Stay with us, Lord
for the day is far spent
and we have not yet listened to your Word
on the lips of our brothers and sisters.

Stay with us, Lord
because our very night becomes day
when you are there.

(Korea)

29   The meaning of the last supper, the arrest, the humiliation
and crucifixion now became one saving story when he, the
risen Lord, broke the bread again in Emmaus.

Until Jesus 'took the bread and blessed and broke it' for
the second time, his followers were left in a crisis of
hopelessness and confusion.

He sat at the table twice for us. In him is found the vital
cohesion; there is no Easter without Good Friday, but
equally certainly there is no Good Friday without Easter!

(Japan/USA: Kosuke Koyama)

30   The astonishing thing in life is the way the most ordinary
happenings suddenly change before our eyes into a glimpse
of God. Emmaus is part of everyone's experience, if they
have eyes to see. Surprise is the human response to God.

Surprise us, Lord.

(United Kingdom)

*'Some time later, Jesus showed himself to his disciples once again,
by the Sea of Tiberias . . . When they came ashore, they saw a
charcoal fire there with fish laid on it, and some bread . . .
Jesus said, "Come and have breakfast."'* (John 21:1, 9, 12)

31 O Lord Jesus Christ who after your glorious resurrection
prepared by the waterside a breakfast of fish for the
disciples who had worked all night long: come among these
your servants who work beside our river day by day to
provide food for their fellows, and bring blessing both on
their work and on their lives. O Lord our Saviour and help
for ever more.
(London: blessing for the workers of Billingsgate Fishmarket)

32 Merciful Father, your risen Son prepared breakfast for the
disciples by the lakeshore. We ask him to bless our
breakfast today.
(Tanzania: a breakfast grace)

33 What joy it is at early morn to meet
Beside the sea, with those who love our Lord
And whom we love; and there to read the Word.
And lay our burdens at our Master's feet.
(Japan: Nagata, a leprosy patient)

34 As the sun was rising, the risen Lord, shattering the
imagination of the powerful, stood at the water's edge. The
young fisherfolk, his friends, who had toiled all night yet
caught not a thing, did not understand that it was Jesus.
When they stepped ashore, Jesus took the broken bread and
gave it to them . . .

Lord, we hear the rumbling of your new life deep
underground in the struggles of the poor and the oppressed;

come upon us, possess us and transform us.
Fill us with the hope of your power
made manifest in your broken body,
the power that breaks in among us today
in the wounded and broken sisters and brothers of our land.
Amen.

(Bangalore, India: from a Eucharistic Prayer)

'Then the righteous will reply, "Lord, when was it that we
saw you hungry and fed you, or thirsty and gave you a drink,
a stranger and took you home, or naked and clothed you?
When did we see you ill or in prison, and come to visit you?"
And the king will answer, "Truly I tell you: anything you did
for one of my brothers here, however insignificant, you did
for me."' (Matthew 25:37–40)

35 O God, grant us grace
to receive Jesus Christ in every person
and to be Jesus Christ to every person.

(Germany: Martin Luther, 1483–1546)

The element of surprise is a very striking feature among the responses of the
followers of Jesus to his resurrection appearances, as it is of those featuring
in one of his most mysterious of stories, who are astonished to discover that
in caring for the needs of the naked, the hungry, the thirsty, the prisoner and
the stranger, they are in reality caring for him.

In the same way, Christ's followers continue to be surprised as he multi-
plies the mysteries of his quiet presence with them; promising to be wherever two or three are gathered together in his name (Matthew 18:19–20),
and assuring them that whenever they engage in caring for the needy
around them, he himself is to be discovered in that activity.

36 Risen Lord,
ever multiplying the mysteries of your presence with your
people,

teach us to look for you and to learn of you,
not only in the lives of the saints,
but also in the cemeteries, the gutters
and the dustbins of your world,
as you promised.

(United Kingdom)

37 God dwells among the lowliest of men and women. He
sits on the dust-heap among the prison convicts. With the
juvenile delinquents he stands at the door, begging bread.
He throngs with the beggars at the place of alms. He is
among the sick. He stands in line with the unemployed in
front of the free employment bureau.

Therefore, let him who would meet God visit the prison
before going to the temple. Before he goes to church let him
visit the hospital. Before he reads the Bible let him help the
beggar standing at his door.

(Japan: Toyohiko Kagawa)

38 Jesus my dear brother
you have returned to the earth;
you have taken the aspect of the other
and I do not recognize you in him.
Teach my eyes to discover the truth,
to recognize you, Lord,
in the small man, in the
humble man that I see.

(Philippines: Pope John Paul II)

39 O God, your Son Jesus shared our life and knows what it is
to be deprived and to be despised. You have made yourself
truly one with all people in all sorts of conditions of life.

Help us to see you.

O Christ, you stand with the nameless crowds waiting
to be hired, you crawl on your knees tear-gassed and
water-hosed, you flee from your ancestral home driven by
landgrabbers and soldiers; you shrink to the bones
consumed by disease.

Help us to see you.

O Christ, help us to see you in all who suffer today that we
may be enabled to share ourselves with them. Amen.

(Korea)

40   Servant Christ,
help us to follow you out of the dark tomb,
to share daily your resurrection life,
to be renewed daily in your image of love,
to be used daily as your new Body
in your service to the world,

Servant Christ, help us to follow you.

(India: Litany of the Disciples of Christ the Servant)

41   Risen Lord, we come to confess our sins. Our hearts are full
of impatience, frustration, and sometimes even bitterness
with one another. We find it hard to be accepting.

Break the seals, Lord, roll away the stone, rip open the
protecting bandages. Breathe the breath of life into our
cold, dead hearts.

Risen Lord, we come to petition you. Our minds are so
often full of doubt and we are shy about sharing the good
news of your resurrection.

Break the seals, Lord, roll away the stone, rip open the
protecting bandages. Breathe the breath of life into our
cold, dead hearts.

Risen Lord, we come to adore you. We desire to know you as living Lord and to experience your vitality within us.

Break the seals, Lord, roll away the stone, rip open the protecting bandages. Breathe the breath of life into our cold, dead hearts.

Risen Lord, we come to worship you. The world waits for your coming through us. We want to be filled with joy and to have the freedom to be your true disciples.

As we come, we thank you that you do break the seals, Lord, you roll away the stone and rip open the protective bandages. You breathe the breath of life into our cold, dead hearts, and by your resurrection we are made new.

(New Zealand)

42   Christ our true God, risen from the dead, whose tomb is brighter than any royal hall, will have mercy on us, and save us, for this is a good God who loves us all.

(El Salvador: words used at a memorial service for Oscar Romero)

18

The Mysteries of Commissioning and Ascension

'The eleven disciples made their way to Galilee, to the mountain where Jesus had told them to meet him . . . Jesus came near and said to them: "Full authority in heaven and on earth has been committed to me. Go therefore to all nations and make them my disciples; baptize them in the name of the Father and the Son and the Holy Spirit, and teach them to observe all that I have commanded you. I will be with you always, to the end of time."' (Matthew 28:16, 18–20)

1   O God of love and mercy, your Son Jesus Christ has commanded us to preach and teach and baptize people in Jesus' name. Help us to carry out this great commission with humble hearts.

(Pacific)

2   Let us thank God for calling men and women to serve his work in the world.
For all faithful prophets, ministers and teachers of the past;
For apostles sent into the world boldly to witness to your deeds of grace;
For pastors who have lovingly gathered and tended your flock;
For those who have led us into the way of faith;

Gracious Lord, we give you thanks
for all saints of the past.

For your coming to earth as a humble servant;
For emptying, and spending yourself for the welfare of all;
For shepherding the lost sheep with unceasing concern;
For your costly obedience, even unto death on the cross;

> Gracious Lord, we give you thanks
> for your ministry of love.

For rising again as living Lord, to continue his task among us;
For calling us to minister in love as your new body;
For giving each one your grace-gifts to carry out this task;
For challenging us each day with new opportunities for service;

> Gracious Lord, we give you thanks
> for your confidence in us.

For bringing us together at this time, each from his own
  congregation and church;
For showing us new possibilities of ministry for this new age;
For daily revealing yourself to us here; and
For your promise to be with us to the end of time;

Gracious Lord, we give you thanks
for the hope with which we can now face the future. Amen.

(India: service of rededication of ministers)

3   O Jesus Christ, as you pace through the earth, even though
     it be by the instrumentality of very imperfect disciples, may
     the people of every land and race pause in their work, look
     up, see you, draw nearer, listen, worship, and turn from all
     their past to follow you.

(Australia)

4   Draw your Church together, O Lord, into one great
     company of disciples, together following our Lord Jesus
     Christ into every walk of life, together serving him in his

mission to the world, and together witnessing to his love on every continent and island.

(Canada)

5   God the Sender, send us.
God the Sent, come with us.
God the Strengthener of those who go, empower us,
that we may go with you
and find those who will call you
Father, Son and Holy Spirit.

(Wales)

6   Our Lord Jesus Christ sends you out in the power and strength of the Holy Spirit to be his faithful witnesses to your family, to your country, and to the ends of the earth.

(Iran: prayer at the end of the Confirmation Service)

7   O Lord, whose Church is from the rising of the sun, grant unto all her peoples, from orient to occident, the light and life that are ever new in Christ. From morning until evening let us praise you, and in your glad presence do our work day by day, through Christ our Master. Amen.

8   Jesus Christ is risen and he is with us as he promised: 'Lo, I am with you always, to the close of the age.'

He is with us now in the Assembly of his Church, just as he stood among his first followers and greeted them: 'Peace be with you';

He is with us in Sacred Scripture as truly as he proclaimed in the synagogue: 'Today this scripture has been fulfilled in your hearing';

He is with us in the Eucharist, really and truly, just as he gave himself in the Last Supper, and hung on Calvary;

He is with us in Baptism as truly as he stood in the river Jordan;

He is with us in Confirmation as truly as he promised the Paraclete to his disciples;

He is with us in Holy Matrimony, as truly as he performed the first miracle in Cana;

He is with us in the Sacrament of Reconciliation as truly as he announced over Mary of Magdala that her sins were forgiven;

He is there in Ordination, as he commissioned those first apostles;

He is there in the Anointing of the Sick as truly as he healed the blind and lame, and cured others;

He is with us each day throughout our lives as truly as he visited the house of Zacchaeus, had a meal with the tax gatherer Levi, and walked the highways of Galilee and the narrow streets of Jerusalem.

(United Kingdom)

9   Lord, help us not to dwell too much on the past,
holding you to the Galilean hills and the streets of Jerusalem,
but to know you more and more
as present Lord and Saviour,
risen, ascended, and always present with us
through the power of the Holy Spirit. Amen.

(United Kingdom)

10   Jesus, you are on the right and on the left
when the sun rises and when it sets.

(Ghana: invocation of Jesus of the Deep Forest)

11   Hear our prayer, O Lord, for those in this and every land
who have only intermittent occasion of Holy Communion,
and slender means of livelihood. Remember all who battle
against heavy odds in order to nurture their young, to attain
dignity, to love truth, to know fellowship, and to find
righteousness. Grant to them the fulfilment of the ancient
promise that as our days are so shall our strength be, in him
who is our peace and joy and hope.

(Prayer for an African land: Bishop Kenneth Cragg)

12   O Father Almighty, and God of all comfort; look with
compassion, we pray, upon the little companies of our
faithful fellow Christians who, in lonely places of the world,
are striving to uphold the banner of the cross. If the
comfort of human sympathy seems far from them, be their
close companion, and pour into their hearts the spirit of
hope; that they may steadfastly persevere, and be of good
courage because of your word, knowing that their labour is
not in vain.

(Prayer of a Ugandan Christian)

13   Jesus Christ is your inheritance,
O you ministers of the Lord:
Jesus Christ is your sole security:
  His name is your wealth:
  His name is your inheritance:
  His name is your income:
  His name is your salary,
A salary not of money but of grace.
Your inheritance is not dried up by heat,
  nor devastated by storms.
Jesus Christ is your inheritance.

(Italy: Ambrose, bishop in Milan, 397. Included in a
collection of prayers for the use of Indian priests.)

14 Almighty God, eternally we praise you for raising Jesus our Lord from the dead on Easter day. We praise you for resurrecting also the life of his first disciples, empowering them to carry your mission throughout the world. Risen Lord, resurrect once again your Church also, that it may follow you in liberating all people from the power of sin and suffering, and in establishing justice and peace throughout the world.

(North India)

'Then he led them out as far as Bethany, and blessed them with uplifted hands; and in the act of blessing he parted from them and was carried up into heaven. And they returned to Jerusalem full of joy, and spent all their time in the temple praising God.' (Luke 24:50–53)

15 Blessed Lord, lifting up holy hands perpetually on behalf of all humankind, by your Spirit, breathe such love into the prayers we now offer, that they may be taken into yours, and prevail with yours.

(France: Jean-Jacques Olier, 1608–57)

16 Almighty God,
as we believe your only-begotten Son our Lord Jesus Christ
to have ascended into the heavens,
so may we also in heart and mind thither ascend
and with him continually dwell;
who is alive and reigns with you and the Holy Spirit,
one God, now and for ever. Amen.

(England)

Apprehensive on account of her impending return to a highly volatile African country, and anxious on behalf of elderly relatives she was leaving behind, one visitor to Coventry's Anglican cathedral found her attention caught and held by the figure of Christ in glory, the subject of Graham Sutherland's magnificent tapestry. Referring to the experience later, she spoke of the renewed assurance of the ultimate triumph of God's rule conveyed to her by that visual image of Christ, seated in glory, hands held high in blessing and prayer upon a needy world; and of the courage, strength and peace of mind which she drew from it for her return to the country in which she worked.

17 O Christ, grant unto us and to your people everywhere such a vision of your glory as will give us strength, courage and vision for every task. Amen.

18 Lord Jesus Christ, as we know that your cross was once lifted in public derision, help us on this of all days to picture your high exaltation over everything, everywhere, always; and to rejoice that our hearts may be lifted and drawn to you now, so that we may dwell in you and you in us; till you bring us to the place you have gone to prepare for us.

19 Lord, a thin drizzle of humility is penetrating us. We are not the axis of life as our self-centredness falsely claims. We travel through life like blind persons; we did not choose life before embarking on it nor do we know the day when we shall depart from it. Life is larger than we are, and your ways extend beyond the horizon of our vision.

(Bolivia)

20 Doña Santa lives in a slum. She comes from the region bordering on the frontier with Brazil. It is obvious that her ancestors came from Africa. She is a widow with many children, grand-children and great grand-children . . . At night she says her prayers and reads the Bible, and every week she goes to a Bible group. One day a theological theme

arose in that Bible group in a slum: 'The presence of God' . . .
Where was God? Was he there? 'But if he is here, why do we
live like this, so poorly?' That had been the theme of the week.
'The truth is', said one woman, 'that he has died and risen, and
now he is in heaven' . . . The conversation continued: 'But he is
still here' . . . 'Yes, of course, he said he would be wherever
two or three . . .' The meeting was a true celebration of God,
of experience, of nearness . . . and of hope. All of a sudden
Doña Santa said: 'I think he's up in the sky. At night, when I
look at the stars, it seems to me that he's there.'

Someone proposed a prayer. The group knelt down, the
silence was pregnant with the Presence, Doña Santa prayed:

Lord, I believe you are in the sky.
When I look at the stars, it seems I can feel you there.
I'm very ignorant, I don't know a thing, I can hardly read.
But when I look at the sky at night, I can see you.
I see you in clear nights with many stars.

Men have got to the moon . . .
and to the sun? I don't know, perhaps . . .
But they'll never get to the stars . . .
that is where God is.

Without knowing it, Doña Santa was entering the line of
the great mystics of space, but her space was the whole sky,
the firmament, the starred dome: a consummation of love in
the open fields, like in the Song of Songs and the Psalms
(Song 7:11–13; Psalm 11:4; 19:1; 139:8).

If we as women – not exclusively, but in a privileged way
– have such an intuition of space as inhabitable, don't we
have a unique, fundamental and indispensable contribution
to make to the *oikoumené*? What would happen if women
all over the world started to project their interior space
into the exterior space? Couldn't we contribute to turning
the space which the war between the great powers is
transforming into a theatre of death and destruction, into
an inhabitable space: the 'sky'?

(Uruguay: Maria Teresa Porcile)

21 Claude has the most illogical mind that I have ever
    encountered so this may be the first and last time that he is
    ever quoted in a book. He may ask such questions as 'What
    time is orange?' or 'How was tomorrow?' But still he does
    have a wisdom all his own . . . Well, one day Claude was at
    the beach with Jean-Pierre and several others of the commu-
    nity. The ocean was at low tide so there was an immense
    stretch of flat, sandy beach. They began making designs in
    the sand. Claude drew a big circle with a couple of marks
    inside that could have been facial features. 'What's that?'
    asked Jean-Pierre. With a big smile Claude replied: 'It's
    Madame Sun.' 'That's good' Jean-Pierre said, 'Now let's see
    you draw joy.' Claude took a look around him at the wide
    beach that stretched out in both directions as far as the eye
    could see, then he turned to Jean-Pierre and said with a huge
    smile but in all seriousness: 'There's not enough room!'

    (France: L'Arche Community)

22 Lord our God
    you have raised your Son to be with you,
    and we sing to you in joy.
    Send your Spirit, as he has promised us,
    to free all people from hatred and from fear,
    and so give us the peace of Christ, our Lord.

    (France: Cistercian, Vespers)

23 I bend the knee in the eye of the Father who created me,
                in the eye of the Son who purchased me,
                in the eye of the Spirit who cleansed me.
    In love and affection, in wisdom and grace,
    with angels and saints,
    each shade and light, each day and night
    I bend the knee in the world of the Three.

    (Celtic: Carmina Gadelica)

24   Go forth into the world in peace, looking up to Jesus, who was wounded for your transgressions, and bearing about in your lives the love and joy and peace which are the marks of Jesus on his disciples; and so may the blessing of God, Father, Son and Holy Spirit be upon you.

(Uganda/Congo: blessing attributed
to Canon Alipayo of Acholi)

19

Mysteries of Pentecost

'The day of Pentecost had come, and they were all together in one place. Suddenly there came from the sky what sounded like a strong, driving wind, a noise which filled the whole house where they were sitting. And there appeared to them flames like tongues of fire distributed among them and coming to rest on each one. They were all filled with the Holy Spirit and began to talk in other tongues, as the Spirit gave them power of utterance.' (Acts 2:1–4)

1   Living God, eternal Holy Spirit,
    let your bright intoxicating energy
    which fired those first disciples,
    fall on us today.

                                        (New Zealand)

Some years ago, in a flurry of publicity in roadside tea shops, on station platforms and in the gathering places of the young, Pakistan launched what was then its newest, freshest, fizziest drink: Bubble-Up. With its thirst-quenching promise of 'a kiss of lemon, a kiss of lime' it was claimed by its promoters to be the answer to the insatiable thirst of the people of that hot and dusty land.

Not unrelated to this, 'Bubble-Up Sunday' is the name that might have been given to that Sunday a very long time ago, when a group of flat, dispirited men and women suddenly became conscious of the availability of vast resources of new life and power bubbling up within them. 'They have been drinking', said public opinion in Jerusalem (Acts 2:13–18). They themselves used other figures of speech – a strong driving wind, and flames like tongues of fire – to put into words this new, sparkling, effervescent experience of life in the Spirit.

In striking contrast to this, were the words often used jokingly by Pakistani Christians to describe the drinking water boiled by foreigners for fear of intestinal upsets; but which in the process became flat, lifeless and insipid. 'Missionary pani' (missionary water) they called it! Words that suggested water that was dull, unappetizing and rather to be despised, despite their understanding of the need for it to be treated in this way.

More uncomfortably for us foreigners, however – especially as Pentecost came around each year – was the realization that not only the water in those missionary jugs, but a great deal of Christian life had been subjected to this same treatment! What ought to have been fresh and thirst-quenching had so often come to be stale and tired and unsatisfying.

Of course missionaries and pastors and teachers of whatever nationality must bear their share of the blame for the unimaginative way in which the faith has been passed on; as must all Christians for the unthinking and unquestioning way in which we have so often accepted things said and done in our name.

What therefore is called for, as our journey continues into and beyond this Bubble-Up Sunday, is 'a kiss of pardon, a kiss of peace'; and the rediscovery on the part of believers everywhere of those rich resources of life and vigour which accompany the faithful following of Christ in all his mysteries: joyful, sorrowful and glorious.

2   O Holy Spirit, giver of light and life, free us from all that is matter-of-fact, stale, bored, tired; all that takes things for granted. Open our eyes to see, and excite our minds to marvel.
(United Kingdom)

3   Lord, we find it hard to see you in India. Your presence seems to be lost amongst the millions of people. Your voice seems drowned among the babble of languages. Your truth seems overwhelmed by other cultures and faiths. Yet we know that you are there, working like hot spices in the cooking pots, having a pervading influence on the lives of your people, liberating, changing, inspiring, questioning, giving new vision. Lord, we know you are there amidst the heat, the dust and the noise, touching the heart of India.
(Prayer for India)

4   Holy Spirit, Spirit of the Living God,
     you breathe in us
     on all that is inadequate
     and fragile.

     You make living water
     spring even from our hurts themselves.
     And, through you, the valley of fears
     becomes a place of wellsprings.

     So, in an inner life
     with neither beginning nor end,
     your continual presence
     makes new freshness
     break through. Amen.

                                             (Sri Lanka)

5   Even as the water falls on dry tea leaves
     and brings out their flavour,
     so may your spirit fall on us and renew us
     so that we may bring refreshment and joy to others.

                                             (Sri Lanka)

6   God of our Dreamtimes, we bring you our dreams.

     You dreamed a new dream in your Eden garden,
     lived through a shattered dream in your Gethsemane garden,
     experienced a fulfilled dream in your Burial garden.

     Through the dreams of your people
     you have covenanted, warned, prepared, promised.

     Plant your strong Spirit of trust and hope
     in our dream gardens, we pray. Amen.

                          (Australia: referring to Joel 2:28–29)

7   O God, our heavenly Father,
      renew our faith, our hope, our love;
      renew our wills, that we may serve you more gladly;
      renew our delight in your word, and in the worship we
          offer you;
      renew our joy in you, and in all your good gifts;
      renew our longing that men and women everywhere may
          accept the salvation wrought by your Son Jesus Christ;
      renew our purpose and our happiness to serve others for
          his sake;
      who came not to be served, but to be the servant of all;
      who having yielded up his life upon the cross for us all,
      now lives and reigns with you, in the unity of the Holy Spirit,
      one God for ever and ever. Amen.

                                                    (North India)

8   Come, Holy Spirit.
      Come, Holy Spirit,
      teacher of the humble, judge of the arrogant.
      Come, hope of the poor, refreshment of the weary,
      rescuer of the shipwrecked.
      Come, most splendid adornment of all living beings,
      the sole salvation of all who are mortal.
      Come, Holy Spirit, have mercy on us,
      imbue our lowliness with your power,
      meet our weakness with the fullness of your grace.
      Come, Holy Spirit, renew the whole creation!

                                                    (Orthodox)

9   To the Wind of God's Spirit
      that blows where it wills, free, freedom-bringing,
      victor over law, over sin, over death.

      To the Wind of God's Spirit
      locked in the heart and the womb
      of a woman of Nazareth village.

To the Wind of God's Spirit
that took hold of Jesus
to send him to preach good news to the poor
and release to the captives.

To the Wind of God's Spirit
that at Pentecost freed the apostles
from bias, self-centredness, fear,
opening wide the doors of the Upper Room,
that followers of Jesus might ever be a fellowship
open to the world,
free in the Word they speak,
crystal clear in their witness,
unconquerable in their hope.

To the Wind of God's Spirit
that constantly banishes
new fears of the Church
and consumes in flames all the authority
that serves not the needs of our brothers and sisters,
and through poverty and martyrdom thoroughly cleanses her.

To the Wind of God's Spirit
that reduces to ashes
presumption, pretence and pursuit of profit
feeding the flames of justice and liberation
– the fiery hearth of the kingdom.

So that we may blow strong in the wind, my friends.

This anthology of the Spirit –
has as much burning passion for the God of Jesus
and the kingdom of God
as it has ashes of frailty and sorrow.

(Brazil: dedicatory poem 'The fiery hearth
of the kingdom' based on Luke 12:49)

10 To me who am but
black old charcoal,
grant, O Lord,
that by the fire of Pentecost
I may be set ablaze.

(Lebanon: after St John of Damascus)

11 In one of the study sessions of the Base Christian
Community in a popular neighbourhood of a big city, the
counsellor, speaking of the Holy Spirit, asked: 'How do you
understand the action of the Spirit? How do you explain it?'

A poor working man, whose job was to gather and burn
the garbage of the city, raised his hand.

'I understand it like this: In my job I have continually to
gather the garbage, pile it up and destroy it. I have been
doing this for years and I try to keep the fire burning
continually; nevertheless, there are times when it seems that
the fire has gone out completely, but I know that,
underneath, a few embers continue to burn. Regardless of
how large the garbage deposit is, the fire is never completely
extinguished. I think that humanity is like the garbage and
that the Holy Spirit is like the fire. The Church must always
act as I do in my work: it must gather together humanity
and put it in contact with the Spirit so as to purify it until it
is no longer garbage.

'The Church should never lose hope, even when the fire
cannot be seen and the garbage is plentiful. She must be
convinced that the fire continues to burn below – that it will
never go out.'

(South America)

12 Come rushing wind; come refining fire;
cleanse us, enliven us and burn within us.
Set us on fire with love for our God
and for the poor of the earth.

(United Kingdom: Christian Aid)

13   If you were content, Lord,
      you would not bother with us.
      But you are restless:
      through anger, through excitement, and through love,
      you will all things to change and be made new.

      So we praise you
      that your restlessness has been born in us:
      as the pain of the world,
          the cries of your people,
          the urgency of your gospel,
          and your Holy Spirit
      upset our easiness
      and require us to respond.

                                        (Scotland: Iona Community)

14   Lord, Holy Spirit,
      you are the kind fire who does not cease to burn,
      consuming us with flames of love and peace,
      driving us out like sparks to set the world on fire.

                                        (New Zealand)

15   Kindle in me a hot heart to love you, my Lord and my
      Saviour, and kindle other hot hearts through me.

                                        (China)

16   O God, who, when you sent down your Spirit upon your
      apostles, caused inhabitants of Iran to witness that great
      event, and to believe; grant that we, the Persians of today,
      finding strength and comfort from the Holy Spirit, may be
      active and fruitful in the tasks of your spiritual kingdom,
      through Jesus Christ our Lord. Amen.

                                        (Iran)

17   You are the healing, the loving, the touching. You are the
laughing, You are the dancing, Jesus, Verb of God – You are
the moving – move in me.

(USA)

18   Lord,
we long to speak effectively in your name,
but our words come out muddled and blunted.
Give us the fresh, new-minted words,
that heart may speak to heart
and a new day begin.

(United Kingdom)

19   We offer you, Lord,
the bustle of each day,
all the energy
created by our work
and the enthusiasm of our eager hearts.

(Nicaragua)

20   I dedicate my life to you, O God.
Take me, pardon me, polish me, keep me.
Use me, O Lord, for the work you would have me do.
And taking me, help me not to resist you.

(Africa: prayer of a young pastor)

21   Forgive us, Lord, we are at it again:
confining your Spirit
to those lovely lists Paul fired off to his friends
in the heat of a polemical moment;
while the Spirit listeth where it will,
disturbingly far from our all-night prayer meetings

and ingenious organizations,
storming our protectively closed minds,
lighting tongues of fire
to dance over heads we are reluctant to anoint.

(India)

22   O Holy Spirit, tongue of fire, descend upon us as you
descended upon the disciples gathered in the upper room
for prayers. Sanctify us, free us from the bondage of sin and
give us your power to speak with one voice.

Rushing wind, sweep over our lands and make your sound
gather again the devout people from every nation under
heaven. Help us manifest together the victory of life over
death given through the Resurrection, making us signs of
the living hope and witnesses of your peace.

Giver of life, abide in us, transform our former selves into a
new life in faithfulness to God's will. Along with all others
with whom we live, with all nations and people, we would
enter a new time, a time of transformation, when hatred is
replaced by love, violence by dialogue, condemnation by
forgiveness, self-centredness by sharing.

Power of unity, help us to move from the Babel of division
due to ethnic or religious boundaries to the Pentecost of
unity in the diversity of our gifts, traditions and cultures.
Make us messengers of the good news, apostles of peace.

(Middle East Council of Churches)

23   Spirit of God, speaking in one language the message of love;
unscramble the babble of international conversation
so that leaders may speak words of trust.
May your tongues of fire purge the tongues of men
    and women
so that the clamour of aggression

be overcome by the spirit of love.
And may your Church proclaim your power
in one voice not many
that the world may believe.

(United Kingdom)

24 O God, who to an expectant and united Church granted at Pentecost the gift of the Holy Spirit, and has wonderfully brought into one fold those who now worship you here; grant, we pray, the help of the same Spirit in all our life and worship, that we may expect great things from you, and attempt great things for you, and being one in you may show to the world that you sent Jesus Christ our Lord, to whom with you and the Holy Spirit, be all honour and glory, world without end. Amen.

(South India)

25 Lord, as you have entered into our life and death, and call us into your death and risen life, continue to draw us, we pray, by the power of your Spirit, into an exchange of gifts and needs, joys and sorrows, strengths and weaknesses, with your people everywhere; that united we may be obedient to your commission, and together enjoy the promise of your presence.

(United Kingdom: CMS)

26 Go in peace.
And may the Holy God surprise you
on the way,
Christ Jesus be your company
and the Spirit lift up your life. Amen.

(World Council of Churches, 1991 Assembly,
Canberra: Benediction)

Sources and Acknowledgements

Where the exact source of a prayer or meditation is unknown, or its origin is indicated in the text, no specific acknowledgement has been made below. Thanks are expressed to all those who have given permission to reproduce their material, and apologies offered to any whose rights have been inadvertently overlooked.

In assembling prayers from many different countries and using words that in some instances have passed from one language into another, it is inevitable that some mistakes will have been made. Such errors are regretted and corrections sought.

Action of Churches Together in Scotland, Dunblane, Scotland (successor to Scottish Churches Council). Used with permission. (17)18

Ambrosian Liturgy. (5)1

Amirtham, Arun and Anjum, Zurich. Used with permission. (8)19

Amnesty International, London. (16, I)10

Andhra Theological College, Hyderabad, India. *Services for All Seasons*, The Revd Dr Eric J. Lott (ed.). Used with permission. (13)14 (18)2

The Anglican Church of Canada, Toronto. From the *Book of Alternative Services of the Anglican Church of Canada*, copyright 1985 by the General Synod of the Anglican Church of Canada. Used with permission. (1)23 (18)4

The Anglican Consultative Council, London. From *Anglican World*, Lent 1995; The Revd Canon John L. Peterson. Used with permission. (16,VI)2

Anglican Province of Jerusalem and the Middle East, Jerusalem. *Grace Cup*, a publication of the Central Synod; Rt Revd Kenneth Cragg. Used with permission. (16,V)3,5

Antoine, Charles. *L'Amerique Latine en Prière*, Editions du Cerf, Paris. (16, III)7

Appansany, A. S. Translation of words of manuscript. (14)25

Audenshaw Papers; Mark Gibbs. (11)76; (16,III)5

Baker, Rt Revd Gilbert. *Occasional Bulletin of the Overseas Council of the Church of England*. (4)5

Bishop's College, Calcutta. *The Priest's Book of Private Prayers*. (18)13

Biswas, Diana. Used with permission from *Lord, let me share*, by Canon Subir Biswas, CMS, London. (4)6 (13)11 (14)23 (16,I)18 (16,IX)18 (16,XI)23
Brazil Committee of Women's World Day of Prayer. (11)77 (16,VIII)6
Byzantine Rite. (13)12

Cairns Publications, Sheffield. *Prayer at Night*; Jim Cotter. Used with permission. (4)4 (16,XIV)17
Calver, Mrs Flora. Prayer quoted in *New Day*, Autumn/Winter 1996, a publication of Leprosy Mission by Clive Calver, Director General, Evangelical Alliance. Used with permission. (11)24
Catholic Commission for Justice and Peace, Sydney. Revd Ann Wansbrough. (13)6
Central Board of Finance of the Church of England, London. Extracts from *The Alternative Service Book 1980*: (2)1 (16,II)8 (18)16 and *The Promise of His Glory* (Church House Publishing, 1990): (4)23 (6)9 are copyright The Central Board of Finance of the Church of England and are reproduced by permission.
Children's Aid Direct, London. (3)20
Children's Society, London. Used by permission of the copyright holders. (8)23
Christian Aid, London. Reproduced with permission: (3)3,17 (11)60; and from the following publications: *Christian Aid News*, (16,XI)21 (prayer poem of Francis Khoo); *Harvest* leaflet, 1986, (6)7; *Paperlines*, 1991, (19)12; *Focus on the Sahel* leaflet, (16,IV)8
Christian Conference of Asia, Hong Kong. Reproduced with permission from the following publications: *Your Will Be Done*, CCA Youth, (1)24 (3)11,12 (8)41 (Father Carlos Miyica) (11)49 (13)2 (14)12 (16,I)8 (16,II)14 (16,XI)9 (Mizuro Genzo) (17)5 (Hong Chong Myung); *Hymnal*, No. 177, (2)3 (D. T. Niles); *Your Kingdom Come*, (11)25 (16,XIV)15 (words based on a painting by Gaumana Gauwrain); *Worship Book* of the 8th Assembly, Korea 1985, (14)5 (17)39
Christian Literature Society, Madras. Permission sought to quote from *Book of Common Worship of the Church of South India*, Collects for: Sunday next before Advent (1)16, Christmas Eve (3)13, Feast of Purification (4)1, Epiphany (5)12, Pentecost (19)24; *CSI Liturgy, 1985*, (14)15, 37; *The Lord's Supper*, rev. 1991, (14)10 (16,XIV)22
Christian Workers Fellowship, Sri Lanka. Reproduced from the *Bulletin*. (3)4
Church Hymnal Corporation, New York. Permission sought to quote from *The Book of Occasional Services*, (16,VI)16 (16,VIII)7; *Lesser Feasts and Fasts*, (6)19 (11)83 (16,XIII)10
Church in Wales, The Board of Mission, Y Bwrdd Cenhadu, Penarth, Vale of Glamorgan. Used with permission. (18)5
Church Mission Society, London. Permission sought to quote from: *Christ the Light of the World Prayer Book*, Highway Press. (1)1,15; *Empty Shoes*, John Carden, Highway Press, (2)9 (5)21 (10)7; *Morning, Noon and Night*, compiled by John Carden, (6)5 (Dom Helder Camara) (8)30,43 (from Christukala Ashram, Tirappatur) (9)12,16 (10)14 (11)65,92 (14)28 (15)23 (16) (Bishop C. K. Jacob of Central Travancore) (16,I)2 (Janet Rwagize) (16,III)8 (16,IV)11 (16,IX)3 (16,X)14 (17)1 (Bishop M. Jiro Sasaki) (18)6,24 (19)16,20; *CMS Newsletter*, Simon Barrington-Ward, 'Jerusalem Diary', (9)15; 'In the shadow of Nine Dragons: Hong Kong Sketches', Eric Hague, (16,XI)11; *Prayer Paper* (10)10 (Rev T. L. Mayer) (11)20; *Prayer Paper, 1994*, (8)39; *Prayer Paper, 1996*, (16,IX)12 (Zepha Mualere Gonahasa); Executive

Committee prayer, 1963/64, (16,IX)16; Executive Committee prayer, 1969/70, (12)25; Interchange prayer, adapted, (19)25; *Yes Magazine*, (8)10 (11)56 (13)17 (16,X)5 (the last three by Heather le Dieu) (19)18 (Revd Christopher Lamb)

Church of the Lord, African Independent Church. (5)6

Church of North India, New Delhi. Used with permission. (5)23 (Augustine Ralla Ram) (18)14 (Most Revd R. S. Bhandare) (19)7 (prayer used in Diocese of Barrackpore)

Church of Pakistan, Lahore. *Lahore Diocesan Prayer Letter*. (4)8 (11)3

Church of the Province of Central Africa, Gaborone, Botswana. Anglican Council in Malawi and Zambia, 'Ukaristia, 1976'. Permission sought. (2)15 (3)15 (7)15 (8)20 (11)19,72 (16,I)9 (16,XI)19

Church of the Province of Kenya, Nairobi. *Modern Services*, 1991. Used with permission. (1)6 (5)10 (8)40,42,48 (11)15 (13)8 (14)36 (16,XIV)14

Church of the Province of Southern Africa, Johannesburg. From *An Anglican Prayer Book, 1989*. Used with permission. (16,I)7

Church of Scotland (Panel of Worship), Edinburgh. From *Pray Now*. Used with permission. (16,XIII)8

Church of South India Churchman. (15)7; *About You and Me*, M. A. Thomas, (16,VI)13; *A Kind of Seeking*, A Seeker, (10)17; *The Realisation of the Cross*, M. M. Thomas, (17)22

Church Times, London. Prayer for Terry Waite and other hostages, adapted. (16,VII)7

Clark, T. and T., Ltd, Edinburgh. *Face to Face: A Narrative Essay in the Theology of Suffering*; Frances Young. Reproduced by permission. (6)2

Coggan, Lady. Used with permission. (9)1 (adapted) (18)9

Collins Fontana. *Treat me cool, Lord*; Carl Burke. (3)28 (8)25,28 (16,X)2

Collins Fount Paperbacks, London. Used with permission from *The Quiet Heart*; George Appleton. (4)16 (8)45 (10)25

Collins Liturgical Publications, London. Permission sought. *Dawn through our Darkness* compiled by Giles Harcourt, quoting from *Prayers for Pagans*; Roger Bush (abridged). (13)24

Collins, William and Sons and Co. Ltd, London. Permission sought to quote from: *Hymn of the Universe: Pensées*; Teilhard de Chardin. (1)4 (11)44 (12)18

Council for World Mission, London. Used with permission from: *God's Candlelights*; Mabel Shaw (London Missionary Society). (1)11; *CWM Prayer Handbooks*. (8)29 (adapted from a prayer by Eleri Edwards) (10)24

Council of Churches for Britain and Ireland, London. Week of Prayer for Christian Unity, 1989, (11)6; Week of Prayer for Christian Unity, 1991, (14)31; Churches' Commission for Racial Justice, (16,V)6

Council of Evangelical Churches in the USSR. Quoted from Georg Petrovich Vins. (16,VIII)9

Coventry Cathedral 1964. (XI)14

Cragg, Rt Revd Kenneth. Used with permission. (7)1 (11)11,88 (18)11

Crooks, Peter J. *Lebanon: The Pain and the Glory*. Used with permission. (16,VII)6

Darton, Longman and Todd Ltd, London. Taken from *A Thousand Reasons for Living* by Dom Helder Camara, published and copyright 1987 by Darton, Longman and Todd Ltd and used by permission of the publishers, (1)14; from *Celtic Fire* by Robert van de Weyer, published and copyright 1990 by Darton, Longman and Todd Ltd and used by permission of the publishers, (16,XIV)3; from *Dare to Break Bread* by Geoffrey Howard, published and copyright 1992 by Darton, Longman and Todd Ltd and used by permission of the publishers, (14)24; from *Out of the Deep: Prayer as Protest* by Gordon Mursell, published and copyright 1989 by Darton, Longman and Todd Ltd and used by permission of the publishers, (10)4; from *The Road to Daybreak* by Henri Nouwen, published and copyright 1989 by Darton, Longman and Todd Ltd and used by permission of the publishers, (6)4; from *Enough Room for Joy: Jean Vanier's L'Arche. A Message for our Time* by Bill Clarke SJ, published and copyright 1974 by Darton, Longman and Todd Ltd and used by permission of the publishers, (11)87 (adapted) (18)21

de Blank, Rt Revd Joost, Archbishop of Cape Town. Autobiography, *Out of Africa*; quoting Reinhold Niebuhr. Reproduced by permission of Christopher Niebuhr. (16,IX)18

de Foucauld, Charles, Journal/Diary, 8 March 1908. (7)3

Dehqani-Tafti, Rt Revd Hassan. Reproduced by permission. (11)40 (16,I)12 (16,VI)8 (16,XI)13

de la Torre, Fr Ed. (9)21

Diocese of Atlanta. *Purple Ink*; Rt Revd Bennett J. Sims. (6)13

Dioceses of Colombo and Kurunagala and Diocese of Ripon link prayer by the Revd Roger Harington. Used with permission. (5)2

Dominican Publications, Dublin. *Proclaiming All Your Wonders* (English edition). Used with permission. (3)14 (4)3 (8)1 (9)6 (10)3 (12)6 (16,XIV)12,21 (18)22

Dwyer, E. J., Rome and Sydney. Permission sought to quote from *Your Hand, God*; Johann Hoffmann-Heneros. (7)13 (13)28

East Asia Christian Conference, Urban and Industrial Mission Committee. Permission sought to quote from *New Songs of Asian Cities*, No. 18; Samuel Liew. (2)8

Ecumenical Christian Centre, Bangalore. Permission sought (manuscripts). (16,II)12 (Rankit Kumar Sathyaraj) (16,VI)14 (Susy Nellithanam) (17)34

Ecumenical Forum of European Christian Women. *Newsletter*, Easter 1990; Marie-Therese Van Lunen Chenbu, (8)51; Assembly, 1990, (17)11

Ecumenical Prayer Book, USA/Canada. (11)50

Edinburgh House Press, London. *In His Name: Prayers for the Church and the World*; George Appleton. (16,V)7

Elean, Ruth F. 'This is the thing I most would hate' from *Christian Century*, USA. Used as the basis of a prayer. (11)16

Episcopal Church of Iran. (5)17 (8)30 (19)16

Episcopal Theological School, USA. *Selection of Prayers* by Henry Sylvester Nash. (8)14

Espinal, Luis, SJ. *El grito de un pueblo*; Centro de Estudios y Publicaciones (CEP), Lima, Peru, 1981. (12)3 (18)19

European Ecumenical Assembly, Graz 1997. Frano Prcela OP. (14)35

Faber and Faber, London. From *Markings* by Dag Hammarskjöld, published and copyright 1964 by Faber and Faber, and reproduced by permission of the publishers. (12)4

Fellowship of the Least Coin. Permission sought. (8)4 (14)27 (16,X)15

Flint, Hilda. (manuscript) (6)15

Forward Movement Publications, Cincinnati, Ohio. Reprinted from the *Anglican Cycle of Prayer*. (5)25 (7)19 (from *Prayers for Worship Leaders;* Arnold Kenseth and Richard

Unsworth) (7)20 (Forward Movement Publications in association with Disciples of Christ USA) (8)12 (11)74 (19)1 (adapted) (19)3,4 (16,II)15 (16,VI)1

Foundation for Theological Education in Southeast Asia, Hong Kong. Reproduced with permission from *Lilies of the Field*; Wang Weifan, translated and edited by Janice and Philip Wickeri. (1)21 (4)2 (5)14 (6)11 (8)21 (9)13 (11)32

Freetown Urban Team Ministry, Literature and Almanac Committee 'Krio Shouts and Songs', (manuscript). Permission sought. (11)34 (13)1 (16,IV)1 (16,XI)17

Friends of the Church in China, London. Reproduced with permission from *Unfinished Encounter, China and Christianity*; Bob Whyte, (16,XII)1,4; *Newsletter*, Summer 1989, (16,VII)10

Friendship Press, New York (Harper and Row, San Francisco). Permission sought to quote from *The World at One in Prayer*, compiled by Daniel Johnson Fleming, (1)2,7 (2)11 (11)64 (12)10,17 (13)30 (14)29,33 (16,III)13 (16,XI)29 (18)3 (19)15; *The Cross is Lifted*, Chandran Devanasen, (1)8 (3)8 (5)13 (16,IV)6 (16,XI)28 (16,XII)5; *I Sing your Praise All Day Long*; Fritz Pawelzik (ed.), (1)13 (7)5; *I Lie on my Bed and Pray*; Fritz Pawelzik (ed.), (5)4 (11)14; *Journey of Struggle, Journey of Hope: People and their Pilgrimage in Central Africa*; Jan Heaton, (8)7

Furlong, Monica. Used with permission. (17)30 (19)2

General Board of Global Ministries, The United Methodist Church, New York. Used with permission from *Prayer Calendar, 1985*. (19)17 (Marilee Zdenek) (19)21 (David Gallup)

Geoffrey Chapman, London (Cassell, London). Used with permission from *Take up your Cross: Meditations on the Way of the Cross*, Engelbert Mveng SJ. (16,II)13 (16,III)6,12 (16,IV)5 (16,V)2 (16,VI)12 (16,VIII)10 (16,X)11 (16,XI)2 (16,XIII)2

Geraisy, Walid. (8)32

Gill and Son, Dublin. Permission sought to use from *Prayers of Life*; Michel Quoist. (11)90 (16,I)11 (16,III)10 (16,IV)10 (16,IX)1 (16,XIV)9

Goldingay, John. *Newsletter No. 61*, December 1993, St John's College, Nottingham. (10)8

Gomer Press, Llandysul, Ceredigion. Used with permission from *Twentieth Century Welsh Poems*, J. P. Glancey (ed.), 'Pigeons' by Gwenallt Jones. (9)3

Greek Catholic Church. *Byzantine Daily Worship*, December Vespers. (2)2

Gregorian Sacramentary. (1)22

Gregory Minster, Yorks. (manuscript) (5)22

Griffiths, The Revd Tudor. (manuscript) Used with permission. (3)22

Grove Books Limited, Cambridge. *Praying in the Shadow of the Bomb*; Mark Mills Powell, quoting from *The Prophets* by Abraham J. Heschel. (16,X)4

Guatemalan Committee for Justice and Peace, 1983. (7)24 (17(8)

Hall, Rt Revd R. O. (12)18 (Prayer of Teilhard de Chardin, found handwritten in R. O. Hall's notebook, and used at his Memorial Service) (16,IX)7

Hampton Institute, USA. *Religious Folk Songs of the Negro*. (16,IX)15

HarperCollins, Publishers, London. Reproduced with permission from *The Liturgical Psalter* in *The Alternative Service Book 1980* (2)1; from *Miracle on the River Kwai*; Ernest Gordon. (16,XI)15

HarperCollins Religious, Blackburn, Victoria, Australia. Prayers from *Australian Stations of the Cross*, copyright Miriam-Rose Ungunmerr Baumann, 1984. Used with the permission of the publisher, HarperCollins Religious, Melbourne. (16,VIII)3 (16,X)1 (16,XI)8 (16,XIII)3

Hathaway, Rt Revd Alden M., USA. (4)15

Hitchcock, Olive. (manuscript) (2)14 (17)24 (16,XIII)5

Hodder and Stoughton, Publishers, Sevenoaks, UK. Permission sought to quote from: *I Believe in the Great Commission*, Max Warren quoting *The Last Temptation*, Nikos Kazantzakis, (16,XI)24; *Kathleen*, E. M. Blaiklock, quoting E. M. Farr, (17)27; *Sermons in Solitary Confinement*, Richard Wurmbrand, (16,IV)12 (16,VI)10; *The Blessing of Tears*, Julie Sheldon, quoting Alison Blair, *Rwandan Diary, 1995*, (15)17

Hope Publishing Company, Carol Stream IL. Aotearoa, New Zealand. Permission sought to use from *Come to this Christmas Singing!*; Shirley Erena Murray. (3)21

Hume, Cardinal Basil. (Prayer based on some words of) (16,VI)11

Hussein, Kamil. *City of Wrong* translated by Rt Revd Kenneth Cragg. Reproduced with permission of the translator. (16,I)4

Image Books, NY. *Creative Ministry*; Henri J. L. Nouwen. (3)16

In God's Image, Asia. (8)6

International Bible Reading Association, Birmingham, UK. Used with permission from *Living Prayers for Today* compiled by Maureen Edwards. (16,IX)10 (Simon Oxley)

International Ecumenical Fellowship, Brussels. 1995 Conference, Cieszyn, Poland, (16,III)1; 1996 Conference, Leuven, Belgium, (12)16

International Missionary Council. 1956 Assembly. (5)26 (adapted)

Inter-Varsity Press, Leicester. *Someone who Beckons*; Rt Revd Timothy Dudley-Smith. (10)21

Iona Community, Glasgow. 'The Killing of the Children' (litany) from *Coracle* (the newsletter of the Iona Community 3 January 1993) by Kathy Galloway, copyright Kathy Galloway, Glasgow, Scotland, (6)16; extract from a longer prayer, from *A Wee Worship Book* (Wild Goose Worship Group, 1989) by John L. Bell, copyright 1989, Wild Goose Resource Group, Iona Community, 840 Govan Road, Glasgow G51 3UU, Scotland, (19)13

Jammes, François, translated by B. C. Boulter. (8)5

Japan Christian Quarterly, Tokyo. (16,XII)11 (17)2 (Misuno Genzo)

John Knox Press, Richmond, Virginia, USA. Permission sought to use from *Prayers from an Island*; Richard Wong. (2)21 (11)46,85 (14)22 (adapted) (16,IX)5

Jyotiniketan Ashram, India, Jerusalem, Hong Kong, Ontario. Used with permission. (5)18 (16,V)4 (manuscript) (16,X)12 (manuscript)

Kauma, Rt Revd Misaeri. National Chairman of The Uganda Aids Commission. (11)27

Kevin Mayhew, Leigh-on-Sea, UK. Permission sought to quote from *Prayers for Peacemakers*, Martha Keys Barker, (12)12; *Let My People Go!* compiled by Michael Evans, (16,IV)13 (16,VII)9,11

Kingsway Publications, Eastbourne, UK, in association with the CPAS. Used with permission from *More Prayers for Today's Church* by R. H. L. Williams, published by Kingsway Publications in association with the Church Pastoral Aid Society, (16,XII)9 (Susan Williams) (16,XIII)9 (Dick Williams); *Prayers for Today's World* by R. H. L. Williams, published by Kingsway Publications in association with the Church Pastoral Aid Society, (12)11 (Stephen Gough) (5)11 (Donald Pankhurst)

Kiplagat, Bethel H. (1)3 (8)50
Koyama, Kosuke. (16,II)10 (17)29
Kuhn, Isobel. (10)23
Kups, Bernard. *Yes to No Man's Land.* (1)19

Latin American Federation of Relatives of Disappeared Prisoners. (16,VII)8
Lees, Janet. Prayers which appeared in the Council for World Mission Prayer Handbook 1994, *Edged with Fire*, published by the United Reformed Church in the United Kingdom copyright Janet Lees 1993 and used with permission. (14)14 (16,X)10 (version of prayer by Nisikana the Witness)
Lehman, Carolyn. (17)6
Leprosy Mission, Peterborough. Used with permission from *Escaped as a Bird: Verses from a Japanese Leprosy Hospital*, (3)10 (11)22 (16,XI)3,27 (17)33; *Ask: Prayer Guide 1990*, (11)23
Lion Publishing plc, Tring, Herts. Permission sought to use meditation of Viktoras Petkus, from *The Lion Prayer Collection* compiled by Mary Batchelor. (17)16
Lutterworth Press, London. *Daily Prayer and Praise* edited by George Appleton. (8)46

Macy, Joanna, *Meditation in Time of War* (manuscript), (16,VIII)8
Marins, Jose. (19)11
Marshall, Morgan and Scott, London, Lamp Press. Permission sought to quote from *The Testing of Hearts*; Donald Nicholl. (14)18
Marshall Pickering, London. *Women at Prayer* compiled by Rachel Stowe. Copyright M. U. Enterprises Ltd. Used with permission. (3)24,25 (4)14 (6)10 (7)9,18 (8)16,24 (16,III)11 (16,VI)7
Maryknoll Priests, NY. (12)5
Maryknoll Sisters, NY. (7)25
Memorial Service for Oscar Romero, Newcastle on Tyne, 1985. (15)28
Methodist Church in Great Britain and the General Committee of the Methodist Church in Ireland (General Purposes Committee). Used with permission from *Now*, June 1988, (9)5 (Yong-shik Moon); *Prayer Manual 1987/8*, (16,VII)2 (Jean-Francois Bill); *Prayer Handbook 1988/9*, (13)4 (Kenneth Street); *Prayer Handbook 1989/90*, (13)21 (Jan Pickard) (16,V)11; *Prayer Handbook 1990/91*, (19)19; *Prayer Handbook 1991/2*, (8)33 (Norman Wallwork) (16,IX)9; *Prayer Handbook 1992/3*, (14)8 (Norman Wallwork, based on words of Michael Ramsey) (15)27 (from the United Church in Zambia); *Prayer Handbook 1993/4*, (18)1; *Prayer Handbook 1994/5*, (16,XI)6 (abridged by Brian Brown from *I am an African*, Gabriel Setiloane); *Prayer Handbook 1995/6*, (16,XIV)7 (quoting 'Kagawa' by William Axling, SCM Press, 1946); Prayer Handbook *Your Will be Done*, (19)4
Methodist Missionary Society. *Women's Work 1963*, translated from the Igbo of Harcourt Whyte. (16,VII)1
Middle East Christian Council, Beirut. Used with permission from *Emmaus Furlongs*. (15)13
Middle East Council of Churches, Beirut. (19)22
Milner-White, Eric. (17)31
Mowbray (Cassell), London. Reproduced with permission from *Celebrating Resistance*; Dorothee Soelle. (16,VII)14
Mozarabic Liturgy. (11)29 (14)30

National Christian Education Council, Birmingham. Reproduced from *Oceans of Prayer*, compiled by Maureen Edwards and Jan D. Pickard, with the permission of the National Christian Education Council. (8)31 (11)45,52 (17)5

New Being Publications, Cal. USA. Permission sought to use from *Prayers for Peace*; Robert M. Herhold. (4)17 (11)57 (13)7 (14)34 (17)17

New City, London. Reproduced with permission, passages from two Meditations by Chiara Lubich. (16,XI)22

Niebuhr, Reinhold. Quoted with permission from *Irony of American History*, Dartmouth College Commencement, Hanover, NH 1951 (USA). (16,IX)19

Nkoane, Rt Revd Simeon, CR. (manuscript) (8)27

O'Casey, Sean. *Juno and the Paycock*. (16,XII)6

Open Book Publishers, Adelaide, South Australia. 'Ancient Gumtrees' from *Australian Images* by Aubrey Podlich, (1)18; 'Carol of the Cleared Field' from *Australian Psalms* by Bruce Prewer, (4)19; both used by permission of Openbook Publishers, Adelaide, Australia.

Orthodox. (3)33 (5)3 (6)1 (11)1 (13)3,19 (14)9 (15)19 (16,IV)4 (16,VIII)1 (16,XIV)2,11,19 (17)12,14,26 (19)8,10

Oxford University Press, Oxford. Used by permission of the compiler from *Alive to God* compiled by the Rt Revd Kenneth Cragg. (16,IX)13 (based on John Bunyan's Pilgrim Song) (16,XIV)18

Pace Publishing, Auckland, NZ, in association with Asian Christian Art Association, Kyoto, Japan. *The Bible through Asian Eyes*; Aboriginal woman. (16,II)11

Palestine Committee of Women's World Day of Prayer, Jerusalem. (12)20 (16,VIII)12 (16,XIV)4

Paternoster Publishing, Carlisle. Reproduced with permission from *Through Gates of Splendour*, Elisabeth Elliot, OM Publishing Edition. (9)18

Paulist Press/Newman Press, Mahway, NJ, USA. *Prayers Written by Lithuanian Prisoners in Northern Siberia*, edited by K. A. Trimikas SJ, Copyright unknown. (16,III)4 (16,VII)3 (16,VIII)4

Penguin, UK. From *Prophet, Madman, Wanderer*; Kahlil Gibran. (16,IV)7

Perrins, Revd Lesley. (manuscript) Used with permission. (3)2

Phoenix, Sybil, MBE. Used with permission from *With All My Love*, Rainbow Publishing 1992. (16,III)3

Presbyterian Church of Aotearoa New Zealand, Department of Parish Development and Mission, Wellington, NZ. Used with permission. (1)12 (17)41

Presbyterians for Lesbian/Gay Concerns, USA. From *A More Light Prayer Book*. (11)26 (15)9

Prisoners' Week Committee on behalf of the Anglican, Methodist and Roman Catholic churches, Ramsgate, Kent. (16,VII)12,13

Private Publication, Egypt. *Whisper in the Pines: A Collection of Verses from Ishmael*; Doris Compton. (16,X)9

Reed Books, Rushden, Hants. Reproduced by permission of Reed Consumer Books from *Italian Neighbours: An Englishman in Verona* by Tim Parks, Martin Secker and Warburg Ltd, (16,IV)9; *Are You Running With Me, Jesus?* by Malcolm Boyd, William Heinemann Ltd, (16,XII)10

Richardson and Son, London. Prayer based on some words of F. W. Faber. (16,IX)17
Rigos, Dr Cirolos A. (15)24
Rikkyo All Saints University Chapel, Tokyo. Used with permission from *Father Tetsu's Collection of Haiku Poems*. (1)20 (12)1 (14)3,11 (15)14 (16,II)5 (16,III)2 (16,XI)20 (16,XII)3
Ross, John. (16,XIV)10
Ruiz, Jerjes, Seminario Teologico Bautista, Nicaragua. (16,V)10

Saward, Revd Canon Michael. Used with permission from *Task Unfinished*. (5)9 (11)61 (16,VI)3
Sayers, Dorothy L. *The Choice of the Cross*. (12)23
SCM Press, London. Used with permission from *We Drink from our Own Wells*, SCM Press 1984, Gustavo Gutiérrez, (11)89; *Sweeter than Honey: Christian Presence amid Judaism*, SCM Press 1966, by Peter Schneider quoting words of Marie Syrkih in *Verdict on Father Daniel, 1963*, (16,XIV)6
Seabury/Continuum Publishing Co. NY. From *A Book of Family Prayer* edited by Gabe Huck. (16,XIV)20
Search Press Ltd/Burns and Oates Ltd, Tunbridge Wells, Kent, UK. Used with permission from *The Valley of God*, John Rayne-Davis. (15)10
Seremane, Joe. Permission sought. (15)6
Sharp, Revd Canon Norman. (Translated from the Persian by) (3)7 (5)16
Shelter, National Campaign for the Homeless, London. (11)78
Smith-Cameron, Revd Canon Ivor. (Prayer based on some words of) (17)36
Sojourners, USA. (10)1 (12)9 (13)10 (14)21
South African Council of Churches, Division of Refugee Ministries. (7)8 (7)14 (Fr Roger Hickley, Catholic Welfare Bureau, Cape Town)
SPCK/Christian Aid, London. Used with permission from *Bread for Tomorrow* edited by Janet Morley. (3)6,18 (3)23 (Gillian Paterson)
SPCK, India, Delhi. Used with permission from *Premananda Anath Nath Sen*, (4)22; *Book of Common Prayer of the CIPBC, 1960*, (5)26 (8)13 (17)19; *Swami Abhishiktananda*, James Stuart, (16,VI)6
SPCK, London. Permission sought to quote from *The Seven Storey Mountain* Epilogue, Thomas Merton, (9)20; *Jerusalem Prayers*, George Appleton, (10)15 (11)71 (12)8 (13)15; *Women at the Well: Feminine Perspectives on Spiritual Direction*, Kathleen Fischer, (17)7; *All Desires Known*, Janet Morley, (6)12 (8)3 (10)2 (11)73,82 (12)13
SPCK, Triangle. Permission sought to use from *Praying with the Martyrs*, compiled by Duane Arnold, (4)20 (Yona Kanamuzeyi) (15)11 (16,VII)5; *Another Day*, compiled by John Carden, (6)18
Stainer and Bell Ltd, London. *Spirit of Jesus* by Brian A. Wren, copyright 1983, 1993, Stainer and Bell Limited, (7)17; *Even the Most Common Changes* by Sydney Carter, reproduced by permission of Stainer and Bell Ltd, (5)19
Syrian Orthodox Church of Kerala. (11)54

Tappa, Louise. *God in Man's Image* from a collection of theological reflections by women of the Third World. (16,VIII)11

Taylor, Rt Revd John V. Used with permission. (11)5
The Ceylon Churchman, Vol. 92, No. 5. (19)5
The Franciscan. Permission sought to quote from *The Hope and the Holocaust*. (16,X)3
The Tablet, London. 21/28 April 1984, (18)8; 1/8 March 1997, (16,XI)25. Reproduced with permission.
The Word and the World. (19)23
Tilak, Narayan Waman. (3)29

United Church Board of World Ministries, Cleveland, Ohio, USA. Used with permission from *Calendar of Prayer 1985/6*, (16,XI)4; *Calendar of Prayer 1986/7*, (11)47 (Sherina Niles)
United Church of Canada/L'Eglise Unie du Canada, Etoboke, Ontario. Used with permission from *Gathering*. (2)13 (adapted) (15)21
United Society for the Propagation of the Gospel, London. Grateful thanks are expressed to the USPG for permission to reprint prayers from a number of publications, and in particular to named authors, as follows: Canon S. D. Batumalai (4)11, Dom Helder Camara (9)7, Gerald Butt (13)26, Bishop Leslie Stradling (17)32, Julie Hulme (16,XI)12, and to the authors of the following prayers who cannot now be traced: (1)10 (4)18,21 (7)11 (10)11 (11)9,37,63 (15)1,2,16,20 (16,I)6 (16,X)6 (16,XI)16 (19)7
United Theological College, Bangalore. Quoted with permission from *Worship in an Indian Context*, edited by the Revd Dr Eric J. Lott, (17)25; and in particular from *A Litany of the Disciples of Christ the Servant*, (9)8 (10)9 (11)35,42 (12)19 (13)31,34 (14)2 (15)29 (16,I)17 (16,II)9 (16,V)1 (17)25,40
The Uniting Church in Australia, Sydney NSW. Used by permission of the Commission for Mission, National Assembly of the Uniting Church in Australia: (11)33 (19)6; from *We Believe*, 1986, (16,II)6; from *Risking Obedience*, (16,IX)6; from *From the Rising of the Sun*, (17)24

Uwa, Hosarea. (8)8
Uzima, Nairobi. Used with permission from *Prayers for Today*. (4)10 (8)15 (11)8,36,41,75,84 (13)20

Warwicker, Bob. Prayers which appeared in the Council for World Mission Prayer Handbook 1994, *Edged with Fire*, published by the United Reformed Church in the United Kingdom, copyright Bob Warwicker 1993, and used with permission. (4)9 (16,II)4 (16,XI)10
Wickremesinghe, Bishop Lakhshman. (manuscript) (14)4
Williams, R. H. L. Used with permission from *Godfacts*, Falcon/CPAS. (16,XIV)8
Williams, Susan. Used with permission from *Lord of our World: Modern Collects from the Gospels*, Falcon/CPAS. (9)9 (11)58 (12)2
Women's Theological Centre, USA. From *Newsletter*. (16,VIII)5 (Kip Tiernan)
World Alliance of Reformed Churches, Geneva. Used with permission from: *Testimonies of Faith*, (16,VII)4; *Worship Book* of 1989 Assembly, Seoul, (17)28
World Council of Churches, Geneva. Permission sought to reprint extracts and prayers from the following WCC publications: *For All God's People*, (16,XIV)13 (Daisuke Kitagawa); *With All God's People*, edited by John Carden, (2)7 (Albert Newton) (2)19 (Kim Myong Shik) (10)6 (10)18 (Thomas Tellez) (14)32 (16,V)12 (Francis Akano Ibiam) (16,XI)30

(16,XIV)16; *Confessing Our Faith Around the World* (vol. III), (6)6 (7)12 (16,XIII)4; *Immanuel*, Hans Rudi Weber, (7)4 (quoting Marie Assad); *Worship Resources: Focus on Refugees*, (7)16; *Lima Liturgy, 1982*, (9)10; *Come, Holy Spirit: Renew the Whole Creation*, (9)22 ('A Prayer to the Holy Trinity', Quias Sadiq); *Christ the Light of the World: Asian Sources*, (13)16; *Jesus of the Deep Forest*, (manuscript), Christina Afua Gyan, (1)9 (5)8 (11)2,21,62 (13)5 (16,II)7 (18)10; *Le tronc béni de la prière* (manuscript), Mamia Woongly-Massaga, (5)5 (8)11 (14)13; *3rd Assembly, 1961, New Delhi*, (11)53 (Bengali hymn, Bishop Nirod Kumar Biswas); *Worship Book of the 7th Assembly, 1991*, Canberra, (19)26; Conference on World Mission and Evangelism, (15)3 (Kristan Stendhall); Conference on World Mission and Evangelism, 1980, Melbourne, (14)16; *International Review of Missions*, 71 (282), 1982. (15)18 (Bishop Colin Winter); *Women in a Changing World*, No 25, January 1988, (16,IV)3; *The Ecumenical Review*, 'Fire and Ashes in the Wind', Pedro Casaldaliga, originally written for *Antologia Espiritual*, Santander, Brazil, (19)9; *The Ecumenical Review*, 38 (1), 1986, 'Solitude and Solidarity', (18)20; *One World*, April 1990, 'Pisgah and Sunday', Stanley Samartha, (16,XIV)5; *One World*, January/February 1992, meditation by Manoushag Boyadjan, quoting Kahlil Gibran, (16,V)9

World Student Christian Federation. Worship Workshop *Women and Men in Asia*, 1976, (16,VI)9; *Living Beyond our Means*, (17)42

York Council of Christian Churches, UK. (13)22 (adapted)

YWCA. *Celebration*, 9th World Council, taken from *Jubilaeum Juvenum*, Rome, 1984. (16,VI)5

The following prayers are by the compiler: (2)5,12,16,17,18,20 (3)9,26 (4)7,12 (5)7,20 (6)3,8,14,17 (7)6,10,22,23 (8)17,18,22,26,34,35,44,49 (9)2,11 (10)13 (11)4,10,17, 30,38,51,68,79,86 (12)21 (13)33 (14)19 (15)8,12,25 (16,II)2 (16,III)9 (16,IV)2 (16,VII)17 (16,X)7,13 (16,XI)5,18 (16,XII)8 (16,XIII)6,7 (17)3,4,15,21 (18)17

Unless otherwise stated all biblical passages are taken from the Revised English Bible, copyright Oxford University Press and Cambridge University Press 1989, and are reproduced by permission of the publishers.

The quotation from Isaiah 53:8 in Chapter 16, Station VII, is taken from the New English Bible, copyright Oxford University Press and Cambridge University Press 1961, 1970, and is reproduced by permission of the publishers.

The quotation from Luke 11:27–28 in Chapter 16, Station VIII is taken from the New Jerusalem Bible, published and copyright 1985 by Darton, Longman and Todd Ltd and Doubleday and Co. Inc., and is used by permission of the publishers.

Index

Aboriginal 205, 243, 256, 265, 279, 291
accuse 17, 72, 112, 180, 192–3, 195–6, 238
action 13, 95, 111–12, 248
adolescence 86–91; see also teenagers; young
 people
advent 4–14
Afghanistan 45, 55
Africa 4–5, 8, 11, 41, 48, 56, 61, 70, 71, 82,
 93, 96, 143, 174, 220–1, 225–6, 250,
 313, 326; see also individual countries
Aids 121–2, 181
Algeria 69
Ambrosian 45
Amnesty International 196
anger 74, 101, 164, 178–9, 184–5, 243–4,
 245, 325
animals 7–8, 48, 80, 152, 154–5, 184
Anna 34, 37–8, 39–40, 44
Annunciation 79–82
anoint 53, 91–6, 99–100, 311–12, 326–7
anxiety 8–11, 127, 182
Argentina 93, 214–15
arrest 186, 188, 195, 238, 279
Ascension 314–18
Asia 56, 82, 280–1; see also individual
 countries
Australia 8, 12, 42–3, 71, 124, 154, 170–1,
 179, 205, 243, 251, 256, 265, 279, 291,
 301, 310, 321, 328
authority 16, 148, 176, 195, 199–200
awakening 6, 42

Bangladesh 79, 130, 178–9
baptism 97–104
barren 110, 133–4; see also desert
Belgium 148
benedictions 14, 33, 177, 255, 272, 293, 318,
 328
bereaved 9, 39–41, 277, 278–9, 287–8
Bethlehem 13, 21, 26, 49–51, 59, 63, 67, 76
betrayal 180, 183–4, 188; see also Judas
birds 62, 82, 97–8, 100, 162–3, 210, 294
birth 30–1, 53, 55, 292
blind 84, 91, 94, 123–4, 222
Bolivia 144, 288–9, 315
Bosnia 66, 123
Botswana 107
Brazil 10–11, 24–5, 59–60, 99, 138, 146, 155,
 233, 244, 322–3
bread 16, 22, 100, 106, 141, 169, 172, 175,
 303, 304–5, 306

burial 53, 278–9, 283, 284–93
Byzantine 155

calamity 127–30, 159
call 43, 80, 90, 92, 97, 143, 220–1, 246–7
Cameroon 169, 206, 210, 212, 216, 220–1,
 231, 246–7, 248, 260–1, 262–3, 278–9
Canada 14, 20, 116, 174, 186, 297-8, 310–11
care 21, 182, 243
Caribbean 41, 90, 130
celebrate 27, 32, 58, 61, 296, 297–8, 315–16
Central Africa 21, 28, 73, 86, 120, 136, 196, 269
Central African Republic 47, 83
change 51, 94, 143, 261, 325
children 8–10, 28–9, 31, 40, 58–64, 67, 74,
 77, 82–7, 89, 93, 107, 147–8, 258;
 see also infants
Chile 29, 203–4, 239–40, 296
China 13, 35, 45, 50, 62, 86–7, 101, 111,
 123, 134, 186, 238, 273, 274, 325
choice 111–13, 147, 187
Christian Aid 30, 61, 133, 163–4
Christmas 13, 23–33, 60–1, 66
Church 79, 95, 135, 181, 228, 310–11, 314,
 327–8
churches 94–6, 140, 167, 252, 309–10; see
 also congregations
city 63, 152–64, 199–200; see also town
cleansing 6, 133, 167, 195, 228, 229–30, 270
climate 9, 10, 30, 53–4, 107–8, 110, 166,
 169, 173, 183, 203, 249–50, 253, 254,
 271, 274, 284, 313; see also seasons
clothing 225, 228, 256, 258–61
clown 201, 205–6, 265–6; see also fool
comfort 20–1, 40, 66, 75, 85–6, 87
commissioning 309–14, 328
communion of saints 22, 39–40, 42–3, 49–50,
 54, 198, 221, 292–3, 300, 301–2, 305–6,
 309–10
companion/companionship 9–10, 39, 63,
 76–7, 90, 254, 313, 328
compassion 14, 21, 94, 98, 160, 161, 222, 228
Congo 176
congregations 85, 95, 135, 141, 171–2, 227,
 239, 309–10; see also churches
conscience 193–4, 195
constancy 37, 39, 43–4, 209–10, 251–3
counting 15–17, 21; see also numbering
courage 33, 53, 81, 90, 110, 114, 136, 142–3,
 145, 178–9, 186, 244, 264, 283, 291,
 297, 313, 315

country 7, 60, 77, 125, 295-6, 300;
    see also land
creation 5, 7, 13, 42, 153, 155, 239, 293, 299
Croatia 65-6, 176
cross 25-6, 49, 69, 112, 144, 145, 146, 147,
    150-1, 166, 180, 181, 189-293, 301, 315
crowd 125, 154, 200, 218, 307
crucifixion 193-4, 214-15, 256, 257, 262-72
Czech Republic 85, 198

dance 5, 57
darkness 4-11, 35, 54, 94, 135, 149, 182,
    186, 278, 281-2, 298
deaf 84, 124
death 10, 53, 55, 61, 63-4, 66, 135-7, 146-7,
    170-1, 238, 278-82, 284-93
delinquents 88, 306
Democratic Republic of Congo 176
Denmark 110
departed 152, 290, 292-3
deposition 278-83
depression 182
desert 8-9, 104, 105-11, 133-4, 173
desertion 186-7
despair 92, 137, 195, 250, 301
devil 111, 123, 124; *see also* Evil One; Satan
dignity 22, 90, 202
disability 84, 162; *see also* handicapped
disappeared 87, 88, 214-15, 237
displaced persons 74-5
dispossessed 18, 20, 22, 63, 227, 269-70
diversity 19, 22, 327
doubt 112-13, 135
dove 97-8
dreams 8-9, 29, 76-7, 321; *see also* vision
drink 66, 92
drugs 264
dying 38, 40-1, 43, 273-7, 291

east 36, 46, 47, 49, 50, 51
education 82-3, 86, 89; *see also* teach
Egypt 5, 21, 68-9, 73, 76-7, 109, 110, 193-4,
    259, 291
Eire 59, 275
elderly 34-44, 74, 97, 107, 138, 228
El Salvador 28, 72, 78, 178, 280, 308
Emmanuel 23, 110; *see also* Immanuel
England 40, 44, 61, 98, 110, 182, 198, 204,
    250, 251-2, 304, 314; *see also* United
    Kingdom
Epiphany 45-56
Eucharist 127-8, 165, 167, 168, 169-73,
    176-7, 313
evangelism 117-19, 135, 167; *see also* mission
evil 48, 49, 112-13, 184-5
Evil One 48, 104, 111, 198; *see also* devil;
    Satan
exaltation 23, 314-17
exhaustion 211, 212, 224, 235

exile 68-9, 71, 73, 77
Exodus 110, 170
expectancy 5-6, 7-11, 13, 96; *see also* waiting
exploitation 19, 20, 61, 99, 164, 269, 293

face 7, 22, 25, 89, 136, 151, 227-33, 273,
    303; *see also* image
faith 13, 22, 33, 35, 37, 82, 98, 137, 169,
    184-5, 209, 235-6, 248, 252, 254, 255,
    287-8, 291, 297, 301-2
fall 208-13, 224, 249-55
family 31, 32, 71, 72-3, 84-5, 87, 91, 137-9,
    140, 141, 172
fasting 106, 108
fear 10, 11, 20, 46-7, 88, 94, 108, 124,
    127-8, 135, 153, 182, 184, 185, 186,
    192, 196, 205-6, 209, 211, 213, 235,
    237, 245, 270, 297-8, 299-300, 302, 317
fellowship 118, 313
Fiji 43
fingerprinting 18, 22
fire 101-3, 145, 322-4, 325, 326-7
flight 9, 68-78
flowers 5-6, 57, 64, 77-8, 107, 152, 155,
    178, 284-5, 294, 295-6, 299-300
following 32, 52, 62, 87, 89, 99, 108, 115-16,
    124, 127, 142-3, 149, 150, 151, 164,
    165, 167, 186-7, 188, 199, 204, 220,
    248, 261, 262-3, 267, 288, 307, 310-11
fool 201-2, 205-6, 265-6; *see also* clown
footwashing 166-8
forgiveness 19, 39, 138-9, 185, 203, 248,
    255, 267-8, 269, 308; *see also*
    reconciliation
fragrance 50, 53, 55, 153, 201, 284, 294-5
France 28, 35, 59, 79, 80, 92, 96, 98, 106, 110,
    142, 143, 145, 196, 211, 218-19, 239,
    249, 277, 288, 290, 293, 314, 317
freedom 48, 82, 98, 99, 297-8

garden 159, 182, 266, 295, 321
Germany 50, 65, 72, 111, 162, 219, 230, 305
Gethsemane 103, 107-8, 112, 127-8, 154,
    178-88, 321
Ghana 8, 10, 47, 48, 56, 70, 115, 118, 120,
    134, 153, 204, 312
ghetto 5, 96, 166, 286-7
gift 33, 40-1, 53, 172-3, 205-6, 309-10, 328;
    see also offering
glory 8, 15, 32, 33, 35, 50, 145-9, 153, 154,
    155-6, 184, 233, 299, 300, 315
grace 10, 27, 35, 36, 40-1, 43-4, 84, 119,
    139-40, 144, 148, 195, 204, 274, 305, 313
grain 100; *see also* bread
gratitude 225-6, 272; *see also* thanksgiving
Greece 148
Greek Catholic 15
Gregorian 13
grief 135, 214-16; *see also* mourning; sorrow
Guatemala 60-1, 77-8, 297

haiku 13, 144, 166, 169, 183, 203, 209, 269, 274, 294
handicapped 62, 142, 169–70, 171; *see also* disability
Hawaii 22, 128, 141, 172, 251
healing 8–10, 30, 63–4, 87, 95, 118, 120–4, 184, 202, 228, 245, 266–7, 280–1, 326
heart 11, 13, 51, 58, 83, 96, 143, 161, 176, 220, 250, 272, 273–5, 278, 307–8, 315, 325, 326
helpless 63, 74, 222
hen 82–3, 162–3
hidden 5, 90, 127–8, 281–2, 298, 299, 302
Hiroshima 146, 147–8, 256–7, 276; *see also* nuclear
Holocaust 13, 15–16, 276, 285–6
Holy Family 9, 68, 70, 72–3, 84, 88
home 13, 31, 84, 140–2, 199–200
homeless 9, 92, 94, 106, 137–9, 142, 159, 199–200, 227, 258, 268
Honduras 78
Hong Kong 161, 230, 251, 266
hope 8–10, 19, 23–4, 27, 28, 33, 49–50, 60–1, 72–3, 82, 88, 92, 98, 110, 159, 161, 169, 170, 251, 255, 285, 287–8, 289–90, 291, 293, 297–8, 304–5, 313, 321
hospitality 66, 70, 118, 138, 140–2, 165; *see also* welcome
hostage 236–7, 285–6
humble 24–5, 27–8, 29, 80, 128, 306
humility 23, 27, 97, 284, 315
hunger 59–60, 61, 62, 92–4, 100, 212, 227, 297

image 21, 164, 227, 229, 230, 231, 257; *see also* face
Immanuel 62, 74; *see also* Emmanuel
immigrant 18–19, 21, 158, 257; *see also* migrant people
India 7, 23–4, 25–6, 32, 36–7, 43, 45, 49–50, 51, 53, 54, 85–6, 99, 100, 108, 110, 124, 127, 131, 134–5, 140, 145, 149, 154, 155, 156, 158, 163, 164, 165, 172–3, 180–1, 188, 194, 199–200, 204, 205–6, 213, 217, 220, 228–9, 232–3, 254–5, 270, 272, 273, 274–5, 285–6, 300, 301, 302, 304–5, 307, 309–10, 313–14, 320, 322, 326–7; *see also* South India
indigenous people 18, 19, 285–6
Indonesia 121
infants 20, 23–4, 25–6, 29, 31, 59–62, 63–6, 67; *see also* children
injustice 24, 59, 61, 99, 164, 178–9, 186–7, 196, 202
innocents 57–67
integrity 193, 197, 301
interruptions 89, 139–40, 171–2
Iran 45, 51, 89, 102, 126, 197, 229–30, 267, 272, 295, 311, 325; *see also* Persia
Israel 5–6, 8, 34, 35
Israel (State of) 65
Italy 90, 175, 184, 202, 218, 270, 271, 278, 313

Japan 13, 22, 26, 119, 120, 125, 133, 144, 151, 166, 169, 183, 203, 205, 207, 209, 211, 261, 263, 265, 269, 271, 274, 276–7, 287, 290, 294–5, 303, 304, 306
Jerusalem 94, 101–2, 109, 136, 145–6, 149, 152, 153–4, 154–5, 157–8, 160, 161, 171, 222, 227, 248, 261, 285, 295
Jordan 70–1, 95, 165, 301
Jordan (river) 98, 99, 104, 112
Joseph 9, 21, 84, 88
Joseph of Arimathaea 55, 278, 283
journey 9, 10–11, 21, 51, 52–3, 54, 69, 76–7, 80, 86–7, 110, 114, 142–3, 211, 213, 254–5, 262–3, 288, 302, 328
joy 12, 27, 33, 34, 35, 43, 58, 95, 163, 213, 217–18, 233, 298, 304, 317, 318, 321, 328
Judas 166, 168, 171, 183–4, 188
judgement 100, 105, 199
justice 27, 63, 67, 82, 92, 93–4, 96, 128, 147–8, 158, 163–4, 175, 180, 210, 222, 232, 263, 280–1, 285, 297, 314

Kenya 6, 38–9, 49, 84, 93–4, 95, 109, 117, 119, 124–5, 126, 137, 141, 154, 159, 176, 290
kingdom 22, 30, 36–7, 42–3, 67, 77, 136, 166, 171, 177, 269, 300, 325
Korea 33, 91, 98, 166–7, 295–6, 303, 306–7

lament 64, 242–8
land 7, 55, 95, 125, 149, 161, 211, 291; *see also* country
L'Arche Community 59, 108, 142, 317
Last Supper 165, 166–7, 169, 169–70, 171, 180–1
Latin America 27, 210, 237, 239–40; *see also* South America *and individual countries*
laughter 19, 37–8, 57, 205–6, 223, 326
Lazarus 135–6
Lebanon 52–3, 104, 217, 224, 236, 269–70, 324
leprosy 26, 120–1, 234–5, 263, 294–5, 304
Lesotho 125
Liberia 67
life 37–9, 46, 111, 120, 132–3, 135–6, 137, 149, 153–4, 164, 170, 173, 178–9, 279, 291, 292, 293, 294–308, 315
light 4, 6–7, 8–11, 13, 25–7, 35–6, 46, 50, 51–2, 54, 70, 94, 103, 147, 149, 185–6
listening 10–11, 126, 144, 282, 294, 303
litanies 6, 8–10, 18–19, 29, 65–6, 82
Lithuania 209, 235, 243, 299–300
loneliness 138, 182, 192, 228, 235–6, 302, 313
love 14, 22, 23, 25, 27, 31, 32, 33, 34, 37, 40–1, 43, 55, 58, 59, 62, 63, 67, 74, 79, 82, 83–6, 147–8, 150, 169, 174–5, 176, 185, 202, 204, 220, 229, 244, 255, 259, 265, 275, 280–1, 283, 285, 301, 314, 317–18, 325, 326, 327–8

Madagascar 89, 127
magic 46–9
Malaysia 39
market 163–4
Martha and Mary 140
martyr 43, 57, 322–3
Mary, the anointer 53
Mary and Martha 140–1
Mary Magdalen 123
Mary, mother of Jesus 5–6, 9, 21, 31, 35, 58, 59–60, 72, 79, 80–2, 85, 88, 142, 214–19, 247–8, 270, 275–6, 278–80
Mauritius 129
mentally handicapped 57–8, 59
Mexico 32, 60–1, 78
Middle East 142, 183, 221, 222, 327; see also individual countries
midwife 30, 31
migrant people 18–19, 20–1, 73; see also immigrant
minister 102, 117, 227, 282, 309–10, 313
ministry 39, 114–43, 309–10, 313
missing 63; see also disappeared
mission 35–6, 46, 112–13, 116, 168, 309–14, 325, 326; see also evangelism
mother 31, 72, 83, 85–6, 88, 162, 216, 270
Mount Tabor 146, 148
mourning 63–4, 159, 161, 278–9; see also grief; sorrow
Mozarabic 122, 174–5
Myanmar 117, 174
Mystery 1–3, 28, 80–1, 85, 99, 145, 156–7, 189–90, 305

naked 92, 256, 257, 260–1, 264
name 15, 17, 18–19, 239–40, 246
Namibia 185
nativity 23–33
nature 5, 7, 12, 13, 299; see also creation
Nazareth 76, 79–96
Nepal 300
New Guinea 11, 146
New Zealand 8–10, 30, 302, 307–8, 319, 325
Nicaragua 110, 145, 224, 326
Nicodemus 190, 281–2
Nigeria 30, 40, 134, 160, 217–18, 225–6, 227, 234–5
night 8–10, 163, 270, 282, 291
north 36–7, 47
North Africa 117, 131, 213, 250, 284; see also individual countries
North America 129; see also individual countries
nuclear 105, 146–8, 256–7, 276; see also Hiroshima
numbering 15–22
Nunc Dimittis 35–6

offering 45, 50–1, 53, 54–6, 208, 326; see also gift
oppressed 91–2, 170, 219, 263, 304–5

ordinary people 24–5, 80, 97, 221
orphans 18, 40, 60, 84–5, 92, 94, 216
Orthodox 33, 46, 57, 115, 131, 152, 159, 168, 175, 185, 216, 242, 284, 289, 291, 292, 298–9, 302, 322
other faiths 5–6, 51, 52–3, 54–5, 157, 285–7, 292
Our Father 55, 179, 203–4, 270
outcast 19, 29, 35–6, 92, 228

Pacific 111–12, 309
Pakistan 17–18, 25, 29, 37, 53, 85–6, 92, 107–8, 115, 120, 134, 319–20
Palestine 65, 83, 149–50
Papua New Guinea 82–3, 243
parents 31, 63–4, 87, 88, 91, 141
Passion 61, 155–7, 174, 178–277
Passover 86–7
patience 44, 81–2, 169–70, 217–18, 265, 287; see also waiting
peace 27, 35, 54, 63, 67, 71, 72–3, 81–2, 96, 98, 105, 123, 128, 135, 147–8, 153–4, 157–8, 161, 164, 167, 174, 175–6, 177, 184, 210, 271, 280–1, 285, 297–8, 300, 301, 314, 317, 318, 325
peace-keepers 76–7, 285
Pentecost 319–28
perseverance 81–2, 110, 169–70, 251–4, 265, 313; see also constancy
Persia 25, 51; see also Iran
Peru 99–100, 142–3
Philippines 7, 14, 21, 45, 103, 129, 149, 174, 186–7, 195, 297, 306
Poland 208
Polynesia 118
poor 24–5, 27–8, 31, 32, 35–6, 60–1, 91, 92, 93–4, 95, 99–100, 108, 142, 159, 170, 220–1, 222, 227, 293, 297, 304–5, 324; see also poverty
Portugal 169–70
poverty 29, 30, 61, 92, 93, 106, 138–9, 180, 185, 199–200, 243, 322–3; see also poor
power 6, 27, 28, 48, 56, 74, 101, 104, 105, 111–12, 116, 120, 126, 127–8, 147, 151, 164, 166, 233, 301, 304–5, 311
praise 12, 35, 51, 82–3, 128, 152, 153, 266–7, 273, 284, 289, 292, 311, 314
preparation 5–6, 8–10, 35–6, 46, 77–8
presence 5–6, 7, 21, 27, 55, 63, 95, 100, 109, 121, 127, 130, 140, 144, 145, 150, 166, 168, 258, 295–6, 299–300, 302, 303, 305–6, 311–12, 315–16, 320, 321, 328
Presentation 34–44, 97
prison 98, 199, 214–15, 234–41, 299–300, 306
prisoners 48, 91, 94, 98, 203–4, 222, 234–41, 285–6
problem 49, 111, 138, 178–9
promise 10, 35, 44, 80, 174, 297–8, 305–6, 309–10, 313, 317, 321

prophets 92, 154, 195, 285–6
prostitute 121, 203, 228–9, 243, 268
protection 21, 46–7, 54, 62, 72, 76–7, 82,
 85–6, 87, 88–9, 127–31, 142, 150, 159,
 235, 302
purify 50, 55, 56, 100–1, 177, 324

question 63–5, 86, 91, 109

racism 162, 170, 222–3; *see also* Holocaust
recognition 5, 7, 27, 35, 36–7, 75, 96, 127–8,
 132, 199–200, 231, 232, 288, 299–30,
 302, 303, 305–7
reconciliation 184, 269, 271, 280–1; *see also*
 forgiveness
refuge 70–1, 142, 225–6
refugees 22, 68–78, 258, 268
rejoice 11, 27, 32, 184, 236, 315
renewal 6, 9, 12, 46, 94, 95, 99, 104, 124–7,
 134, 135, 167, 178–9, 180, 268, 297–8,
 307–8, 319–28
repentance 17–18, 39, 75, 93, 104, 118,
 138–9, 174, 180, 184, 185, 187, 205, 269,
 290, 307–8, 326–7; *see also* forgiveness
rest 124–7, 140–1, 293
resurrection 27, 136–7, 146, 147, 149, 155–6,
 269–70, 285–6, 288, 294–308, 314, 327
risk 51–3, 81–2, 96, 166
road 66, 149, 150, 151, 288; *see also* journey
rosary 80–1, 219, 246–7
rubbish 8, 159, 258, 301, 305–6, 324
runaways 87–8
rural 90, 118, 160, 212, 262–3
Rwanda 39–40, 43, 74, 140, 184–5

Sahel 106
Satan 71, 106, 108; *see also* devil; Evil One
Scotland 63–4, 65–6, 282, 300, 325; *see also*
 United Kingdom
scourging 199, 204, 207, 218
seasons 13, 38, 42, 128, 217, 250, 292–3;
 s ? als clim_te
seekers 35–6, 54, 148
Serbia 65–6
servant 79, 92, 99, 108, 124, 127, 149, 163,
 164, 165, 166–7, 169–70, 188, 199, 204,
 220, 307
serve 14, 33, 80, 89, 95, 144, 166, 167,
 174–5, 180, 222, 227, 300
sharing 28, 29, 93, 100, 133, 166, 169–70,
 170–1, 175, 177, 259, 303, 306–7, 328
shepherd 21, 25–6, 27, 33
sick 9, 61, 107, 120–4, 228, 306
Sierra Leone 88, 124, 152, 214, 252, 269
silence 43, 126, 166, 192–3, 201, 220–1
Simeon 34, 35–6, 37–8, 44
Simon of Cyrene 220–6
Singapore 17, 128
sleep 8–10, 178, 179, 180–1, 192
Somalia 65
song 13, 76–7, 77–8, 223

sorrow 57–67, 137, 213, 217, 219, 245–6,
 328; *see also* tears; weeping
south 36–7, 47
South Africa 19, 71, 72–3, 74, 88–9, 180,
 184, '95, 22ɔ, 235, 240, 255, 257,
 259–60, 264, 268, 281
South America 324; *see also* Latin America
 and individual countries
South India 6, 11, 27, 34, 49, 94, 102, 131,
 152, 167, 168, 170, 177, 190–1, 293, 328
space 84, 98, 143, 159, 278, 315–16, 317
Spain 122, 174–5, 179
squatters 72–3, 129, 199–200
Sri Lanka 15, 20, 46, 55, 80, 128, 166, 169,
 187, 261, 280–1, 301–2, 321
star 46, 48, 49–50, 51–2, 54
stone 70, 90, 111–12, 153, 162, 296, 307–8
storm 127–31
stranger 7, 75, 118, 132–3
strength 14, 27, 35, 46–7, 71, 81, 109, 122,
 136, 209–10, 250, 297, 300, 311, 313,
 315, 328
stripping 256–61, 264
struggle 92, 96, 106, 108, 110, 184–5, 252,
 293, 297
Sudan 31, 72, 85
suffering 19, 57–67, 123, 142, 144, 148, 149,
 159, 181, 189–277, 306–7
surprise 36–7, 297, 303, 305, 328
Switzerland 150

Taiwan 27, 136, 236
Tanzania 304
teach 86, 89, 117, 309
tears 19, 144, 223, 242; *see also* sorrow;
 weeping
teenagers 31, 89, 256; *see also* adolescence;
 young people
temptation 71, 108–9, 111–13, 127–8, 210
testing 109, 188
Thailand 65–6, 268
thanksgiving 8, 25, 26, 27, 3:, 37–9, 43, 70,
 83, 85, 124–5, 172, 176, 225–6, 251,
 309–10
tired 36–7, 38–9, 41, 126, 132, 208, 209;
 see also weariness
torture 60–1, 199, 204, 207, 219, 238, 263
touch 22, 36–7, 120, 121–2, 123, 173, 231,
 281, 300, 326
town 65–6, 158, 160, 167; *see also* city
Transfiguration 58, 97–8, 145–9, 180–1, 233,
 266–7
travellers 21, 39–40, 76, 150, 302
trial 112, 192–200
trust 44, 46–7, 81–2, 144, 153–4, 321, 327–8
truth 25, 105, 109, 175, 188, 195, 197–8,
 198–9, 232–3

Uganda 25, 30, 62, 71, 118, 122, 143, 167,
 192, 253, 313, 318

Ulster 160
unborn 292
unemployed 8–10, 93–4, 159, 162, 306
United Arab Emirates 45
United Kingdom 21, 23, 29, 32, 35–6, 37–8,
    46, 48, 49, 51–2, 54, 63, 66, 72, 80, 87,
    90, 95, 97, 99, 101, 105, 106, 109, 111,
    116, 132–3, 134, 136, 137, 138–9, 140,
    144, 146, 147, 151, 153, 158, 159, 160,
    162, 163–4, 168, 173, 179, 182, 186, 188,
    193, 195, 196, 198–9, 200, 201, 202, 207,
    209–10, 212, 219, 228, 229, 231, 236–7,
    238, 239, 252, 253, 254, 257, 265–6,
    266–7, 268, 276, 282, 287–8, 299, 303,
    305–6, 311–12, 320, 324, 326, 327–8;
    see also England; Scotland; Wales
unity 91, 95, 98, 135, 148, 155–6, 157–8,
    167, 174–6, 271, 310–11, 327–8
unknown people 165, 172, 181
unlikely people 36–7, 52–3, 132
Upper Rooom 154, 165–77
Uruguay 102, 185, 315–16
USA 17, 31, 41, 63, 67, 73, 75, 84, 88, 89,
    102, 103, 105, 119, 121–2, 132, 137,
    140–1, 147, 154, 172, 176, 181, 205, 223,
    228, 233, 243–4, 244–5, 253–4, 255, 256,
    257, 263, 276, 283, 292–3, 300, 303, 326
useless 92, 106, 218–19

Veronica 227–33
Via Dolorosa 151, 189–293
victim 29, 63, 65–6, 67, 147–8, 176, 256
violence 63, 66, 147–8, 176, 188, 243, 276
vision 23–4, 28, 35–6, 63, 76–7, 90, 123–4,
    133, 159, 228, 301, 302, 303, 315, 320

waiting 4–14, 35, 44, 214, 237, 254, 284,
    285–6, 287–8, 290
Wales 97–8, 311
war 147–8, 159, 170–1, 245;
    see also weapons
watchfulness 11, 114–15, 142–3, 188, 214
water 99, 132–5, 266, 321
weakness 80, 92, 209, 210, 222, 271, 328
weapons 147–8, 153–4, 176, 245;
    see also war
weariness 21, 108, 126, 180–1, 210, 212–13,
    217–18, 220–1; see also tired
weeping 27, 63, 64, 65–6, 144, 157, 158, 159,
    160, 217, 242–3, 246–7, 278–9;
    see also tears
welcome 11, 20, 37, 136, 140, 142–3, 165
west 36–7, 46, 47, 49, 56
wholeness 120, 151, 244
widows/widowers 39–40
wind 105, 128–30, 173, 319–20, 322–3, 324,
    327
wise men 9, 33, 45–56
women 20, 24–5, 30–1, 39–40, 63, 79, 80,
    82, 149, 153, 214–15, 230, 242–8,
    258–9, 268, 281, 284–5, 295, 296–7,
    298–9, 315–16
work 92, 93–4, 124–5, 159, 254–5, 284, 304,
    311
worship 45–56, 95, 152, 163, 186, 307–8,
    317

young people 74, 87–9, 90, 91, 306; see also
    adolescence; teenagers

Zambia 188